"Michael Cosby brilliantly captures t
father. He was a free-spirited man loved
the pieces of my dad's life into a coherent biography is a daunting undertaking that Cosby masterfully accomplishes. I will treasure this book and so will you."

—**Thales Panagides**

"The value of hidden treasure cannot be measured until it is uncovered and shared with the world. Michael Cosby has done just this with the compelling story of the life of Dafnis Panagides! From a corner of the world where a rich and textured history is often overshadowed on the world stage by events and places of broader notoriety comes the story of a man whose life was spent in the service of others and at the same time in the sacrament of living life to its fullest. Take a moment and learn from Dafnis about the balance of these things in times of profound hardship and in times of peace!"

—**Rick Granger**, author and global nomad

"Michael Cosby's captivating account of the life of Dafnis Panagides captures the fascinating personality of the man and causes readers to ponder the meanings of paradox, passion, and activism. This honest portrayal demonstrates the unconventional leadership of a vibrant heart. It enabled me to think more about my own life and also how to view others' lives nonjudgmentally. I love the focus on love and justice in this very inspirational narrative. I learned much by reading *Storyteller*, for it deals with the human condition, cultures and history. Magnificent!"

—**Dennis Plies**, Professor Emeritus

"Saints are inspiring, but storytellers are often more interesting. *The Storyteller from Kalo Chorio* recounts the rollercoaster life of Daphnis Panagides, along with the joys and frustrations of being his friend. Mixing biography with travelogue and personal reflection, this story of a life well lived will delight anyone interested in eccentric characters or the wonderful island of Cyprus where Panagides lived."

—**Douglas Jacobsen**, author of *The World's Christians*

"Cosby's account of travels in Cyprus with its native son, revolutionary turned peacemaker, Dafnis Panagides, was engrossing from the start. The life of Dafnis, told through the eyes of an American, reveals the rich tapestry of this intriguing island with its inimitable braiding of religion and politics. Cosby is a consummate storyteller himself. His fluid writing style and light-hearted humor will engage lovers of creative non-fiction everywhere. I highly recommend this book!"

—**Terri Smiley**, leadership consultant and bibliophile

"There are two lead characters in Michael Cosby's new book. One is the enigmatic and spirited Dafnis Panagides. The other is Cyprus itself, a rugged Mediterranean island with a dramatic history and a complicated present. Cosby deftly interweaves the life story of Dafnis with vibrant descriptions of the place that shaped and inspired him, inviting readers to experience the island's charms and complexities for themselves."

—**Kathryn Jacobsen**, William E. Cooper Distinguished
University Chair, University of Richmond

The Storyteller from Kalo Chorio

by Michael R. Cosby

STONY RUN PUBLISHING
Grantham, Pennsylvania

The Storyteller from Kalo Chorio

Stony Run Publishing
P. O. Box 343
Grantham, Pennsylvania 17027

http://www.stonyrunpublishing.com

PAPERBACK ISBN: 978-0-9824774-3-4 (0-9824774-3-0)
EBOOK ISBN: 978-0-9824774-4-1 (0-9824774-4-9)

Cataloguing-in-Publication data:
Name: Cosby, Michael R., author.
Title: The Storyteller from Kalo Chorio / by Michael R. Cosby.
Description: Grantham, PA: Stony Run Publishing, 2022.

Identifiers: Paperback ISBN 978-0-9824774-3-4 (0-9824774-3-0)
EBook ISBN 978-0-9824774-4-1 (0-9824774-4-9)

BISAC Subjects:
BIO002040 BIOGRAPHY & AUTOBIOGRAPHY / Cultural, Ethnic & Regional / Arab & Middle Eastern
HIS026000 HISTORY / Middle East / General
REL049000 RELIGION / Christianity / Orthodox

Cover photo of Dafnis Panagides by Lynne Cosby. Processing of cover photo by John McCubbin. Cover design by Geoffrey Isley.

Author's website: https://www.michaelrcosby.com

To our dear friends in Cyprus,
particularly the family of Dafnis Panagides

Contents

Illustrations

Color versions of all photos available
at michaelrcosby.com/storyteller/photos

Foreword

After I read *The Storyteller from Kalo Chorio*, I wrote to Michael Cosby, "Congratulations on a book that managed to capture the wind, because Dafnis is totally like the wind, blowing here, there, and everywhere. At first, I thought it would be an insurmountable challenge, yet not only did you capture this brilliant, complex man but you also managed to present a portrait that is very close to reality. You do not flatter him, nor do you exaggerate his shortcomings, but the final picture that you present to your readers is one of a truly remarkable person, loved by nationalists and communists, clergy and laypersons alike, an almost impossible task in the highly charged climate of Cyprus. Only Dafnis could have achieved it. You have my unconditional respect and admiration."

While Cosby lived in Cyprus in 2011, researching the development of beliefs about St. Barnabas, patron saint of Cyprus, he fell under the spell of Dafnis. In 2017, he returned to Cyprus to conduct extensive interviews as the first step in writing the biography of a unique and extraordinary character. Dafnis captivated many people, and his art as a storyteller even inspired this American Fulbright scholar to spend years of his time researching and writing a book about him. Cosby rightly portrays Dafnis as a complex character who does not fit into any mold.

I am far from being impartial about Dafnis, because my husband and I spent much time with this mysterious trickster who proudly called himself "unpredictable, spontaneous and incorrigible." The Storyteller, as Cosby calls him, appropriated the viewpoint, "Why let truth get in the way of telling a good story?" He freely admitted a tendency to exaggerate and pepper stories with hyperbole. He reacted to many situations playfully, mischievously, and humorously, yet with good intentions and an open heart. The life story of this contemporary Cypriot Odysseus, a leader in environmentalism and human rights and an activist for peace and justice, exceeds Nikos Kazantzakis's fictional Zorba the Greek in complexity, charm, and mysteriousness.

Michael Cosby's biography of Dafnis Panagides offers a brilliant portrayal not only of his protagonist's strengths and weaknesses but also of Cyprus's troubled history. Cosby paints a compelling depiction of life in a rural village, Kalo Chorio, where Dafnis was born, and covers in detail his active participation in the 1955–1959 armed struggle for independence from British colonial rule. He also describes vividly the staggering first steps of the newly created, independent Republic of Cyprus in 1960 that subsequently led to further conflict and eventually to a Greek military coup and a Turkish invasion in 1974.

In his younger days, Dafnis was a patriot who not only participated in the armed struggle against the British, but he also hid Colonel Grivas, the leader of EOKA—the major anti-colonial organization—in a hide-out dug under his machine shop. He eventually got caught by the British, was tortured and then imprisoned for 28 months. In 2017, however, Dafnis admitted to Cosby that EOKA tragically destroyed the social fabric of Cyprus by legitimizing violence in an otherwise peaceful society. Paradox and contradictions were major threads running throughout Dafnis's entire life, and Cosby beautifully captures this reality.

Cyprus's foremost philosopher, Zenon of Kition, founder of Stoicism, proclaimed a philosophy of paradox, and Dafnis embodied paradox in almost everything he did, as Cosby aptly reveals in this book. Dafnis was the son of a priest, yet his views on Greek Orthodoxy were unorthodox, because he embraced all people, even those who belonged to different world religions. He sometimes prayed with Bahá'ís, non-Orthodox Christians, and Muslims—much to the chagrin of a Greek Orthodox monk in a monastery on Mt. Athos who told him he could not receive holy communion until he got re-baptized for having denied the Orthodox faith when he prayed with Muslims. Dafnis objected, saying he prayed only Christian prayers, not Muslim prayers. But the monk held firm. Yet, that very monk later came looking for him in the church, during a vigil in the darkness of night, to say that the Holy Spirit revealed to him that Dafnis should receive communion.

This ethnographic study of the life of Danfis Panagides is both fascinating and captivating. *The Storyteller from Kalo Chorio* offers an authentic presentation, depicting Dafnis's adventurous life, drawing not only on his lofty side but also on his shadow side: struggle and turmoil, mischief, wit, humor, goodness of heart, generosity to a fault, the opening of his house to everybody, a prankster, a devout Greek Orthodox not confined by conventional rules and regulations, a totally free spirit within Greek Orthodox tradition and culture, a paradoxical Cypriot at heart! Our life has been much enriched by knowing Dafnis, for whom we have great love and affection; and we believe that Michael Cosby's colorful portrayal of Dafnis will inspire and enrich the lives of readers everywhere.

Emily Markides
January 17, 2022

Dr. Markides has served as Interim Director of the Peace and Reconciliation Studies Program at the University of Maine, where she still teaches courses on Ecology and Peace while actively involved with these issues in her native country of Cyprus—see www.ecocityproject.com

Preface

My wife and I first journeyed to the eastern Mediterranean island of Cyprus in 2011. As a Fulbright Fellow, I was conducting research on the Apostle Barnabas, whom Cypriots revere as their founding saint. While living on this lovely island, we met Dafnis Panagides and were captivated by his art as a storyteller. Born in 1929, he was an eyewitness to the history of modern Cyprus. Indeed, he was instrumental in the birth of the Republic of Cyprus and served in its first parliament. We met other fascinating people during the four months we lived in Nicosia, but Dafnis was the most intriguing—a national treasure.

We returned to Cyprus in 2017 with a digital recorder and a Nikon camera to record interviews and images that I would painstakingly organize into a chronicle of his life. Dafnis had been hesitant to grant permission for me to write his biography, because he felt uncomfortable with my exploring his past. But grant permission he did, and he clearly stated that no subjects were off limits. We could ask him or the other people we interviewed any questions we wanted. He emphasized that he would not censor us in any way. "Let the truth be told," he said. And, to the best of my ability, I have done exactly that. As with any account of someone's life, details surfaced that surprised and sometimes shocked us. I have not sensationalized such revelations, nor have I left them out of the account. I have included them in the book in obedience to Dafnis's own mandate: "Let the truth be told."

Every time I interviewed people, I always asked for and received their permission to use what they told me in my biography of Dafnis. A few times, interviewees asked me to turn off the recorder before they made comments they did not want me to use in my book. I respected their requests and complied with their wishes. All of the quotations included in the book were offered freely by those we interviewed. For certain characters, I have used pseudonyms. For other people, however, I have used their actual names in the narrative, after receiving permission to do so. Keeping the book to a manageable size forced me to be selective in what I included—leaving out interesting stories to conform to length requirements.

As with any oral history project that includes the voices of many people, dealing with divergent accounts of the same events can be difficult to navigate. Indeed, Dafnis regularly gave different details if he told the same stories to us more than once. Sometimes the differences are insignificant. Sometimes I note such disparities in the narrative. Almost always, I retain his exact words when quoting him. On a few occasions, I slightly modify his words to make them grammatically correct. Oral speech does not employ the same precision as written speech, and we all make mistakes on occasion while speaking. Although I adjusted a few words in a few places for readability, I never altered the meaning of the person who was speaking.

We made some of our recordings in challenging circumstances with considerable ambient noise. Transcribing these interviews could be painstaking and involve listening to the same comments repeatedly before we were sure we understood the speaker's words. Also, when the interviewee spoke in Greek and Dafnis or someone else functioned as translator, I cannot guarantee the accuracy of the translation. I have kept all of the recordings, so if there is ever a question about wording, I have the interview. I doubt that anyone will ever challenge the translations, but know that I have striven for complete accuracy in all of my uses of interviews.

Certain aspects of Dafnis's personality and life repeatedly emerged from the interviews. Over and over, we heard how wonderful he was—how he loved people regardless of their ethnic backgrounds or their places in society. His love for others and desire to help them revealed much about the man. People were attracted to his charismatic personality. He loved to tell stories and be the center of attention. But he was also adept at doing menial tasks for others in a selfless manner. His tireless advocacy for foreign workers endeared him to those he saved from abusive employers. He cared about the welfare of others, and he expended considerable time and money seeking to help them have a better life.

Dafnis also loved the environment. He was an unabashed tree hugger and lover of all things natural. His idealism and innovative ideas provided major motivation for environmental movements in Cyprus. At a meeting of the Cyprus Sustainability Initiative in Paphos in 2017, we witnessed grateful leaders of the Initiative present Dafnis with an award designating him as the Father of Environmentalism in Cyprus. His tireless efforts resulted in an enlightened environmental movement on the island. He sought to provide a better life for island residents—both human and otherwise. All life was sacred for Dafnis.

Listening to and recording the oral accounts given by Dafnis and his friends was an enriching experience. We learned a great deal, and because we asked many questions, some things came to light that even his long-time friends did not know. One of Dafnis's friends who read the book manuscript wrote the following response:

> Your work is a real gift about a unique life that is reminiscent of a contemporary Odysseus.... Reading your book made me nostalgic of the great encounters with our friend, even though like you he caused us to feel exasperated! But I do feel that our life has been richer by knowing this colorful character. Thanks for doing it. I am amazed at the details you uncovered in such a relatively short time making it so lively for the reader —particularly for those of us who knew him. I learned so much about Dafnis that I did not know before no matter how much time we spent

> with him.... So, Michael, thank you for the great gift you gave us all with your study of the "The life and times of Dafnis Panagides."

Indeed, Dafnis was wonderfully loveable, and studying his life has enriched ours. As you read his biography, you will encounter a complex and contradictory individual whose stories provide inspiration for pondering the best ways we can pass our years on planet earth—lovingly caring for the earth and all of its inhabitants. Such was Dafnis's motto. Such was his legacy.

Michael Cosby
February 2022

Acknowledgements

Stories told by Dafnis himself form the backbone of my narrative; but without the input of numerous individuals, I would not have been able to do justice to his biography. I am grateful to Kyriacos Markides for introducing me to Dafnis in 2011 when I journeyed to Cyprus to conduct research on St. Barnabas. His introduction ultimately resulted in a deep friendship between Dafnis and my wife, Lynne, and me. In 2017, we spent *many* hours listening to Dafnis tell stories of his long and influential life. He introduced us to his children and cousins and friends, all of whom were incredibly gracious and helpful. His son, Thales, repeatedly gave of himself in such practical ways. He became a close confidant and has remained a great source of encouragement as I have labored over telling the life story of his father. I owe him a large debt of gratitude. Thales's lovely Brazilian wife, Glauci, was also quite hospitable and helpful.

While we were in Cyprus, Dafnis's second daughter, Louisa, and her husband, Antonis, often invited us to join family dinners hosted in their home on Sundays. Louisa is a great cook known for her hospitality. She also made available to us a large number of family photos she has collected. Oldest daughter, Lydia, provided important family information and also discovered a collection of letters that Dafnis and his wife, Maroula, wrote to each other while he was in a British detention camp. These letters added a dimension to our understanding that we did not gain from recorded interviews. Lydia's husband, Pantelis, is often the life of a party, leading in singing songs.

We did not meet Dafnis's youngest daughter, Dora, and her husband, Michael, until 2019. Unlike her siblings, Dora does not live in Cyprus. But she and Michael recently purchased a home near Limassol; so in the not-too-distant future, all the siblings will live in the same general area of their beautiful island homeland. Lynne and I extend our thanks for the way Dafnis's children treated us as adopted members of their family. Thanks to all of them for their valuable feedback on my biography of Dafnis.

In the summer of 2017, we got to know Dafnis's brother, Stahis, and his wife, Joy. We are grateful for their friendship and hospitality—and for what they taught us about the Panagides family. In 2019, we stayed with them in their home in the small village of Kalo Chorio, located in the mountains north of Limassol. Years ago, Joy had organized a major renovation of their house, so that it retains the external appearance of a traditional village structure but inside has modern amenities. We slept downstairs in a bedroom that once was a stall for the family donkey.

On our numerous trips with Dafnis, we met and interviewed his cousins. All were warmly hospitable and gracious. They shared stories about Dafnis and

Maroula and included us in various community events. In particular, Petros and Androula Petrides are delightful hosts, and Petros provided a detailed genealogy he wrote of the descendants of Michalis Petrides, grandfather of Dafnis and Petros. We spent special time with Petrakis and Koralia Ioannides at their home in Kalo Chorio, and they kindly gave tickets to us for a concert performed by a choir in which they sing.

Thanks to Dafnis's dear companion, Maria, for her hospitality and for often serving as driver on our excursions around Cyprus. She and Dafnis shared a deep love for the environment and were both marvelous sources of information about the plants, animals, and ecology of Cyprus.

Dafnis introduced us to various friends, some of whom we met at meals served in his home. Conversations with these people provided insights into Dafnis and Cypriot history and culture. The meals we ate at Dafnis's house were prepared by Vietnamese women whom he allowed to stay in his home as a place of refuge from abusive Cypriot employers. These women gratefully called Dafnis "Daddy."

Elfrida Calvocoressi made a special trip from London to Cyprus to tell us stories about the long-standing friendship between Dafnis and her husband, Roy, a peace activist who deeply influenced Dafnis's thinking on conflict resolution and peacemaking. Elfrida also located correspondence between Dafnis and Roy and allowed me to scan these documents and use quotations from them in my book.

Thanks to Joseph Farah, long-time friend and colleague of Dafnis. Joseph was generous with us in practical ways that facilitated our work on Dafnis's life story. We also enjoyed outings with him. Our trip to Omodos and the ancient Venetian Kelefos Bridge was quite a lovely excursion.

Katy Goldsmith met Dafnis in 1954 when she attended an ecumenical work camp at Kakomallis led by Dafnis. She became a life-long friend of the Panagides family, and she graciously shared scans of letters she wrote to her parents in 1954—letters that paint vivid word pictures of her experiences in Cyprus.

Thanks to Andreas Karyos, historian and Director of The National Struggle Museum in Nicosia, for helping me to understand events that occurred during the years of the EOKA rebellion—especially important aspects of Dafnis's relationship with Andreas's grandfather, Andreas, after whom he is named. Thanks also to Renos Lyssiotis for sharing important insights into the circumstances of Dafnis's arrest and detention by British forces in the 1950s. Renos, who earned his law degree in London, was arrested by the British shortly after they arrested Dafnis. He and Dafnis shared a cell at the Omorfita interrogation/torture center. The two men became friends during their incarceration. Renos kept meticulous notes on conditions in the detention camp.

Thanks to the following people who read all or part of the book manuscript and provided suggestions for improving the text: Dafnis's children (Lydia, Louisa,

Dora, and Thales), Stahis and Joy Panagides, Kyriacos and Emily Markides, Michael Chommie, Kathryn Jacobsen, Dennis Plies, Wayne Cosby, Rick Granger, Douglas and Rhonda Jacobsen, Bob Gorinski, Terri Smiley, Beth Mark, Laurie Babcock, and Beth Transue. Receiving diverse comments from people representing different backgrounds allowed me to glimpse different responses readers have to the story of Dafnis and thereby modify my narrative for greater clarity.

Most of all, thanks to my wife, Lynne—freelance editor extraordinaire—for the hours she spent editing the manuscript. We read the text out loud to each other several times, because we know that ears often catch things the eyes do not. I have no idea how many hours we spent together discussing what to add, what to delete, what changes would make the narrative flow better, and how readers might understand the meaning of particular sentences. Few books have had more thorough scrutiny than *The Storyteller from Kalo Chorio.*

We thank Dafnis's family and friends for their warm hospitality and for making our stays in Cyprus a source of pleasant memories and opportunities for learning about their culture. Know that we appreciate you even if your name is not in this list. Our lives have been enriched by all these encounters.

CHAPTER 1
Trying to Catch the Wind

A Dark and Stormy Day

At dawn's first light the dead man's son contemplated the dark clouds and heavy downpour: *This weather certainly sets a somber tone for the day.* A few hours later, however, his sister reminded him that, according to local customs, rain on the day of a funeral indicates the death of a good person. On the arid, Eastern Mediterranean island of Cyprus, rainfall is almost always considered a blessing, and the rainy winter of 2018–2019 ended a decades-long drought.

A meaningful life deserves to be commemorated, and the ominous weather did not prevent 700 people from packing the Orthodox Church of the Holy Trinity in Limassol, Cyprus. Numerous dignitaries, relatives, and friends gathered to bid farewell to a man who helped and befriended a multitude of people. After they were all in the church, the rain abated. The funeral resembled the changing weather, combining somber elements and light-hearted reminiscences. During the memorial service, son-in-law Michael began his eulogy on a sad note by saying,

> Daphnis Solomon Panagides… passed away in his sleep. He was just days away from turning 90. We were set to celebrate this milestone with him in Cyprus, along with the concurrent launch of his book. Instead, we had to cajole Aegean Airlines to allow us to fly earlier so we can attend his funeral service in Limassol… . We are still in a state of shock, but look forward to celebrating his life with family and his legions of friends, admirers, and maybe even a foe or two.

Michael concluded his eulogy with a remark that elicited knowing laughter from the crowd.

> Even the most exquisite Persian carpets have a flaw and Daphnis had one as well: he was a lousy driver! He would constantly cheat death by barreling through single lane mountain roads with one hand on the wheel and the other on a comically large cellphone. I was certain he would die in a car accident. Instead he left us quietly, in his sleep.

Those who knew Dafnis well could point out flaws in addition to reckless driving that were woven into the complex tapestry of his life. On several occasions, he said to me, "I am no saint."

Dafnis had granted my wife and me permission to write his life story and had given us unlimited access to his life—well, sort of. He was open yet also guarded in what he told us during the many hours of interviews we recorded. Always an aura of mystery surrounded him. Always we had to speculate on how much he told us was truthful and how much was simply what he wanted us to believe. He agreed with advice I have heard on occasion from my oldest son: "Dad, never let truth get in the way of telling a good story." How do you write the biography of a man who deliberately obscures details of his life? Cautiously.

Can you know a man by his friends?

During the funeral, an astounding sixteen Greek Orthodox clergy, including bishops, monks and priests, participated in the liturgy; and the diversity of the assembled mourners illustrated the breadth of Dafnis's influence. Numerous high-ranking officials attended the funeral, including politicians representing opposing views. Right wing Greek Cypriot nationalists came to pay their respects. Left leaning, atheist Communists openly grieved his passing. Members of the Baha'i faith were among his good friends gathered at Holy Trinity. Even Turkish Muslims from the occupied northern third of Cyprus drove through fortified checkpoints to come and pay their respects to this man who looked past simmering ethnic hostilities to embrace the common humanity of both Greeks and Turks. The variety of people in the church that rainy winter day reflected Dafnis's amazing ability to foster friendships with individuals regardless of their beliefs or ethnic backgrounds.

Others longed to attend the funeral but could not. Vietnamese and Filipino workers with questionable legal status in Cypriot society deeply felt the loss of a man who worked tirelessly to protect foreign workers from abuse by unscrupulous employers. When the women's shelter he helped to establish was full, Dafnis allowed some abused women to live in his home, sheltering them from the circumstances they had fled and from a legal system that would readily deport them for not remaining in their designated places of employment. These women, who called Dafnis "Daddy," were frightened to attend the funeral for fear of exposure. Suddenly, their world had changed. What would happen to them now that he was dead? Where would they go?

My wife, Lynne, and I had concocted an elaborate plan with Dafnis's children to journey to Cyprus without his knowledge so that we could surprise him at his 90th birthday party. His younger brother, Stahis, had made even more intricate plans to appear unexpectedly at the celebration. Instead, Dafnis surprised us. On 5 February, he died in his sleep of thrombosis. We learned about his death the following day.

After we received the shocking news, we asked ourselves, "What shall we do? Shall we cancel our trip to Cyprus or go for a very different purpose than we anticipated?" We could not change our travel arrangements to be able to attend the funeral. In a somber conversation with Stahis in Bethesda, I asked, "What do you suggest?" As the new patriarch of the Panagides clan, he more ordered than advised, "Stay the course." As adopted members of the family, we obeyed. And, although we missed the funeral, we heard detailed reports from a number who attended.

Only love Remains

In a eulogy delivered during the funeral, Dafnis's son, Thales, quoted part of a chat he had with a woman named Sofia in Kalo Chorio, the mountain village where Dafnis was born: "At the end of our conversation, she concluded by saying, 'μόνο η αγάπη παραμένει, τίποτα άλλο.' 'Only love remains, nothing else.'" Her words echoed the philosophy of the man in the casket. Thales gazed at the crowd of mourners and said, "I look at you all and I see people from all walks of life—different races, religions and beliefs. You've all come to pay your respects to a man who loved people unconditionally. As one of his friends said, 'He said yes to everybody.'" The most memorable moment for Thales came when a friend approached and, instead of saying "My condolences," said "Congratulations for having such a magnificent father."

At the gravesite later that day, while 100 people gathered around the tomb, a group of wizened warriors—Dafnis's elderly comrades in arms—spontaneously broke into patriotic songs. These members of EOKA (*Ethniki Organosis Kyprion Agoniston* or National Organization of Cypriot Fighters), survivors of the 1955 to 1959 bloody fight for liberation from British colonial rule of Cyprus, sang nationalistic songs from their youth. Tears filled the eyes of some mourners gathered around the grave as they listened. Others, however, considered the songs to be completely inappropriate. Following the rebellion against Great Britain, Dafnis had become a pacifist, rejecting all forms of violence. What would he have thought about his old friends singing stirring, militaristic songs? Would he have enjoyed them or been alarmed? Or both?

Dafnis's friends represented diverse religious and political perspectives, and he adeptly navigated these differences. He tried to treat all people with dignity, even those who annoyed and frustrated him. Yes, he could deliver sharp verbal confrontations, but people knew he cared deeply for other human beings.

A master storyteller, Dafnis often was the center of attention at social gatherings. People enjoyed being in his presence, even though his free-spirited lack of concern with schedules frequently frustrated them. It is safe to say that, if possible, Dafnis would have been late for his own funeral—or he might have just decided on the spur of the moment not to come.

Mediterranean Mayhem

Kyriacos Markides, a Cypriot sociologist at the University of Maine, introduced us to Dafnis. In 2011, in preparation for my journey to Cyprus to conduct research on the Apostle Barnabas, I had read Kyriacos's *The Mountain of Silence* (New York: Doubleday, 2002), and I had emailed him to say how much I learned about Eastern Orthodoxy from his fascinating book. He thanked me for my endorsement and forwarded my email to Dafnis as a means of putting the two of us into contact. Kyriacos explained that Dafnis was the character Lavros in *The Mountain of Silence.*

Markides told me Dafnis Panagides was the son of a priest, was part of the violent Cypriot resistance movement against the British in the 1950s, was elected to the first parliament of the Republic of Cyprus in 1960, was a pioneer in environmental protection of the island, was well connected with Eastern Orthodox monastics, and was a personal friend of Athanasios, Bishop of Limassol, as well as Chrysostomos II, Archbishop of Cyprus. Dignitaries like the president of Cyprus regularly called Dafnis to get his input on political matters. Obviously, such details influenced my preconceptions of the man.

On 9 August 2011, I sent the following email to Dafnis.

> I have just finished reading a very kind email from Kyriacos Markides, in which he advised me to contact you. I understand that he forwarded my message to you regarding my research on St. Barnabas. As I was reading *The Mountain of Silence*, I remember thinking that Lavros must be an interesting man. I did not consider the possibility that I might meet him (you).
>
> My wife and I look forward to our time in Cyprus and all that we will learn during our stay. Any advice that you have for me will be deeply appreciated.... From what Kyriacos said about your involvement in politics during the tumultuous 1960s, you must be a gold mine of information about Cypriot politics as well as theology. I look forward to talking with you personally—perhaps over a cup of tea.

Designating Dates

To conform to the European way of specifying dates that Cypriots employ, I follow their form of giving first the day, then the month, and then the year. It keeps notation consistent with their correspondence and speech patterns.

His response was warm and inviting—and went well beyond merely having a cup of tea.

> How wonderful, in these unrestful times, to meet people like you! Thank you for your email but let me say that Kyriakos in his enthusiasm may have said things which stimulated your expectations of how helpful I may be to your research.

> Of course I look forward to meet you and your wife, not over a cup of tea, but over a full Mediterranean meal, here in my house in Limassol.... I shall put you in touch with key personalities in the Church, the Monastic and the Academic environments, who, I believe will provide you with valuable information for your research.

I smiled as I read the words "a full Mediterranean meal here in my house."

After we had been in Cyprus a short time, I emailed Dafnis—and waited a few days. I called his phone number and left a message—and waited a few more days. Dafnis finally returned my call and cheerfully invited Lynne and me to visit him in Limassol and spend a night at his house. He seemed very busy for a man his age. His invitation seemed unusual by our cultural standards, because he knew little about us. But we had previously experienced such generous hospitality elsewhere in the Middle East. We would later learn that Dafnis frequently entertained guests in his home. His generosity was almost legendary—even by Mediterranean standards, where their model of hospitality extends to all aspects of life, not just the "offer the visitors a cup of coffee" model typical in the United States.

The day finally came for us to meet Dafnis. On Friday, 2 September 2011, Lynne and I stood in the mid-day heat outside a McDonalds near the motorway in Limassol, our overnight bags perched on the sidewalk. We fidgeted as we waited for Dafnis to pick us up at a prearranged time and take us to his home. He was late. Had he forgotten? Were we at the wrong McDonalds? Should we be worried? While we baked in the sun, pondering our options, I felt sweat trickling down my back. And I noticed beads of perspiration on Lynne's face.

As seasoned travelers, we are flexible in other cultures. But we had been in Cyprus less than two weeks, and everything still seemed strange. Furthermore, the woman who had driven us to Limassol from Nicosia looked annoyed. She was part of a small caravan of vehicles transporting professors and students to an archaeological dig in Paphos. The other cars were already en route to Paphos, but she was reluctant to leave before Dafnis came. She stood in the heat, glancing at her watch, impatiently waiting for an 82-year-old man to arrive in his SUV.

Suddenly, a mud-spattered Mitsubishi 4x4 stopped near where we were standing. The driver did not bother to pull into a parking space; he stopped behind parked cars. The vehicle looked like it had been on an off-road excursion and returned to Limassol with several pounds of dirt stuck to it. A scruffy man wearing rumpled clothes got out and walked toward us. Several days of white stubble decorated his face around his goatee. Our driver and Lynne looked nervously at me and then at the elderly man. I smiled in the direction of Mr. Scruffy, and he broke into a wide grin. "You must be Michael and Lynne Cosby. I am Dafnis Panagides." His warmth and confidence did not match his appearance. I immediately noticed a trace of humor. Laughter lurked behind those eyes—and something else. What was this amiable old man thinking as he sized up two Americans with sweat running down their faces?

Our driver from Nicosia soon slipped inside her clean, small sedan, backed out of her parking space, and disappeared into Limassol traffic. With a grand little flourish, Dafnis gestured toward his muddy Mitsubishi. He had fashioned seat covers out of old T-shirts, so each seat looked like it was wearing a T-shirt with a headrest poking out of the neck hole. We grabbed our overnight bags and climbed into the vehicle. Out of long habit, we automatically fastened our seat belts. Good thing! Dafnis roared out of the McDonalds parking lot and onto the motorway, heading toward his home—wherever that was—careening east on Highway A6.

Cypriots are fairly laid back people—until they get behind the wheel of an automobile. At that point they morph into a different species. True, they are not as dangerous as drivers in some other Mediterranean countries. Taking a taxi in Cairo, Egypt, is a terrifying experience. And we seriously wondered once while in a taxi in Turkey if our two sons would soon be reading our wills. Dafnis was not that extreme, but he had this way of weaving through traffic while talking rapidly, gesturing wildly with both hands, and periodically fumbling around trying to find his mobile phone when it blared a variety of tunes. I gripped the armrest and kept my feet wide on the floorboard to steady myself as we sped down crowded streets filled with other drivers behaving like Dafnis. Motorcyclists, with barely enough space between cars to squeeze through, maneuvered to the front of the line at stoplights—leaning left and right to avoid hitting rearview mirrors. When they reached the stoplights, they often did not wait for a green signal. If they could proceed, they did. I winced as I watched the Mediterranean mayhem.

An Island of Green in a Sea of Cement

I relaxed when Dafnis turned onto a quiet street and parked his SUV in a narrow enclosure by an old, Cypriot farmhouse surrounded by a multitude of trees and bushes. His property looked like an island of green in a sea of cement. Apartment buildings and commercial shops crowded in on his home—a solitary relic from an earlier era. In 1955 when his father purchased the farm, this house was isolated. The outskirts of Limassol lay well to the west. Now Limassol has engulfed the land that once was their farm, and the city limits extend far to the east of the old farmhouse. Metropolitan Limassol has a population of around 240,000 people and is growing steadily.

Dafnis explained that he was an agronomist, and he pointed out some of the exotic plants that proliferated around his house. "This one is from South Africa. I got it when I was there on my 80th birthday trip. This beauty is from Saudi Arabia, and this one is from Brazil." Tucked under some bushes was a small sign that read, "Beware. Turtle Area Ahead." As we listened to him speak, we quickly became aware of Dafnis's infectious sense of humor.

Figure 1. *Dafnis's house is nestled in the trees, a green island surrounded by modern apartment buildings. Note the common Cypriot practice of parking cars partly on sidewalks to compensate for the narrow roads.* ***Color versions of all photos available at michaelrcosby.com/storyteller/photos***

Sitting on his veranda drinking tea, shaded by vegetation, we felt a sense of seclusion—except for the constant traffic noise from a busy street nearby. Dafnis enjoyed telling stories about his experiences during the tumultuous 1950s, including the fact that Colonel Grivas hid from British troops for three months in a room dug under Dafnis's machine shop near the house. Once, while talking in his office, he pointed to the chair on which Lynne was sitting and said, "Many times Grivas sat in that very chair." He casually mentioned that British soldiers arrested and tortured him, and then incarcerated him in detention camps for almost three years. Pointing to the chirping birds in a large birdcage on the veranda, he said,

> My father, Solomon, loved birds, and he always kept a variety of them in that cage. He enjoyed watching them and listening to them sing. Just before the British granted independence to Cyprus in 1960, they freed us detainees from their concentration camps. I rode a bus home from Nicosia, and the driver stopped here at the house. When I stepped off the bus, my father opened the aviary and let all his birds go free.

Tears wet his eyes as he recounted his father's symbolic act. Lynne and I got tears in our eyes as we listened to the story and pictured the scene in our minds.

For the rest of that day, Dafnis regaled us with stories. I realized that he was a living witness to the modern history of Cyprus, which I had been studying for months. He explained that, after independence, voters elected him to serve in the first parliament of the Republic of Cyprus. But his former comrades in arms began fighting each other for power. Dafnis grew weary of polarized politics as the new republic spiraled downward. He wanted out.

He mentioned doing graduate work in agronomy at Iowa State University, recounted some funny incidents about working among Bedouin in Saudi Arabia, and he told a hysterical story about sitting next to Colonel Sanders on an airplane. During the days we spent with Dafnis, we listened to an almost non-stop

Figure 2. *The author with Dafnis at his Limassol home in 2011.*

recitation of his fascinating experiences. We realized that we were only scratching the surface of an amazing life journey, and his stories kindled our curiosity about where all Dafnis had lived and what all he had done. We also realized that this old man did not merely sit around reminiscing. He mentioned driving to the Ayia Napa area the previous week with a lawyer. Together, they were involved in a court case, seeking justice for two women who were foreign workers being mistreated by their Cypriot employer. Dafnis was busy. The mud on his Mitsubishi resulted from a recent excursion into the Troodos Mountains, where he had lead a group of people on a camping trip to teach them about ecology—pretty ambitious for an 82-year-old man.

Ice Cream and Feral Cats

Dafnis said that his wife, Maroula, died in 2002; and he admitted he was so slovenly as a widower his children decided he must have a housekeeper. They hired Vicki, a Filipina who did an efficient job of cooking and taking care of the house. She affectionately called Dafnis "Daddy." One afternoon, we heard her animated conversation via Skype with her husband and four children, ages six through sixteen. She only got to return home every year or two, yet she seemed happy to support her family with the wages she earned from Dafnis.

Following a nice dinner served by Vicki, Dafnis led us on a leisurely walk to the nearby Mediterranean Sea. "I want to take you to a café by the seashore to get ice cream," he said. "A friend of mine owns it, and the setting is nice." As we walked toward an empty table, he stopped to say "Hello" to a cousin who was sitting with a Greek Cypriot couple from Wisconsin. We enjoyed eating ice cream and listening to the waves lap against the shore as Dafnis entertained us with more stories of his younger days.

Dafnis summoned the waitress, pointed to his cousin, and said, "Tell the three people at that table to order whatever dessert or drink they want, and I am paying for it." A few minutes later, the waitress returned and said to Dafnis, "Sorry, but the gentleman at the other table has already paid their bill and has also paid for your ice cream." The cousin flashed a satisfied smile and waved. Dafnis blushed and waved back. The whole hilarious event illustrates Cypriot generosity. Paying bills at restaurants is a competitive sport that Dafnis rarely lost.

As we walked back to his home, we startled cats scavenging trashcans, and they scampered away. Others, hissing and growling over garbage, paid no attention to us. I hesitate to estimate how many feral cats roam the streets of Cyprus. When we reached Dafnis's house, he bid us good night. "I get up early," he said. "So I am going to bed." By early, he meant 4:00 or 5:00 a.m. We had no intention of arising that early. I turned on the little air conditioner in our bedroom to drown out the nocturnal screeching of feline disputes so that we could sleep.

Meeting an Indian and a Monk

While we were eating breakfast the next morning, an Indian man called Sami stopped by the house. Dafnis had met Sami, whose actual name is *Swaminathan*, in Saudi Arabia in 1989. Sami told us with a heavy Indian accent that he was starving in Saudi Arabia, because his wealthy employer refused to pay his wages for long periods of time. Unfortunately, abuse of foreign workers by Saudis is common. But Dafnis, who worked for a prince of the royal family, used his influence to liberate Sami and get him back to India. Later he arranged employment for him in Cyprus. Sami called Dafnis *Baba* and named his first son after his beloved benefactor. He proudly told us, "My son is the only man in southern India named Dafnis." Evidently, Dafnis had been involved in a lot more than agricultural work. And from what Dafnis said about his friends who were Orthodox clergy, it was clear that Eastern Orthodoxy was an important feature of his worldview. Because of my research project, Dafnis announced that he would take Lynne and me to speak with a monk so I could ask questions regarding Orthodox beliefs about Barnabas.

He did not simply give us directions to the monastery and wish us well. He insisted on taking us personally to introduce us to his friend, Father Gennadios, and to function as our translator. Dafnis drove his muddy Mitsubishi 4x4 into the hills north of Limassol to the Holy Monastery of Archangel Michael where we had our first experience of interviewing an Eastern Orthodox monk trained in the traditions of Mt. Athos, the center for archaic Orthodox spirituality. Gennadios explained that humans cannot *understand* God; we can only *experience* God by practicing spiritual disciplines, through which we become more like God through a process called *Theosis*. He was critical of the attempt by Catholic theologians to explain God's attributes. He was even more critical of Protestant health and prosperity teachings and insisted that suffering is a vital part of becoming like God.

After our fascinating interview of Fr. Gennadios, Dafnis drove back to his house and took his daily nap. While he slept, Lynne and I discussed our trip to the Monastery of Archangel Michael and what we heard about Eastern Orthodoxy. Later that afternoon, Dafnis drove us to a nearby bus stop where we waited for a bus to Nicosia. Finally it came. We arrived in Nicosia late that evening, and then we walked approximately eight blocks to the archaeological center where we lived. Even at night, we remained alert when crossing streets.

Cypriots drive on the left—fast. If you forget this fact, you might step in front of a vehicle speeding down the street; because you are looking the other way out of habit, expecting cars to be driven on the right. Driving on the left is one of many differences between Cyprus and the United States. We embraced and appreciated the norms of the culture in which we temporarily resided and realized that what seems normal to us might be quite foreign to our new friends. We did not want to be whiny Americans, insisting that the way

Dilemma of transferring Greek Words to English

Transliterating Greek names into equivalent English sounds is problematic. The Greek *phi* (ϕ) used to be transliterated into English with a "ph," but more commonly today an "f" is used. Modern maps of Greece read Del*f*i instead of Del*phi*, and Greek Cypriots pronounce the town *Thelfi* (th sound as in *then*, not as in *thermal).* To avoid confusion for English readers, I use "d" for *delta*, "g" for *gamma*, and so forth, even though this approach does not match the way Cypriots pronounce words. They give the gamma (γ) a "y" sound, and the delta (δ) a "th" sound. Consequently, for the name Dafnis Panagides (Δάφνης Παναγίδης), Cypriots usually say *Thafnis Panayides*. They pronounce *Gennadios as Yen-nÁ-the-ōs* (the a sounds like the a in father). Such linguistic changes are common. For example, English speakers form the sounds for both *t* and *d* by placing the tongue against the ridge behind the front teeth. I tend to pronounce *seventy* as *sevendy*, but I never say *twendy* for *twenty*. The *th* sound is made by placing the tongue against the back of the front teeth. Thus, the transition from a *d* to a *th* involves a minor change in tongue placement.

things are done back home is the way things *ought* to be done. My one exception to that rule was complaining about crazy drivers.

Warrior and Peacemaker

When we returned to the United States, we kept in touch with our new friends in Cyprus, especially Dafnis. Although we had not spent a lot of time with him when we were living in Nicosia and I was conducting research on Barnabas, we considered him to be the most interesting person we had met during our four months in Cyprus. My research as a Fulbright Fellow focused on how, over centuries of time, leaders in the Eastern Orthodox Church had transformed Barnabas from a peacemaker in the early church to a warrior saint for modern, Greek Cypriots. I painstakingly tracked down how a leader known for formulating creative solutions to ethnic tensions in the early Christian movement became a champion for one ethnic group—a saint to whom Greek Cypriots pray to expel Turks from the island.

The contrast between Barnabas and Dafnis intrigued me. Barnabas the peacemaker was co-opted for political purposes and converted into a warrior saint. Dafnis, on the other hand, fought against the occupying British forces when he was a young man, but later he became a pacifist and renounced all violence. He concluded that Jesus' command to love your enemies precluded killing them. Dafnis transformed from a warrior to a peacemaker—the opposite of what happened in Orthodox traditions with St. Barnabas.

My curiosity grew. What transformed Dafnis? Did his transformation in any way affect the modern history of Cyprus? At that time, I knew only a few details about Dafnis's involvement in the freedom struggle against England in the 1950s, his work as an elected representative of the first parliament of the Republic of Cyprus in the 1960s, his academic studies in the United States, his work among the Bedouin in Saudi Arabia, and his activism against human trafficking in Cyprus. I knew nothing about his young life. I did not yet know that, during his retirement years, he accomplished more for his country than he had during all his previous working life. But I knew enough to be convinced that his diverse experiences were worth exploring for life lessons.

As I pondered my next sabbatical, I wanted to do something outside my specialty of New Testament scholarship. Taking on new challenges appeals to me, and that tendency had inspired my research on Barnabas. One morning, as Lynne and I were drinking Cyprus frappé, she asked what I wanted to do for a sabbatical research project. I set down my cup and said, "Honestly, I would like to write a biography of Dafnis Panagides." She did not expect that pronouncement, but she had been pestering me to return to Cyprus; so my idea thrilled her. Foremost in my mind was the question of what members of the faculty committee responsible for awarding sabbaticals would think about a New Testament scholar seeking to write the biography of a Cypriot peace activist. I needed a compelling proposal for this project. I needed to study methodology pertaining to researching and writing oral history. But first, I had to gain consent from Dafnis.

I emailed Dafnis and told him that I would like to write his biography, because I believed his life story would provide valuable insights for readers. I told him I understood that my request placed him in the awkward position of having foreigners scrutinize his life. It would require him to spend many hours with us recording interviews. I recommended that he take his time making a decision and discuss the matter with his family members and with Fr. Gennadios, his spiritual father. I heard nothing from Dafnis for weeks, and I feared he would say, "No." But one morning, there was a message from him. He had spoken at length with Fr. Gennadios, who encouraged him to grant permission. He also discussed the matter with his children, because a biography might affect them. He was nervous about the whole project, but "Yes." He would do it.

Good. Next, I had to convince the faculty committee that my research project was worthy of a sabbatical. They endorsed my proposal. Then the real work began.

Chaotic Return to Cyprus

In preparation for returning to Cyprus, we needed to rent a flat (an apartment). Dafnis assured us that he would find a reasonable place for us to stay in Limassol. We appreciated his desire to help, but we discovered that only looming deadlines motivated him. As our departure date approached, he

"Coffee Time"

A habit we adopted while living at the Cyprus American Archaeological Research Institute (CAARI) in Nicosia is taking a break mid-morning. Around 10:30 a.m., Phodoulla would step into the library and announce, "Coffee time." We would all move to the lobby, where Phodoulla served each of us whichever form of coffee we requested. It was a time for free-flowing conversations about whatever topics arose—great for camaraderie and keeping up with each other's research. I *never* drank coffee before our time in Cyprus. I did not like the bitter taste. But the director of CAARI had warned me *not* to offend the CAARI staff by refusing their coffee. On our first day at the center, I listened carefully to my choices. I wanted to avoid the strong Cyprus coffee served in small cups, something Lynne loves. I decided to try Cyprus frappé, because it was cold and half milk—which I figured would dilute the bitterness. Phodoulla delivered her artistic frappé with its distinct layers due to frothing the water, coffee, and sugar before adding the milk. I discovered that I actually enjoyed the drink, and it became my staple during "Coffee time." Indeed, I still drink a frappé most mornings during a coffee break that Lynne and I enjoy together.

suddenly became intent on finding a flat. Every few days he had a new idea of where we should stay. We would prepare to rent a flat, but then Dafnis would say, "Wait! I found something better." Finally, he wrote to say that he had lunch with a Cypriot woman who lived in Washington, D.C. She owned a flat close to his house that she only used a few months each summer. He told her that she should rent it to us for our stay during fall 2017. Dafnis could be very persuasive. She agreed to meet us for lunch in Maryland, and only then did she feel comfortable about renting her property to strangers. We signed a rental agreement and began to focus on other trip details.

Of the tasks we needed to accomplish in preparation for an extended stay abroad, the most vexing was convincing Dafnis to provide a list of the people we should interview. I wanted names and contact information prior to our departure, so that I could write to these people and explain the nature of our research on Dafnis's life. I wished to provide advance notice so they could let me know whether or not they wanted to participate in the oral history project. It would maximize what we could accomplish during our limited stay on the island. But the list never came. Indeed, Dafnis did not begin to assemble a list until *after* we arrived in Limassol. We tried not to be anxious about what was not happening.

Adjusting expectations is always challenging. We had learned from our stay in Cyprus in 2011 that relationships were an important first step toward getting anything done. We would meet someone who had a friend who knew someone who could help us with gathering information about a particular matter. All my Barnabas research progress except for what I did in the library in Nicosia came as a result of developing relationships. We met Fr. Gabriel, the abbot of the Monastery of Apostle Barnabas, because the battery on Lynne's MacBook died and we had to go to an Apple store in Nicosia to get the battery replaced. The shop owner knew someone who was a spiritual child of Fr. Gabriel, and he called this man—who owned the Chevrolet dealership a block away—and arranged for us to meet him. That man then called a lawyer friend of his who set up a meeting with Fr. Gabriel. And Fr. Gabriel directed one of his spiritual children to drive us to the Monastery of Apostle Barnabas. Such relationship-based contacts opened doors for my research.

Now, however, with the oral history project, Dafnis was the self-appointed funnel through which *everything* flowed—or didn't flow. He had an amazing number of friends and contacts, and his personal influence was essential for our work. Because of my time as a Fulbright Fellow in 2011, we knew the island and had grown to love the culture. The frustration in 2017 was that we could not control our schedule. We met wonderful people and had delightful experiences. We learned a great deal about Dafnis's life—and we did a lot of waiting on Dafnis. Transcribing all of the interviews after we returned home was time intensive. Assembling the information into a coherent sequence was a massive undertaking. What kept us moving ahead on the project was our goal of telling the story of a man who made a difference in his country by the way he lived. Given the end result, I am tempted to say our time was *well spent*; but as Dafnis asserted, my western concept of *spending time* is out of sync with the Mediterranean concept of *passing time*. "Time," he said, "is not a commodity to be purchased or sold."

Trying to Catch the Wind

During the months we spent in Cyprus conducting interviews, we had to cope with Dafnis's chaotic lifestyle. He greeted each day with his spontaneous approach to life. His plans constantly adjusted to events that arose. What he said we would do and what we actually did often differed dramatically. One problem was his mobile phone—with which he had a love/hate relationship. Many people called him, and he was notorious for not answering. He described some of his friends as *TW*s—Time Wasters: "I have better things to do than spend all day talking with these people." But his children voiced the same complaint about his not answering his "mobile."

Dafnis ignored calls if he wanted to focus on a sudden trip he decided to make to a field in the foothills to fix an irrigation pipe or go to the airport near Larnaca to pick up someone—or maybe he got a message from a friend in Ayia Napa or Paphos, so he dropped everything to drive across the island to see that person. Cyprus has a maximum length of about 150 miles (east to west) and a maximum

Figure 3. *Dafnis, an accomplished storyteller, enjoyed an audience.*

width of about 60 miles (north to south). He could go west from Limassol to Paphos in about an hour, or east from Limassol to Ayia Napa in less than an hour and a half; so he thought nothing of such spur-of-the-moment trips. We soon realized that he knew numerous people in government, and it was not unusual for the president of Cyprus or the archbishop to call him to confer about something. Of course, he answered phone calls from these individuals. Usually.

After we arrived in Cyprus in August and began recording interviews, Dafnis decided to eliminate the distraction of people calling and emailing and dropping by his house to visit. So, he sent a message to hundreds of people saying that he would not be available for three months. But he could not stick to that plan. His habits were too deeply ingrained. He tried to set up a schedule, but conforming to it restricted his lifestyle. Our attempts to organize interviews failed. To schedule Dafnis was like trying to restrain the wind. We entered his whirlwind life and quit worrying about how much we were not accomplishing.

We wanted to gather more material about Dafnis's activities after he retired and returned home from Saudi Arabia. But EOKA loomed large in his memory, and many of his friends whom he had us interview spoke at length about their EOKA experiences. Those years from 1955 to 1959 occupy an immense place in their memories. Therefore, we have more information about that brief time period than we do about most of the rest of Dafnis's life. Nevertheless, we were able to capture the multiple textures of his complicated lifespan. What emerged is a fascinating portrait of an intelligent, imaginative, creative, persistent, generous, endearing, flawed, and frustrating individual who by his actions made a lasting impact on Cyprus. Reflecting on the positive contributions of his disorganized life reveals that, for him, the Western concept of time management is largely irrelevant.

Spending Time versus *Passing* Time

Our months in Cyprus demanded modification of our attitude toward time. The relationship-based approach to life and business in Cyprus continually frustrated my need for a schedule and a plan for completing my research. So did Dafnis's pride in his own spontaneity. After a number of non-productive days, I told him, "We have limited time in Cyprus. It is imperative that we organize interviews to maximize the time we have available." But scheduling interviews in advance went against Dafnis's DNA. With predictable regularity, he would tell us in the evening the people we were going to meet the following day and that he had made all the necessary arrangements.

The problem was that Dafnis rarely called anyone on his list until the morning of the day he told us we would be meeting them. In the evening, he would say things like, "I will call Andreas tonight and remind him that we are coming to see him at 9:30 a.m." But Andreas would have no knowledge of any 9:30 a.m.

appointment, because Dafnis had not yet talked with him about it. And when he did call the next morning, he would say something like, "Hello, Andreas. What are you doing today at 9:30? Two Americans are here and they want to talk to you." Andreas might have no idea who the two Americans were or why they wanted to talk to him. If Andreas said, "Sorry, that will not work for me," Dafnis created Plan B or Plan C. When we arrived later that morning, we would discover that the schedule he announced the night before had changed considerably—and it might change several more times during any given day. To save face, he seldom divulged why we were not going to do what he had told us the day before.

Figure 4. *Dafnis's research assistant passing time.*

I almost begged him to let me contact the people on his list, but he insisted that he needed to be the one to call them. Dafnis was the patriarch, and everything had to go through him. He would not let anyone else organize things, so each day we waited for this unorganized micromanager to cobble together a chain of events. Several times, Dafnis told us, "I am unpredictable, spontaneous, and incorrigible." Once, he added, "And Maria (his long-time companion) says, 'Unreliable.'" He did not apologize for his lifestyle. "You need to be spontaneous," he said. "It will help you to live longer." Maria did not agree. She chastised him for his behavior—but to no avail. He was who he was. Deal with it!

Dafnis had multiple ways of defending his actions. After one particular day when nothing happened according to "plan," we discussed the topic of time. Dafnis emphasized the difference between Western and Mediterranean concepts of time: "You Americans ask, 'How did you *spend* your time today?' You look at your watch as if time is a commodity you must not waste. We never speak that way. We say, 'How did you *pass* your day?'" For Dafnis, each day was an adventure that unfolded in response to whatever circumstances arose. Lynne and I had to adopt his mindset of *passing* time rather than *spending* it. Here is one example.

We awakened in the mountain village of Kalo Chorio, where we had spent the previous night after a harrowing ride in Dafnis's little car over narrow mountain roads to reach his ancestral village. By 2017, he had sold his Mitsubishi 4x4—which did not get good enough gas mileage—and purchased a tiny, two-door sedan. We had difficulty getting in and out of the vehicle. Crawling into the backseat was especially challenging. The car was so underpowered that Dafnis could not maintain speed driving up hills. To compensate, he drove rapidly downhill so that he could slingshot up the next hill. The problem was that often there was a curve at the bottom of a hill, so the tiny two-door sedan with two Americans scrunched inside screeched around these curves as Dafnis attempted to gain speed for the coming grade. His 88-year-old reflexes were not the best, and we feared that we might end up trapped in a twisted pile of scrap metal at the bottom of one of the steep gullies. He ignored our hints that maybe he was going too fast around the corners. He seemed to enjoy frightening us Americans on the mountain roads.

His plan for this particular day was to drive in the cool of the morning up into the forest to Kakomallis, where his father had started a church camp in the 1930s. I had my camera and digital recorder ready, so that we could conduct an extended interview on site at Kakomallis and take photographs of the campground. When I entered the kitchen that morning to make a cup of tea, Dafnis was talking loudly in Greek on his mobile phone. When he finished his conversation, he said he was unable to find anyone in Kalo Chorio who made frappé, so he found an owner of a coffee shop in Limassol who agreed to send an employee on a motorbike with a frappé for me. "Right!" I smirked. "Someone is going to drive 30 kilometers up here just to bring a frappé!"

Dafnis looked offended and chastised me for my lack of gratitude. He said that he had gone to trouble and expense to get a frappé for me because he knew I liked them—and he did not like the way I was being dismissive of his efforts. Cypriots emphasize hospitality, and I did not want to be insensitive to his cultural norms. What if he actually did arrange for someone to bring a frappé to me? It seemed too bizarre to be believable, but Dafnis appeared genuinely offended. As a result, I backed off from viewing the whole thing as a joke.

Humor as Social Critique

Dafnis liked to tell jokes that lampooned societal trends, especially the way Saudis have foreign workers–especially from the Philippines–do their work for them. Here is one example.

Survey of Work and Sex in Saudi Arabia

A firm did a survey of wealthy men in Saudi Arabia, asking the following question: "How would you characterize sex? Is it work, or is it pleasure?" Initially, all of the men questioned said, "Pleasure." Finally, one prince said, "This is an important question. Let me think about it." A few days later, he called back with his answer: "After giving much thought to your question, I have concluded that sex should be categorized as pleasure; because if it were work, we would have to have a Filipino do it."

After breakfast, we contorted ourselves into his compact car and he sped down a narrow lane in the old village of Kalo Chorio. The lane, a paved donkey path, squeezed so tightly between the houses on either side that the stones of the homes threatened to scrape the car's rearview mirrors. I was still wondering about the frappé. As he drove south toward Kakomallis, he had to go through the village of Louvaras, where Dafnis spotted his friend Panicos, the Mukhtar, or mayor. Dafnis stopped in the middle of the street and had a lively conversation in Greek before continuing on up the road. "Panicos invited us to his house for coffee," said Dafnis, as he passed some men working on a masonry project along the street. "We will just stay a few minutes and then be on our way."

Panicos greeted us at his veranda, which was covered in grape vines heavy with fruit. We sat down to visit in a setting surrounded by olive and fruit trees, and pots of basil and rosemary and lavender. Soon his mother appeared and asked us what we would like to drink. Dafnis was speaking loudly to Panicos in Greek and periodically looking over his shoulder at me. Both were laughing.

By the time the mayor's mother brought coffee for the others and a frappé for me, two of the workers we had passed appeared, wanting to know who these strangers were and why they were visiting the Mukhtar. Panicos's mother served them coffee also and set out sweets and fruit. Now Dafnis was holding forth in animated Greek to Panicos and the two workmen, and they also were laughing. Dafnis enjoyed having an audience. Lynne and I smiled and sipped our drinks and tried not to look too awkward.

After a little while, Dafnis turned to me and said he was just explaining that this American professor is so gullible he will believe anything. He told them that I actually believed that no one in Kalo Chorio or Louvaras made frappé so he ordered one to be delivered from Limassol. They all got a good laugh at my expense. So much for trying to be culturally sensitive! But Panicos's mother made a good frappé, and I enjoyed it in spite of my being the butt of a practical joke.

Lynne and I sat and listened to the men talking on and on. We had no idea what they were saying, but we were getting better at not feeling frustrated while we waited for Dafnis to finish his favorite pastime—conversing with people. If only we understood Greek, the wait would have been less tedious. Finally, the men decided the little party was over. Our unplanned stay in Louvaras lasted at least an hour—and it was not over yet.

When we crawled back into his tiny car, Dafnis explained, "Yesterday was the Name Day of Saint Mamas, so I need to see Father Mamas to pay my respects. We will only stay a few minutes." Orthodox Christians in Cyprus place more importance on the Name Day of the saint after whom a person is named than they do on the person's actual birthday. Over the centuries, the Orthodox Church assigned a specific day for special veneration of each saint—called the saint's Name Day. Some of our Orthodox friends in Cyprus have a book that provides for each day of the year a short description of the saints who are honored on that day. This book serves as a devotional guide for venerating saints on their name days. And, because churches are named after saints, every year church members hold a special celebration to commemorate the Name Day of the saint after which their church is named. The name day for St. Mamas is 2 September, so Dafnis felt obligated to pay his respects to his friend, Fr. Mamas.

He drove back down the road into the village to the retired priest's house. Fr. Mamas invited us to sit with him under the grape vines shading his veranda—after proudly showing us his fruit trees. His Filipina housekeeper supplied us with more coffee, but before she had time to bring out some fruit, a Greek Cypriot couple from Australia appeared unexpectedly for a visit. The wife, Maria, had grown up in Louvaras, but she and her husband immigrated to Australia after Turkey invaded Cyprus in 1974. She had brought Fr. Mamas *baklava*, which he promptly shared with everyone. His housekeeper then brought out more sweets and fresh fruit. Time *passed*.

We listened to Maria and her husband recount their pilgrimage. He grew up in the Karpas Peninsula of northeastern Cyprus. Shortly before their planned wedding in 1974, the invading Turkish army captured him and held him captive for five months. When the Turks released him, he searched until he found Maria in Athens. They married there and then moved to Australia to settle in Sydney, where they raised a family. Their children and grandchildren are all down there. Maria said they return to Cyprus frequently to visit relatives. We heard numerous sad stories of displacement following the Turkish invasion. Numerous Greek Cypriot refugees had to build new lives for themselves in other countries after losing everything to Turkish invaders.

Fr. Mamas seemed sad. After a while, Dafnis translated for him and explained that his wife had died of Multiple Sclerosis a few years earlier. Fr. Mamas got teary as he told about his beloved wife. After two hours of conversation, we said our goodbyes, leaving with a bag of fresh peaches from a tree by the front gate.

After at least three hours of unplanned visiting in Louvaras, we held on for dear life as Dafnis drove up the mountain road devoid of guardrails to the Kakomallis camp. After a series of switchbacks, the camp came into view—a tile-roofed, stone building nestled in the pines. At last, we had arrived, and we would be able to sit down and record our interview of Dafnis.

But Dafnis said, "Would you like to see the view from the top of this mountain, where the fire lookout tower is?" We said, "Yes," and he drove right past the camp on a gravel road that got increasingly bumpier as we made our way up—the kind of road more appropriate for pickup trucks. When we reached the top of the mountain, Dafnis parked his car and walked slowly with his cane over to the tower. The watchman, a little man with a big moustache, called down to Dafnis from the top of the tower. We climbed the stairs to meet the man, who had worked at the fire lookout tower for 30 years. He spent his shift chain-smoking cigarettes and using huge binoculars to search for any smoke rising from the mountains. The irony was not lost on us.

Lynne and I walked around the observation deck, enjoying the view of the surrounding area. To the south, through the haze, we saw Limassol and the Mediterranean Sea. We could even see the large, hideous-looking Russian building called the *Oval* because of its circular shape. We took pictures and waited for Dafnis to finish talking with his friend. He was obviously in no hurry and was clearly enjoying conversing with the man.

Finally, we said our goodbyes and Dafnis drove back down the road from the tower. However, when the Kakomallis camp came into view again, Dafnis said. "Well, it is getting a little bit late… I think we will come back tomorrow. Now we will go back to Stahis and Joy's house in Kalo Chorio for a bite of lunch, and we will take our rest." And thus ended our plan to *spend* time that day recording an interview of Dafnis at the Kakomallis Camp, letting him explain how his father had overseen the construction of the camp—and recount the history of the place. After the unplanned conversations, Dafnis decided it was too late in the day. He drove down the mountain to Kalo Chorio so he could take his nap.

On that day, we *passed* an hour waiting for Dafnis to chat with Panicos and the two workers, *passed* another two hours sitting in the shade at the home of Fr. Mamas, drinking coffee and eating sweets, and then *passed* another hour while Dafnis chatted with the little man with the big moustache on the fire lookout tower. Then we returned to Kalo Chorio without conducting the interview, which was the main reason we had come to this area in the first place. We did not *spend* time doing organized work. We *passed* time with Cypriots, and we were richer for it. I just wish that we spoke speak Greek so that we would know what in the world was happening during those four *passed* hours!

Criminal Mastermind

In 2017, Dafnis repeatedly quipped about contacting President Donald Trump to bolster Trump's remarks about the FBI's incompetence. He said, "I am going to write to Trump himself through the American Embassy, and I shall tell him how stupid the FBI is." He paused and added, "But listen now, about this story, there is some truth in it." Those words "some truth" alerted us.

Dafnis began by claiming that a BBC report in 1956 called him "one of the most dangerous terrorists on the island." He shook his head and said, "This was the *first* time I was described as a dangerous terrorist." He continued.

> The second occasion [when I was labeled a terrorist] is that there is an Internet site—I don't know who posted it. Maybe it is the Intelligence Service, maybe the CIA. A good friend of mine who used to work for the

German Secret Services alerted me of this [Internet] page. So, I visited this page, and the title is "The 100 most dangerous terrorists on the island of Cyprus." You can find this list right now if you look it up. But I could not locate the source, even though it is there, posted on the Internet. It is a public document. And I am listed among the 100 in this document. I am not in the top ten, but I think that I am maybe 66 or 67 out of the 100 most dangerous.

I later searched for such an Internet site but never found anything resembling what Dafnis described.

By now Dafnis was on a roll. "The most honorable title given to me by the USA, I don't know [by whom], Home Office or Department of Immigration, or whatever—I don't know—is that they consider me as a *persona non grata*, and my visa to enter the United States was *revoked*." I interrupted Dafnis and asked what would happen if he wanted to come and visit us in the United States. "No," he said. "I cannot do it. I cannot get a visa. When I asked about it, they gave me various explanations when Bush was president. Finally, they told me a very interesting idea: I was one of the *major* masterminds of the nuclear program of Iran." Dafnis shook his head dramatically and looked completely baffled by this accusation. I was laughing, and he asserted, "No, but this is serious, Michael." He continued,

The closest I came to nuclear power—the closest I came to knowing something about it was while I was attending Iowa State University. We lived about five miles south of Ames Lab at Iowa State, which was experimental for the Ames Nuclear Engineering Department. There was a small reactor for students in nuclear engineering. I never visited this department, and I have no idea whatsoever about nuclear power. But the lab is there.

Well, that made no sense, but we continued to listen. Dafnis rolled his eyes, and said,

I laugh when I think about this. I get a good laugh myself. But I am also sarcastic about the matter. Some friends of mine who are hardcore members of the Communist Party and who really hate the United States come and go freely in the United States, but I am denied a visa to enter the United States.

Dafnis was having a jolly time telling us about his visa woes. He continued,

Now, because I get some pleasure out of all this, like now that I am relating it all to you, I have *not* found it necessary to take steps to have this case cleared. But now I am taking it seriously as I am getting old and getting to know you. Maybe it would be good to go back to the States to visit. I am thinking of writing a letter to President Donald Trump, and I have been playing with this idea—I have drafted the letter, actually—

> because during his campaign he made some derogatory comments about the CIA and Secret Services. I shall use these examples [of their blunders with me], and I will tell Trump that he was right, and I would tell him my story so that he could use it as an example [of their incompetence] in his speeches.

We were laughing at Dafnis's sardonic wit. I summarized: "So you are not just a terrorist but you are a terrorist mastermind who is an expert in nuclear physics? This accusation is good. It will increase the sales of your biography."

Dafnis was not only a great storyteller, he was also cunning in what he said and did not say. Sometimes important information only came out after more prodding. On this occasion, he took a deep breath and finally came clean on the matter of the visa, basically admitting that everything he had been saying was totally fabricated: "Okay, maybe I should tell you what I *really* suspect caused the CIA to blacklist me."

> When I was in Saudi Arabia, my boss was a very respectable prince of the royal family. One day Prince Faisal called me to his office to introduce me to a Lebanese banker named George.... George and I became friends, although he was a banker in Jeddah, and I lived and worked in Riyadh. Then I left Saudi Arabia and came to Cyprus, and two or three years later, George came to visit me, bringing a young Lebanese with him.... They told me, "We have a proposal for you. We bought at an auction some spare parts made by General Electric for nuclear plants. But these spare parts cannot be sold anywhere except Cyprus. They can be exported to Cyprus because it is not on the prohibited list. If we bring them to Cyprus, we can look around and see which countries have nuclear plants. There are some in Russia and some in the Balkans. There are 15 containers [In another telling of the story, Dafnis said "18 containers of spare parts for nuclear reactors"], which we have bought already; and because you are a Cyprus citizen, we shall bring them in your name and we shall store them. Now, we are talking about millions from their sale. We can export them from Cyprus."
>
> I was impressed that they would trust me with property worth, I think, $30 million. How could they trust that I would not go and sell them myself? Anyway, they had second thoughts. I don't know how they did the thing they did, but they finally did bring the containers and stored them in the free zone in Larnaca. The year was about 1998 or 1999.... A few months later, I received a call from Interpol in America. The man said, "Is this Mr. Dafnis?" [Obviously, an American would say "Mr. Panagides," but in Cyprus it is always "Mr. Dafnis"] I said, "Yes I am." The man asked if I knew Mr. Habib and George. I said, "Yes, I do." The man

> said, "Can you tell us something about these spare parts?" I said, "Yes, I can tell you that they produced for me an original bill of lading, stamped with a stamp of the U.S. Department of State that said, 'Good for export to Cyprus.'"
>
> Do you know what this Interpol man told me? He said, "Yes, we know. That stuff was fake." I told him that I did not know what happened. I know they came. They disappeared. They brought the parts to Cyprus, but they did not use my name. I did have contact with them, but that was it.
>
> A few weeks later, I received another call, this time from the Cyprus Minister of Foreign Affairs. He said, "Dafnis, can you come to Nicosia tomorrow to meet with me for a very serious matter?" I said, "Yes, but can I know what this is all about so that I can be ready?" He said, "It is about the spare parts and the Lebanese who brought them. I want to know what happened."
>
> So, I went to Nicosia, and the Minster showed to me a letter from the United States saying that these containers were illegally exported. The license was forged, and the containers should be immediately confiscated by the Cyprus government. Otherwise, the United States would take drastic measures against the Republic of Cyprus.

In another telling of the story, he said, "The United States government threatened the Cyprus Republic that they would sever relationships with Cyprus and impose sanctions on the Cyprus government because of these containers of nuclear spare parts." Dafnis could exaggerate and fabricate details with complete abandon, so knowing exactly what people in his stories actually said is impossible. He went on to quote the minister:

> He said, "Do you know what it means? It means that Cyprus will be blacklisted by the United States. Whatever you know, you must tell us." So I told him the story about George and the spare parts. I wrote a report about the incident and brought it with me to Nicosia. I explained how I met with Mr. George and later with Mr. Habib and how they brought the containers to Cyprus. I know the gentlemen. I know that they stayed in the Sylva Hotel. They left without paying their €16,000 bill. They disappeared. I put in the report everything I knew. I suspect that my connection with these Lebanese men is what makes me one of the masterminds of the Iran nuclear deal.

Perhaps I should have asked Dafnis how he knew these details if he had nothing to do with George importing the spare parts. The Sylva Hotel is only a few blocks from Dafnis's home in Limassol. He knew the owner and would have talked with him. Did he exaggerate the size of the bill? Perhaps. The precise role Dafnis played in the scheme to sell spare parts for a nuclear power plant remains unclear, and the circuitous way he told his story raises questions. The United States probably had legitimate reasons for revoking Dafnis's visa.

Moving Forward by Looking Backward

When I write my own memoirs, I will spend a lot of time carefully assembling a timeline of my life. I will struggle to remember the exact years in which memorable events happened, so I will compare various sources and consult with my siblings. I recognize that my ability to state how old I was when something happened can lack clarity—particularly if it was when I was a kid. But memory lapses are not limited to when I was young. "How old was I? Now, let me think. When *did* that happen?" Our memories sometimes play tricks on us. Occasionally, it is embarrassing.

For decades, I was convinced that the Selective Service system in November 1968 conducted its first lottery to determine by birthdate the order in which it would draft men in the USA. I remembered watching the live broadcast of the lottery on a TV in the dorm with other freshman basketball players at the University of Wyoming. Each of us held his breath as the official reached into a large bowl, selected another capsule, took out a slip of paper on which was written a day of the year, and read that date. The order in which one's birthday was drawn determined how early or late his name would come up in the draft. To my great relief, my birthday was drawn at number 211, and the official estimate was that the military would draft men through about number 185. I immediately cancelled my student deferment so that I would be in that year's draft. "The only way they can get me next year," I reasoned, "is to draft everyone in next year's lottery and then return to this year's pool. And that probably will not happen unless we are in all-out war—in which case it will not matter."

Recently, however, while reading about the first draft lottery conducted in the United States, to my horror, I saw that it occurred in 1969. But that simply could not be! I refused to believe it. I remembered where I was when it happened. When I checked other Internet sites, however, every one of them said "1969." The story I had told and totally believed for decades was wrong. The lottery happened when I was a sophomore at the University of Montana, where I had transferred. Somehow, my mind had created an entire scenario at Laramie, Wyoming, that never happened. I was in Missoula, Montana, at the time. I did not live in a dorm but alone in a trailer house off campus. I did not even own a television, so I probably just listened to the lottery proceedings on a radio—by myself. How could I have gotten such an important event in my young life so wrong? I was embarrassed. I began to wonder what other memories I have modified. It happens: sometimes accidentally; sometimes on purpose; sometimes innocently; sometimes deliberately. I have witnessed people telling stories they know are lies, but after telling these stories enough times, they came to believe them. Humans have a tendency to modify and even create memories.

Dafnis did not share my interest in taking time to track down the exact year and circumstances in which any particular event happened. He was not that precise. He sat down with us, typically at a small, plastic table on the veranda behind his house, and he answered our questions. He enjoyed telling stories about his life, but he was 88 years old at the time, and numerous events he described happened years earlier. Although he spoke with complete conviction, he was certainly not accurate in everything he said. Sometimes our recordings of his interviews reveal that he disagreed with himself, providing different details for the same stories. No doubt, some of his mistakes resulted from memory lapses. Most of us would be embarrassed by our own inconsistencies if we listened to multiple recordings of ourselves describing past events. Sometimes, however, Dafnis deliberately misled us. He was by his own admission a crafty individual, and he had his own agendas when he spoke with us.

Dafnis's stories were wide ranging. During any particular session, he might recount events that happened the previous day or sixty years earlier. Much of what he told us was stream of consciousness. Consequently, I had to reconstruct the metanarrative of his life. My raw material for this narrative consisted of oral interviews of Dafnis and his friends and family, plus a few archival sources, such as letters written by an American student in 1954. To allow these people to speak with

Figure 5. *Table where we conducted many interviews of Dafnis.*

their own voices, I had to abandon any attempt at providing a seamless narrative of events in exact chronological order—or harmonizing their divergent accounts of the same events. If one interviewee spoke of events that happened over a five-year period, and the next interviewee spoke of the same five-year period, I simply could not weave the two accounts together. I needed to follow the descriptions provided by both. Consequently, when presenting what different people said, I had to stitch their accounts together in a loosely chronological sequence. You must be prepared to shift slightly forward and back in time as I move from one narrator to the next. Keep in mind that I have done most of the work for you. My task in writing this book resembled putting together a giant jigsaw puzzle without having a picture on the puzzle box to use for deciding approximately where each piece should go. If I were writing a novel instead of a life story, I could simply fabricate the plot line and have the characters say what I wanted them to say. But I did not have that luxury. History is much more complicated and messy.

CHAPTER 2
Early Life in Rural Cyprus

If you want to understand a man,
carefully consider his childhood.
—Michael Cosby

In the Shadow of Solomon

Some people feel a close connection with their ancestors. Others feel disconnected. My mother and father were vagabonds, alienated from my grandparents, frequently moving from job to job, never escaping themselves. I don't remember ever being around my mother's parents, and I only spent a few days with my father's parents. I grew up in the western part of the United States with little appreciation for family traditions. My wife, Lynne, who grew up in the South, had a much more wholesome experience. She feels a deep connection to her extended family and a strong appreciation for their traditions. We all have our own histories, and our family of origin exerts a strong influence on us. Growing up, I often heard the saying, "You can pick your nose; you can pick your friends; but you can't pick your family."

Overall, Cypriot culture promotes family connections. The small size of the island means that family members typically live nearby. War and displacement of Cypriots from their ancestral lands resulted in a diaspora, but Lynne and I noticed a persistent connection with extended family. Cyprus has less fragmentation of families than does the United States. Families maintain a tradition of gathering for meals and socializing. This holdover from village life persists in spite of urban sprawl in population centers like Limassol.

Dafnis's nuclear family provided positive influences worthy of passing on to future generations. But dark secrets lurked in the past, things that his father, Solomon Panagides, had to overcome. Some people remain permanently crippled by dysfunction in their family of origin; others shake off the impediments, move on and reinvent themselves. Solomon moved on. He emerged from poverty and a broken family to become a respected leader. Born near the east coast city of Famagusta, he became a visionary in his views on farming and education in Cyprus. His achievements came not from a position of privilege but through tenacity and hard work. He distinguished himself in school, and others saw potential in this young man and helped him at key points to get the education he craved.

Dafnis explained that when Solomon was a small boy, he prayed, "Please, God, help me when I grow up to become either a teacher or a priest." Dafnis added, "He became both, eventually." Solomon's innovative leadership, first as a schoolteacher and then as a priest, exerted a positive influence on society in the Limassol area and beyond.

Successful men often devote so much effort to their work that they have diminished time for home life, and Solomon was no exception. We tried unsuccessfully to probe Dafnis's feelings about his father's limited time at home. Dafnis was the firstborn child of Solomon and Maria Panagides, and his relationship with his father remains a mystery. He was guarded in what he said. At times in our conversations, he expressed resentment toward his father, but not about Solomon's absence. Usually, he conveyed abundant admiration for Solomon's achievements; and we became increasingly aware of the influence his father had on Dafnis.

Dafnis adopted some aspects of Solomon's parenting style—often away from home on work-related activities. He also embraced his father's ecumenical mindset on religious matters, his philosophy regarding workers' rights, his insistence on equitable business practices, and his fondness for communal farming and banking. To a point, the old saying, "Like father, like son," applies. However, some aspects of Dafnis's life differed distinctly from those of his father.

Their relationship was complicated. On the one hand, Dafnis admired Solomon. Indeed, many Cypriots in the Limassol district revered the man, and after his death they erected a monument to him in the courtyard of the Church of the Holy Trinity in Limassol, where he served as priest. Yet Dafnis chafed at his father's control over his life, especially with respect to denying his desire to go to college. Solomon was a visionary thinker, but he was also a product of the patriarchal Cypriot culture of his time.

Saved from the Waters of Baptism

In 1928, at age 35, Solomon married his former student, twenty-two-year old Maria Socratous, a daughter of the mayor of Kalo Chorio. By that time, Solomon had known Maria about eight years. Dafnis said their age difference posed no problems: "To be a priest or teacher at that time was a very prestigious thing. And to have the teacher become a member of your family was a great honor." The mayor was pleased to have Solomon as a son-in-law.

A year later, on 17 February 1929, with the aid of a midwife, Maria gave birth to Dafnis in a house in Kalo Chorio. Dafnis explained, "My passport has my birthday as the twentieth. It's wrong.... People at that time used to write important dates on their walls, usually behind the doors. Whoever wrote when I was born did not write the seventeenth. He wrote the twentieth. So until now, I am listed as three days younger than I am actually." In Cypriot villages, midwives helped

Figure 6. *Maria and Solomon Panagides.*

deliver babies—in homes, not hospitals. Parents did not view precise birth records as essential, and few parents in 1929 Cyprus pondered the possibility that their children might need exact information for documents like passports.

In America, people in past generations often wrote important dates (births, marriages, deaths, etc.) in the family Bible—which served as a concise record of family members. Mistakes are common in such registers. Cypriot citizens did not own big, family Bibles. They had other traditions for keeping family records. Rural Cyprus in 1929 had no governmental structures in place to keep precise track of birth and death dates. Churches were often repositories for community data. Also, most Orthodox Christians name their children after saints. For example, lots men in Cyprus are named Andreas after St. Andrew, the saint to whom women pray if they have trouble with their pregnancies. Parents often name their boys Andreas as a means of honoring and thanking St. Andrew for his aid in childbirth. The fact that Solomon did not name his baby boy after a saint or a male relative reveals much about the personality of the man. He named his son after the laurel tree.

In Greek mythology, Dafnis, a shepherd from Sicily, was the child of the god Apollo and a beautiful nymph. She left her baby under a laurel tree, where shepherds found him and named him after the tree. I cannot help but wonder what Solomon's wife and her family thought about his decision to give his son a botanical name with mythical connections. But Solomon did not mind breaking some traditions, no matter how deeply held they were in Cypriot society. His daughter, born in 1931, he named Chloe, which means a "green sprout"; and his second son, born in 1937, he named Stahis, which in Greek means a "head of grain." Solomon loved botany.

Dafnis told us that, when Solomon and Maria had him baptized, the inexperienced priest who officiated the baptismal liturgy had never before baptized a baby. He immersed Dafnis in the water to the point he almost drowned the child. Fortunately, the godfather grabbed Dafnis out of the priest's hands and shook him to get the water out of his mouth and lungs. When telling this story, Dafnis said, "We have a saying here that, if someone is a little bit off from normal, we say, 'Sure, he was baptized by a silly priest.'" He laughed and added, "It applies to me, I think."

No Running Water, but plenty of donkeys

Understanding the rural Cyprus environment in which Dafnis grew up provides insights into his adult life. His early years revolved around agricultural rhythms—as well as the Orthodox calendar. In the small village of Kalo Chorio, houses on the hillside are packed together, and Dafnis experienced life in the extended family of his mother, Maria. When Dafnis was a boy, the village had no electricity, no indoor plumbing, and no telephones. Villagers did not own farm machinery or automobiles. They accomplished farm work by hand or with donkeys. They could take a bus to Limassol, but roads between villages were often little more than paths. Villagers seldom saw a doctor, so some died due to the absence of basic medical care.

Village life was mostly self-contained. Folks raised their own food and led a simple existence. Relationships were central to daily life, and encounters with others happened constantly on the narrow paths between homes. Children ran freely from house to house. Literacy was limited, and few people owned books. In their communal existence, everyone shared coffee, tea, food, and wine with neighbors. The Orthodox Church was at the center of everything, the cultural and spiritual anchor that not only provided a meeting place but also gave villagers a sense of identity and purpose. Eastern Orthodox traditions permeated all of life.

Today, Kalo Chorio is remarkably quiet. Many residents are elderly—some are retired British expatriates. We heard very few children. But when Dafnis was a boy, the village was full of life, and children were everywhere. He said, "They had everything they needed to sustain the family throughout the year. They worked all day in the fields." They had vineyards and olive trees; they planted vegetables; and they had goats, pigs, and rabbits for meat.

Everyone was expected to participate in the family's livelihood. Dafnis said, "Children helped their parents in the fields

Universal Ignorance

During a town meeting a few years ago, the mayor of Kalo Chorio asked Stahis to translate for the British residents. He said that the first question came from an elderly British lady: "What can the Mayor do to keep the pigeons from pooping on my veranda!" Examples of such cluelessness seem to be ubiquitous among human cultures.

irrespective of age. They started early, at five or six years of age." The modern mode of children having few responsibilities other than schoolwork and a few chores did not apply at that time. Everybody worked. Education was basic and limited, especially for the girls. Mostly, they needed to learn how to perform the daily duties of village life.

Last Donkey of Kalo Chorio

In the mountain villages of Cyprus, roads were constructed with donkey carts in mind, not automobiles. Houses are crowded together on hillsides and the walkways between them are adequate only for human foot traffic or donkeys. Measures taken to make some of these paths usable for motorized vehicles sometimes borders on hilarious. Cypriots are accustomed to narrow spaces and navigate them without stress.

When driving on some of these narrow lanes, I folded in the side mirrors on our rental car to avoid scraping them on the rock walls of houses on either side of a lane. A few times as I was inching my way forward, I saw another vehicle rapidly approaching from the opposite direction. My heart rate elevated, and I muttered about driving on paved donkey paths. I had to decide who would back up—and how far it was to a place wide enough for two vehicles to scrape by each other. Lynne devised an appropriate attitude for driving in villages. She said, "I compare it to driving into our garage. There is not much space on either side of the car in our garage, and I don't fret about that. So, I transfer this mindset to dealing with roads in mountain villages: I tell myself, it is just like driving into our garage." That strategy works best when another car is not approaching from the opposite direction!

Figure 7. *One of the narrow walkways between tightly packed houses in the village of Kalo Chorio.*

Before the advent of automobiles in Kalo Chorio, villagers

used donkeys to transport all sorts of things. These important work animals easily navigated the paths in town and the steep trails to the terraces where Cypriots grow their trees and vines. Sturdy and surefooted, donkeys were an integral part of village life. In the home where we stayed in Kalo Chorio in 2019, we lived downstairs in the space that originally functioned as a stable. In the walls of our little bedroom were niches—built-in feed troughs for donkeys. A renovation of the lower level of the house turned the space into a lovely living area complete with a bathroom. But when Dafnis was a boy, the house had no electricity or running water, and the toilet was an outhouse up the hill a ways. In 1929, using the lower level of a house as a stable for one's animals was standard architecture.

Donkeys are social animals, and they like to "talk" (i.e., bray) to each other across the hillsides, especially in the mornings when people used to take the animals out of their little stable spaces underneath the living areas of the houses. In 2017, Dafnis took great delight in telling us about the last living donkey in Kalo Chorio, which belonged to an aunt of his. He said that, over the years, the donkey population steadily declined because of mechanization. Machines replaced the function of the donkeys, so villagers no longer needed these little beasts of burden. Consequently, their numbers thinned until only one was left in the village—Dafnis's aunt's donkey.

Dafnis said that his aunt called to tell him the sad story. She was up on a hillside terrace with her donkey, and the poor animal lost its footing and fell over the ledge and died as a result of the fall. Dafnis snorted and said to us, "I don't believe for a moment that the donkey accidently fell down the hillside." By this time he was very animated. With a twinkle in his eye, he said, "Donkeys are the most sure-footed animals I know. They never lose their footing and fall like that. I am convinced that he got so lonesome because he had no other donkeys to talk to that he simply committed suicide."

One Telephone per Village

The pervasive presence of mobile phones today makes it difficult for younger people to understand a world without such communication devices. When Dafnis was young, letter writing was the primary means for families to keep in touch with relatives who lived elsewhere. Although those who lived in mountain villages experienced colder winters than their relatives who lived in cities close to the Mediterranean Sea, they enjoyed cooler temperatures in the summer—which made life more pleasant. Prior to the advent of air conditioning, during the blistering hot days of summer, relatives from coastal cities came to Kalo Chorio and spent extended time with their kin in the mountains. According to Dafnis, "After schools closed, the village population doubled, because people from the towns would go and spend the summers."

Figure 8. *Mosaic of a woman and her donkey in the village of Louvaras.*

The postal service enabled people to communicate with relatives in preparation for these summer pilgrimages. Koralia, a cousin of Dafnis from Kalo Chorio, explained that each morning, someone at the central post office in Limassol placed a bag of mail—one for each village along the bus route—onto the bus that drove through the villages. Every village had a small post office where the driver stopped and deposited the bag of letters, and then he picked up any mail to be taken back to the central post office. In those days before junk mail, getting letters was exciting.

Koralia went on to say that, at some point, Kalo Chorio got a single telephone. She explained how it worked.

> There was only one phone box in the middle of the village. If someone from Limassol wanted to speak to Papa Markos, he called the telephone box of Kalo Chorio, and someone passing by would answer it. The caller would say, "Can you say, 'Papa Markos come to the phone?'" Or, "Tell Papa Markos…." Or, the most usual was that the person in the village who answered the telephone—for example, if the caller wanted to speak to Dafnis—the man in the phone box would step out and holler, "DAFNI!! COME TO THE TELEPHONE!!" During the colonial years, the colonial powers had telephones installed in the cities where they had their offices. Of course, the rural areas were abandoned—neglected.

Language of Direct Address

When Greeks speak directly to each other, they do not say the last letter of the name if it ends in an s. When talking to Dafnis, they say, "Dafni."

Her last statement was a complaint, yet she grew wistful and added, "We lived a good life. We ate healthy foods without chemicals, no GMOs, and all these things. But we did not have electricity, running water, etc." In part, she longed for the simplicity of the village life of her youth. Suddenly, her mobile phone rang, and she interrupted our interview by speaking loudly to the caller—oblivious to the rest of us in the room. Her husband was embarrassed by the way she stopped what we were doing to chat with her friend. The digital recorder I used for the interview captured the entire event. Whoever said that life is not filled with paradox?

Weddings and Baptisms

Village life revolved around the Orthodox Church calendar, and community members experienced a sense of belonging to a larger whole. Of course, neighbors can be frustrating, especially when houses are packed together; but most people did not feel lonely or alienated. Social gatherings formed the fabric of life. Sunday meals after liturgy were occasions for extended families to gather. Children played with their cousins. The advantage of living in a village is that you know everyone. The disadvantage of living in a village is that everyone knows your business. The positive side is that people feel part of the whole. The negative side is that privacy is minimal.

Rites of passage were important in village life. In Cypriot society weddings celebrated transition from adolescence to adult status, and marriage ceremonies were community events. Petrakis, one of Dafnis's cousins from Kalo Chorio, told us,

> When there was a wedding in the village.... people were playing the violin and *lauton*—like a mandolin, only bigger—during all the days of the wedding. The wedding started on Friday evening and the festival continued for five days: Friday through Tuesday.... People prepared a big meal of special food made of wheat and meat, as well as many other small meals. The whole village would be singing, and there was special wedding music. And always there were prayers to God for the happiness of the couple and their families.

Although weddings were costly rites of passage, the whole community contributed to and participated in the celebration. Villagers had much more of a feeling of belonging than do many people in the United States, where adult children often leave their home towns to go to college and move on to a distant location for employment. Social isolation is frequent experience in America, and couples often invite only close friends and family to their weddings. The idea of a wedding being a village-wide celebration seems like something out of the distant past.

Another important rite of passage in Cyprus involving festivities is the baptismal liturgy when children receive their first communion. Although the baptismal celebrations today involve the same liturgy that has been used for centuries, modern modes of dress and behavior have changed substantially. When the "silly priest" baptized Dafnis, the people in attendance would have dressed modestly. Today, what Orthodox Christians consider appropriate dress for such solemn occasions has changed dramatically. We were invited to witness the baptism of a baby girl in an Orthodox church in Cyprus, and we felt honored to be asked. While the elderly priest worked his way through the lengthy baptismal liturgy, people chatted with each other. They revealed no concern to listen quietly to what the priest was saying. I noticed a striking contrast between the archaic robes of the old priest and the tight miniskirts worn by scantily clad women in the church. The ancient symbolism in the church building and the centuries-old liturgy seemed profoundly out of sync with the modern clothing and behavior of those who attended.

The Profound and the Profane

Easter is a major event in the Orthodox calendar—more significant than Christmas celebrations. Interestingly, their celebration of Carnival occurs on the Sunday prior to the season of fasting associated with Lent. Carnival is a less extreme version of the *Mardi Gras* madness that occurs in New Orleans. *Mardi Gras* in French means "Fat Tuesday," the day before Ash Wednesday, which initiates the beginning of Lent, when Christians fast in preparation for Easter. In Catholic tradition, Fat Tuesday is the final day to eat rich foods until after Easter. First you party; then you fast.

Solomon Panagides disapproved of Carnival festivities, so he did not allow his children to attend what he considered to be a decadent celebration. Instead, he organized large family gatherings in Kalo Chorio for alternative celebrations. According to a cousin of Dafnis in Kalo Chorio, "During those days, we had a big celebration with five families together in one yard at one of the houses. And there were about ten [of these family] groups in the community." These family celebrations provided a more wholesome celebration than Carnival.

Orthodox calendars differ from Western calendars, so they celebrate Christmas, New Years, and Easter at different times than Catholics and Protestants. And, because Orthodox Churches are named after saints, Name Days of saints also provide important occasions for communities to celebrate. Some of these festivities conclude at a reasonable time; others last long past midnight.

Some celebrations of saints are somber; others have carnival type festivals. For example, Dafnis, Maria (his long-time companion), Lynne, and I drove to the Monastery of the Holy Cross (*Stavros tou Agiasmati*) on 14 September 2017, the official day to celebrate the Holy Cross. This small, UNESCO church built in the 1400s high in the Troodos Mountains was full of Orthodox Christians; and more gathered outside to listen to the lengthy liturgy. Neophytos, Bishop of Morphou, delivered a powerful sermon on the necessity of love in the Christian's life. The entire event was somber, although vendors did set up booths and tables relatively near the church for people to purchase food and drink after the conclusion of the liturgy. We sat down at one of the tables, enjoyed a light snack from one of the vendors, and listened to Dafnis summarize the homily by Neophytos.

Next, Maria drove her SUV down the mountain to another Church of the Holy Cross (*Timios Stavros*), located in the town of Omodos. By this time, the morning liturgy at the village church was over and the atmosphere in the town was like that of a state fair. The main street through Omodos was loud and boisterous with all sorts of vendors displaying their wares. One booth displayed skimpy women's underwear. The spectacle seemed obscene, especially as a way of celebrating the Holy Cross. I asked Dafnis why this vendor was selling women's underwear to people walking toward a monastery. He said it was because of European Union restrictions against discrimination. One man selling religious trinkets was dressed like a priest, but he obviously was not one. Monks selling tourist trinkets manned booths closer to the monastery.

We entered the monastery church where folks lined up to kiss the icons and see relics of the holy cross and the holy rope that tied Jesus to the cross. There is also on display part of the skull of the Apostle Philip. Although the origin of these relics is dubious, the reverence that Orthodox Christians give to them is, for the most part, sincere. Overall, the crowd of people in Omodos seemed to enjoy themselves, buying food from vendors, paying devotion to holy relics, and perhaps purchasing sexy bras and panties. Something for everybody!

On a more personal level for me, Orthodox Christians honor Archangel Michael on 8 November, so that is my Name Day. When Greek Cypriots celebrate their Name Days, they typically invite friends and members of their extended family to come to an open-house sort of party. People attending the celebration often bring small gifts. For Greek Orthodox folks, their name days are typically more important than their birthdays. So far, I have not yet hosted a party on 8 November, but perhaps next year I will correct this deficiency.

Public Education kills Creativity

When Dafnis was a baby, Solomon Panagides was still a village schoolteacher who had not yet been ordained as a priest. His educational training, although modest, set him apart from the villagers of Kalo Chorio. They respected him because of his education, but his modern ideas about farming, nutrition, and personal hygiene puzzled these rural farmers who accepted the wisdom of their traditional ways. Years passed before they began to embrace his ideas.

Bishop Nikodimos Milonas, head of the combined districts of Larnaca and Limassol, became aware of Solomon's talents. In 1930, a year after the birth of

Dafnis, the bishop offered Solomon a management position. At that time, the bishopric was located in Larnaca, and Milonas appointed Solomon to be his deputy, putting him in charge of all the churches in the district of Limassol and relegating to him the responsibility to conduct an annual audit of the finances of each church. For his new position, he was ordained as a priest, becoming Father Solomon, and was delegated responsibility for the ecclesiastical family court. During this time, therefore, the second part of his childhood prayer, to become a teacher or a priest, became a reality.

When Solomon moved his family to Limassol, they left behind the supportive, close-knit environment of their small village. On the farm he rented east of Limassol, his family was more isolated than they had been in Kalo Chorio. Their new location was beautiful, and the fruit trees surrounding their home gave the place an almost idyllic setting. But leaving the tightly packed living conditions of the mountain village involved considerable adjustment. Solomon loved the agricultural possibilities of the farm, but his duties as a priest kept him from spending much time there. Maria grew into her new role of running their home and farm.

Dafnis had a happy childhood with loving parents and lots of room to explore. Solomon taught him about plants and animals and farming. His father's fascination with nature exerted considerable influence on Dafnis, who said that he, Chloe, and Stahis "grew up on this farm, which was *way, way* out of [Limassol]. We had animals, we had horses and pigs and hens and lots of flowers.... Father was prejudiced against formal education... so he said, 'No, you will do home schooling.'" He hired a family friend who was young and unmarried at the time. She came to their house three times a week for two hours to teach Dafnis Greek, mathematics, and other basic lessons. Solomon had Dafnis read books on history and other subjects, and he instilled in Dafnis a love of reading.

Figure 9. *Father Solomon Panagides after he became a priest.*

After three years of home schooling, Dafnis attended public school for a while. One of his main memories involved transportation to school: "[World War 2] was not over, and I enrolled in the fourth grade of the public elementary school. And I would commute every day to school in a carriage... because there were no cars at that time; and we had a carriage and a horse."

Unfortunately for Solomon and Maria, the owner of the farm they rented sold the property. The Panagides family bought a farm farther east of Limassol, which increased their commute to town. Dafnis explained their system.

Problem with Public Education

Dafnis agreed with his father that public schools kill creativity. He preferred a movement started by a German educator that does not use a standard curriculum but emphasizes developing students' creativity and ability to analyze and think. Starting in kindergarten, teachers help students to *create* rather than merely *memorize* information from textbooks.

> My grandfather moved to town and lived with us, and he took care of the horse and the carriage, and he took us back and forth to school. He also took my father, who had by that time become a priest.… And three or four nights of the week, Solomon had to stay in town, so we were alone on the farm.

I asked Dafnis if the transition to public school was a problem, and he assured me that it was not. They had family connections at the school, and he quickly integrated into the classroom.

Because WW2 was raging, students practiced running to an underground shelter. Lynne asked, "Was it like a game?" Dafnis replied, "It was fun. And every morning we had to assemble, and after prayer we had to sing the national anthem of Great Britain." At this point, he broke into a raucous version of "God save the Queen." Then he added, "But we did not recite the exact words. We would modify the words and sing—in Greek, of course—'God kill the queen.'" Even at a young age, Cypriot children were aware of resentment toward the British.

Solomon steered his son toward knowledge of agriculture, and Dafnis took correspondence courses in beekeeping and farming. Dafnis explained, "When I graduated from high school, my father said, 'You will continue the family business and become a farmer.'" By this time, Dafnis was reading farming books from the United States, because his English skills were more advanced than most Cypriots his age, largely due to his contacts with English speakers who lived nearby.

Indian Soldiers and Reincarnation

During WW2, Cyprus was spared a German invasion; but during the war a contingent of Indian soldiers lived in tents on the Panagides's farm. British soldiers also bivouacked near their farm, and Dafnis remembered a man from Scotland who became a good friend of Solomon. "The two would talk for hours," he said. Unfortunately, the Scottish man was killed in North Africa in the fight against Rommel's army.

Frequent interaction with these soldiers helped Dafnis improve his English, and his exposure to them included observation of people with different religious beliefs. The men in the Indian contingent were Brahmans—strict vegetarians. Dafnis said that sometimes during the night they would dance around a big fire, celebrating their rituals. One incident seemed quite significant to Dafnis. When the main Indian spiritual leader visited their farm one day, he saw Dafnis's grandmother slaughtering a chicken. Dafnis remembered the man's visceral, almost horrified reaction to the sight. I asked Dafnis how these Indian soldiers dealt with the horrors of slaughtering human beings in warfare. He did not know.

Sometimes while recounting stories, Dafnis expressed surprising beliefs. He said that a priest among the Indian soldiers analyzed his possessions and told him that he had lived in Germany in the 16th century. When Lynne chuckled at his comment, he grew serious.

> And now I see you are smiling. I am telling facts now. He said, "You lived in Bavaria on a farm near the edge of the Black Forest in Germany…." Years later, for some reason, I was always interested in German things. In German agricultural machinery. I studied the German language. I have German friends. For unexplained reasons, I had German feelings during the war. Then, on my first trip to Germany, when I went to an international ecumenical camp, a friend drove me through the Black Forrest. And all of a sudden we came to a small village. And there was a church there. And I said, "STOP! Stop here!" And then I said, "I know this place. I have been here before. This is exactly the place I used to come."

He looked deeply into my eyes and asked, "How do you explain this?" I declined to get into a discussion on reincarnation—although I almost mentioned that the Indian man's assertion about Dafnis being in Bavaria could easily have implanted thoughts that grew over time in his young mind. I also chose not to joke about his once having been a German Lutheran, or worse yet, from an Orthodox Cypriot viewpoint, a German Catholic. He shrugged and returned to his story of the soldiers, saying he was sad when they deployed to North Africa. Such encounters with people from other cultures intrigued Dafnis, and exiles from England added to his diversity training.

End Times Cults with Teleporting Prophets

In 1946, when Dafnis was 17, John Sebastian Marlow Ward (born 22 December 1885) led a group of twelve followers from England to Cyprus. Ward wrote about Masons and other secret societies, traveled widely, and claimed to have psychic powers. His first wife, Eleanor Caroline Lanchester, died in 1926, and Ward married Jessie Page in 1927. With her, he founded the Confraternity of the Kingdom of Christ (he also fathered a son with another woman, named Ursula

Cuffe, shortly before his death). Ward wrote books on prophecy, made numerous predictions about future events, died of a stroke on 2 July 1949, and was buried in an unmarked grave in the Church of St. Nicholas cemetery in Limassol.

Dafnis was fascinated with this communal group. He said,

> They called themselves The Confraternity of Christ the King. John Marlow Ward and his wife, the Holy Mother as they called her, led this group.... He was a 33rd degree Mason: the highest level. But one day, John Ward denounced Masonry, and he revealed some of their top secrets. So the Masons put him on their wanted persons [list] to be exterminated for revealing their secrets. And the Masons got assistance from one of the top executives of the Electrolux Company.... His daughter, Bridgette, was very young—about 20 or 22—and she joined the Confraternity. Her father and mother deeply opposed her doing so. They wanted to find this Ward and *exterminate* him. And they paid a lot of money to kill him.

Historically, the situation was not that violent, and Dafnis got the girl's name and age wrong. A businessman named Stanley Lough became furious with Ward for enticing his *sixteen-year-old daughter, Dorothy,* to join his end-times sect. Lough launched a court case against Ward, who was found guilty and fined £500. Perhaps the Confraternity people told Dafnis that Lough put out a hit on Ward. Perhaps Dafnis invented that detail for drama. He continued,

> So, Ward and his wife took this group of twelve people, and they secretly moved to Cyprus. They always claimed that an angel guided them. They had direct communication with this guardian angel. According to them, the guardian angel told them, "You must buy this farm next to Father Solomon." And they did. We became very good friends, and this helped me a lot with my English. I was far above my age group as far as English was concerned.

Ward was an archaeologist, and he and Dafnis traveled together around Cyprus. Dafnis added that Ward asked him many questions about how to farm and be totally self-sufficient during the last days—a detail that seems odd, given that Dafnis was only a teenager.

Dafnis also narrated a prediction by the group's guardian angel of dark days to come.

> One night they came over—this was in 1952. And they said, "Dafnis, terrible things are going to happen to Cyprus, and the highest danger is for British people. It will not be a safe place for us to stay. The angel told us to leave Cyprus as soon as possible, and we invite you to join us." "Well," I said, "I cannot join you. I would love to." I always had some interest in communal life. I spent some time in a Kibbutz. I was interested in Soviet collective farms. I had an interest in living in a commune. Anyway, I said,

> "No. I am getting married. How can I go? I have to stay. Just please pray for me." And they left Cyprus and moved to Kenya in east Africa. Shortly thereafter the EOKA rebellion broke out.

Because Ward died in 1949, such a visit from Confraternity members would have happened after his death. Dafnis became engaged to Maroula in May 1953 and married her in November 1953. His next story illustrates the problems he had with memory of past events.

Dafnis described a divine message that Ward gave to Maroula to reassure her because Dafnis had been away on a business trip and Maroula had not heard from him in three weeks.

> She talked to John Ward, and he told her, "Maroula, just pray, and I shall soon bring you news of Dafnis." And guess what. He went back, and he told her, "Don't worry. Dafnis is having coffee at the train station in Zürich, Switzerland." And I was there. He had extra-body experiences. I was having coffee at the Barnes Station, as they call it, in Zürich. And he said, "Tuesday, four o'clock in the afternoon. He is in good health. And he is okay." And because Maroula trusted him more than I did, she felt very comfortable.

The fact that Ward died four years before Dafnis and Maroula married makes his story implausible. Also, the Barnes Station is not located in Zürich but in southwest London. However, in his book, *ΠΙΚΡΟΔΑΦΝΕΣ (Bitter Leaves of Laurel)*, Dafnis wrote that Ward's *wife*, Mother Mariam, told Maroula that Dafnis was in the train station in *Geneva*. In his book, he specifies the date as 1954 and says that he was on a trip to Germany on business. I do not know why he called Jessie Page "Mother Mariam."

Dafnis told other stories that revealed his belief that angels and saints communicate with people. For example, on 8 September 2017, as we approached the Church of Elijah perched high in the mountains, Dafnis told us about driving to this church years earlier, when the roads were much less passable. He said a woman called him from Australia and told him that Elijah had appeared to her mother in a vision and directed her to have someone light a candle in his church in Cyprus and she would be healed. The daughter called Dafnis and explained the situation. To the woman's surprise, he replied that he was almost to the Church of Elijah at that very moment. Dafnis went on to say he lit a candle in the church for the woman, and she got well. As he was talking, I thought that, if this event actually happened, it could not have happened too many years earlier, because it presupposed his having a mobile phone. Were the roads still that primitive if he had a mobile phone?

He asked what I thought. I took the easy way out and said, "I don't know." He smirked and concluded that he thought Elijah knew he was on his way to

Figure 10. *Church of Elijah in the mountains north of Limassol.*

the church and therefore appeared to the woman in a vision. He seemed sincere, although with Dafnis, I never knew for sure. At times, he promoted a scientific belief system with empirical checks and balances, expressing interest in historical verification. And at times he expressed beliefs in teleportation and supernatural interventions. I could never predict what he would say next. I do not think he ever integrated his eclectic worldview into a coherent belief system. But he did believe in *Eros*.

Discovering *Eros* in Italy

Solomon knew that Dafnis was unhappy about not being allowed to attend a university with his friends from the Cyprus Christian youth movement. To make his son feel better, Solomon let him travel—which he grew to love. Before Dafnis died, he had toured extensively around the world.

One of his most formative trips happened soon after he graduated from high school. Solomon let him spend a month at an ecumenical, Christian work camp in Italy where youth from different countries converged. Dafnis was nineteen at the time, and this experience changed his life—especially with respect to women. He said,

> It was the first time I ever met young women—you know, Greek, Germans, Dutch, Americans, and Italians. It was a completely new world

> for me. And that was another strong influence. My exposure to multinational, multicultural, and multi-religious experiences shaped my spiritual thinking.

In 2017, Dafnis spoke as if his memories of the month in Italy were still vivid.

> In 1949, I, with a friend, Evgenios, traveled to Italy. At the time we went, it was like Columbus embarking on the trans-Atlantic exploration. I grew up on the farm, and I was a very innocent boy *at that time. At that time!* And we went to north Italy, and there was this small community building an international, Christian youth center called *Agape*. It is still thriving today. Evgenios and I stayed there one month.

Dafnis admitted that he was not an innocent farm boy by the time he left Italy. He evidently first experienced *Eros* (physical intimacy) during that month.

Dafnis's interactions with youth from multiple countries opened his eyes to other ways of thinking and diverse forms of Christianity. And two British participants snubbed him.

> During the camp in Italy, we decided we wanted to have a group picture taken. But two young men from England said, "We refuse to be in a picture with people from the Colonies." And they stepped out. It was very anti-Christian, of course, but this generated a lot of discussion and a lot of support [for us]. Gretchen from Holland and a German girl protested very strongly. They said, "We want these people to be expelled." I did not know Gretchen very well before this event. I was young and very shy also. But after this incident, we became friends.... Until last year, Gretchen used to come here every summer to spend one month with us. She studied Greek and ended up fluently speaking eight languages, and she worked as an interpreter in Strasbourg, in the European Parliament.

For decades, Gretchen regularly came to Cyprus to see Dafnis, and Dafnis went to Holland to see her.

At the end of the month-long camp in Italy in 1949, Dafnis decided to travel through war-devastated Europe. Evgenios did not accompany him, because he needed to return to Cyprus to help his father with the family business. Dafnis boarded a train and traveled solo to areas of Germany that were destroyed in WW2. He determined his itinerary as he went along. He ended up in Switzerland, where he realized that he was completely out of money. He had his boat ticket to return from Italy to Cyprus, but he did not have enough money to buy a train ticket from Switzerland to Italy to board the boat.

> I was young. I ran out of money. I had my boat ticket to get from the port city of Genoa, Italy, to Cyprus, but I needed to buy a train ticket to go from Geneva to Genoa. I started crying. I said, "I'm stranded, and I know nobody here." I sat on the steps of a Catholic church in Geneva, crying.

> Then the Catholic priest came, and he said, "What is your problem?" I told him I came from Cyprus. I don't know if he even understood where Cyprus was. I said, "My problem is that I ran out of money. I have my boat ticket, but I cannot go from here to Genoa. I need 30 Franks for the ticket." He said, 'I shall give you the 30 Franks." I said, "No. I just want you to make me a loan." He said, "No. I will give you 50." So he gave me 50 Franks, which I sent him after I got back to Cyprus. I was able to get to Geneva and from there I came to Cyprus.

Presumably the 50 Franks allowed Dafnis to have money to buy food on the way from Geneva to the seaport. In other versions of the same story, details differed. On another occasion he said that he was crying *inside* the church and that he had a ticket on a boat out of *Bari*, not *Genoa*. He also said, "I found an open church there, and I stepped *into* the church and I started praying and praying—and crying. And then the Catholic *vicar* came and said, 'What happened my young man?'" Dafnis elaborated different points depending on what he wanted to emphasize. For example, once he said, "He gave me the Franks. I said, 'Father, as soon as I get home, I am going to transfer this amount to you.' He said, 'Never mind. Forget it.' But I said, 'Give me your bank details, and I will make sure.' And I did. When I came back, I transferred the money to him." Such differences do not detract from the main points of the account, but they do raise the question of how much the story changed over time.

Traveling to other countries opened Dafnis's eyes to different religious traditions, but he had already begun that process when he was a child. Dafnis said, "Next to our farm was a Turkish [Muslim] family with six or seven children, and some of their children were my age. We grew up together—playing together. So these things helped me accept people." Dafnis said, "I began to wonder how one can justify rejecting any person, any religion, any nationality and still believe that the rule is LOVE." Over time, his views became increasingly eclectic.

> There is a very good book that I often refer to—written by a Jesuit priest [Juan Arias]: *The God I Don't Believe In* [St. Meinrad, Indiana: Abbey Press, 1974]. And I found this book very meaningful. This author says, "Okay, let us examine ourselves and decide whether we can be called Christians really.... Do we Christians have a law? Do we have a constitution? Eventually, we shall be judged, and we know who the judge is. Are we going to say, 'We don't know the rule by which we are going to be judged?'" This Jesuit priest said, "I tell you that the rule is spelled out in Matthew 5. The judge tells everybody how he will judge."

Dafnis came to believe that God judges all humans on the basis of how we have loved others—which is revealed by how we have responded to their physical needs (Matthew 5). One of his favorite biblical passages was "Let us love one another."

300,000 Workers with no Salary

In spite of Fr. Solomon's popularity in the Limassol region, people criticized him for not sending Dafnis to a university. Farming was not a prestigious career—unlike Solomon's own vocations as a teacher and a priest. Why did he not want his son to have a position with esteem—to become a doctor, or a lawyer, or a professor? Farming was for villagers with no education. But Solomon stood fast and in so doing created tension between himself and his oldest son.

Solomon insisted that Dafnis learn practical skills from Cypriot farmers, and he apprenticed his son to people who could teach him different agricultural techniques. One of the first methods he learned was how to dry figs. Solomon sent him to Pyrgos, the center of fig drying in northwestern Cyprus. In the late 1940s, traveling to Pyrgos from Limassol required at least two days. Dafnis grew pensive as he said, "I went there and I felt very lonely. I was young and away from the family for the first time. But there I learned how they fumigate and dry figs." After he understood the technique, he returned home and began to dry figs on their property.

Dafnis also learned how to order seeds, and he and his father began to plant flower seeds. They were the first to introduce the Black Beauty eggplant to Cyprus. Dafnis added, "Of course, you never become rich by selling vegetables. But we survived, although my father's salary was very small for a family." They figured out how to grow flowers, harvest their seeds, and export flower seeds to England and Holland. Growers in these countries shipped the parent stock of their hybrids to him in Cyprus because of the long, Mediterranean growing season. He grew Zinnias, and this business became profitable. Some of his other farming projects failed miserably.

Solomon and Dafnis attempted beekeeping. Dafnis took a course for beekeepers at the agricultural school in Morphou, but he had no money to purchase beehives. As a result, he had his first experience of trying to get a loan—the very practice that kept his father continually in debt.

Dafnis went to the bank to see George Madrides, an uncle of a good friend. His description of the conversation is vintage Dafnis.

> So to help me make my first bank loan, which was £20 at that time: £20, in contemporary terms, maybe it is some thousand dollars. And Mr. Madrides said, "Okay, what are you going to do?" I said, "I am going to buy beehives and start beekeeping." He said, "Beekeeping? We never made a loan for beekeeping. We do loans for trading, for industries, and things like that, but bees? No." And then I said, "I am surprised you don't, Mr. Madrides. Because give me an example of a business where you have maybe 300,000 workers working free, without a salary, day and night, producing honey for you?"

This story may well have grown over time. I can imagine Dafnis telling it to a group of people and someone in the group making a quip about 300,000 bees working for free—and the next time Dafnis told the story this quip became part of the account. Who knows? Stories develop. It is a fact of oral traditions. Dafnis *did* warn us to believe only 50% of what he said.

Anyway, in Dafnis's description, Mr. Madrides was surprised by this astute statement from a young man and replied, "Okay, list your assets." Dafnis said, "What do you mean. I don't understand." Madrides replied, "Do you have any movable or immovable property?" Dafnis said, "I don't know. What is moveable and immovable property?"

> He explained to me and I said, "I have nothing except one bicycle which my father bought for me for 25 shillings." So he wrote down, "One bicycle." Then he wanted to know what else. I said, "Books. I have almost 300 books, and they're valuable." He pulled his pencil out and made a big X there. "Books! Who cares about books as a security! If they were old newspapers, I would assign some value, because I could give them to Herodotos to use in his grocery." Herodotos was a good friend of my father, and he was the godfather of Stahis. He was our grocer and he used old newspapers to wrap cheese. Anyway, Madrides said, "What shall we do? Twenty-five pounds? You cannot get 25 shillings. You need to have a guarantor." Okay, I felt very down, but my future father-in-law, who was keeping an eye on me, he was keen to offer to guarantee me; and I got the loan, with his signature.

That last statement raises time problems. Dafnis's description of the bee story indicated that he was involved in this effort soon after high school (c. 1949), but he did not get engaged to Maroula until 1953. I cannot determine a precise date for this venture, but I can say that Dafnis briefly became a beekeeper. The Panagides family even had their own label to place on jars of honey. However, he concluded his story on a somber note about the bank loan: "I never got out of debt ever since."

Marriage—Not College

Father Solomon's considerable intellect, his love of reading, his love of nature, and his eagerness to implement modern farming practices all influenced Dafnis in profound ways. But Dafnis admitted he grew frustrated by not being able to leave Cyprus to attend a university with his friends and to explore the intellectual life of the mind in an environment structured to that end. Dafnis was a dreamer. For a time, he wanted to join the work of Albert Schweitzer in Gabon, Africa. Solomon shut down such dreams. Dafnis explained,

> He had in mind to find me a wife like my mother: a village girl. He did not care about education or wealth or a big name from town—only a

> simple girl who grew up in the simple areas in the village family environment. And that is how he spotted my wife. He had three on his short list, and Maroula, if she [were] with us today, she would say she was the lucky one. I cannot say.

By 1953, Solomon's search for potential candidates to marry his son had focused on Maroula Loizou, a daughter of the mayor of Kalo Chorio. Dafnis was not ready to settle down, but he obeyed his father. "It was a different time," he told us. "Children did what their parents said." I pressed him on this matter: "Did you resent your father for denying you the opportunity to attend college." "No," he said. "That is just the way it was back then." We sensed residual turmoil in the 88-year-old Dafnis, but we do not know what the 24-year-old Dafnis thought. People change.

Dafnis claimed that officers of the Colonial Government in the Department of Agriculture offered him a scholarship to go to the Commonwealth Agricultural Bureau in Oxford to study tropical agriculture. But by that time his parents were pressuring him to get married and settle down. He said they did not want him to abandon the farm and go to England to study. But perhaps they had other reasons.

Different views exist among family members on why Solomon would not send his oldest son to a university. We know, for example, that Solomon later paid for the education of his daughter, Chloe, and her husband, Andonis, at a university in Athens. We also have a diary entry by Stahis from August 1954 in which he lamented his family's bankruptcy that was causing the loss of their lovely property where he spent the first 17 years of his life. Interestingly, Stahis wrote that Solomon sold their land for £10,500, and then deposited £1,000 in a bank account for Stahis's university studies. Why did Father Solomon refuse to let Dafnis attend a university yet during a financial crisis set aside that much money for Stahis's education? Theories vary.

I do not know why Solomon did not want Dafnis to follow in his footsteps and become a teacher or a priest. Most likely, multiple factors came into play. From Dafnis's viewpoint, however, his parents simply had marriage plans for their oldest son and set about to make them happen.

The Marriage that almost wasn't

Dafnis said one of his aunts conspired with his parents on how to get him interested in Maroula, who worked in her father's little store in Kalo Chorio. Dafnis said his aunt made up reasons to send him to the store so that he would encounter Maroula frequently, and he wondered why she suddenly needed so many things from the store. I did not think to ask why he was in Kalo Chorio. After all, his family moved to Limassol when he was small. Perhaps they were spending a summer in Kalo Chorio. Given the way Dafnis told his stories, it is difficult to know; and I can no longer ask him.

He explained that his parents and the aunt put on a charm offensive. They boasted that Maroula was a student of Evrena, an accomplished woman who taught Maroula how to cook and how to keep the house spotlessly clean. The strategy finally worked, and they set a date for Dafnis to sit down with Maroula's family in her home for a special meal. As a prospective bride, Maroula needed to demonstrate her competence by serving a special kind of egg and lemon soup. Dafnis loved to tell this story. We heard it at least four times.

> On the twenty-first of May, that was the day of St. Constantine and St. Helena, my parents organized a luncheon to meet my future wife—and to finalize the deal. It was a big event, because the parents and the relatives, aunts and uncles from both sides, and of course my parents and her parents gathered around this big table to eat the traditional soup for feast days, which is the *Avgolemono* soup. And Maroula was young, very attractive, with long hair, and a very nice blue dress. Very thin. And she was beautiful—*by Cypriot standards* (Dafnis's emphasis).
>
> ...Solomon and the parents of Maroula were at the head of the table, and I was also sitting at the head of the table with my father—nicely dressed of course.... I was a handsome young man of 24 years. And the poor girl had this bowl of soup. First she went to my parents and served, and then her parents, and then she came to serve me. And she dropped the bowl of soup on my suit. The poor girl [Maroula] started crying and crying. And everybody was so embarrassed that the whole thing failed. It was a real crisis. It was finished! The marriage is destroyed! That was the end! We would walk away and no deal. However, despite this disastrous mistake, I decided to marry her. And I made the right decision, and I was happy ever since.

"How long," I asked, "did it take before Maroula could laugh about spilling the soup on you?" "We never brought it up," he said.

Dafnis also loved to tell a follow-up story about their first kiss, which was repeated so often that it took on a kind of legendary character. We even heard a version of it from one of his nephews. He said, "Maroula used to tell us a story. She said, 'We were engaged, and he wasn't kissing me, and I was waiting for him to make the first pass.' He was either shy or maybe he didn't want to. And then one day, Maroula just grabbed him and kissed him." He went on to say, "Maroula told us this story several times. She got fed up with waiting and waiting for her fiancé to make a pass, so she made the first move."

Dafnis's version included more details. He said,

> We were engaged, and her aunt, who was the mediator, told her, "Maroula, Dafnis is a very shy boy"—I *WAS*, but years have changed me very much... I am corrupted in many ways.... I can safely say that I am corrupted. At that time, I was still innocent. And my aunt knew me very

> well. So she called Maroula and told her, "You are now engaged and you will go to town for a few days with Dafnis, who will be your husband. Most probably, Dafnis will not kiss you. He is too shy to kiss you. If after a few days he does not, take initiative yourself." Which of course happened. She was such a shy village girl, but she followed the advice of her auntie. And she kissed me in the field with the Zinnia flowers. I was so embarrassed.

In light of his intimate experiences at the Ecumenical camp in Italy when he was 19 years old, one might wonder about his insistence that, when he got engaged to Maroula at age 24, he was such a shy boy that did not kiss her.

The 88-year-old Dafnis often blended stories of his younger days with accounts of more recent events—in a stream of consciousness sort of way. Speaking of Maroula kissing him triggered his memory of another event that he recounted repeatedly as a favorite. The story pertained to his walking along the beach in Limassol, holding hands with a younger woman, and his sister scolding him for his behavior. In one version, he said,

> Today they accuse me that I am seen with Filipinas, with Vietnamese, with Sri Lankans, with Indians, with all the nationalities. One day, Chloe called me aside and said, "Come here. I want to talk to you. Don't you understand that to bear a name you must be careful? You will ruin the reputation of that name. I have a report that last night you were seen at the beach walking with a young girl"—which was true. I walked along the beach with a young girl. She said, "People will start gossip about you." And I said, "Wait. Do you want people to gossip about your brother's relationship with a young girl or with a boy? Which do you want?" Ohh, we had good memories.

He told the story in a humorous way, glibly dismissing Chloe's concern for the family's reputation.

Although Dafnis loved to tell the stories about Maroula spilling soup on him and about her initiating their first kiss, he never said anything about their wedding. We know that they married on 8 Nov. 1953, but we heard no description of the festivities. Maroula would have given us details, but she died in 2002, almost a decade before we met Dafnis. Maroula could also have provided information about the transitions she had to make when she married Dafnis. For example, she left an economically stable home and entered a financial disaster. Maroula's father, in contrast with Solomon, was a shrewd and prosperous businessman. Although people in the Limassol area greatly respected Father Solomon for his teaching and church work, he was inept with finances.

When Dafnis brought his new bride to their lovely farm by the sea, she might not have known about the financial distress of her new family. Soon she did. And all was not well with the newlyweds. Leaving Kalo Chorio and moving to Limassol caused an identity crisis for Maroula. Dafnis explained the situation from his perspective.

> Usually in marriage the first few years are the happiest. In my case, it was the opposite. When we came to the town, Maroula started developing an inferiority complex. She moved to Limassol from the village to a completely different environment. My father had his contacts: prominent lawyers and bankers, and journalists. Her education was elementary school, very simple. So she started feeling that she did not belong in this environment. I sensed she was very unhappy.

Figure 11. *Wedding picture of Dafnis and Maroula.*

Educated people came to the Panagides home, and sometimes they conducted their intellectual conversations in English. Politics were an important topic of discussion and debate, especially the matter of freedom from England. Maroula could not speak English, and she felt marginalized, both because of the language barrier and also her lack of education. In Kalo Chorio, the six years she attended elementary school were sufficient to be a good wife, but life was different in Limassol.

Don't bet the farm on Castor Oil

Dafnis and his father made another disastrous decision when a friend told Solomon he could get rich growing castor beans. The man said, "The oil of these seeds sells at very high prices because they are used in the newly invented jet engines." The friend added that castor beans come from a poisonous plant: "If you eat five seeds, you get a good sleep. Over five, you sleep permanently." In fact, castor seeds are poisonous *if* you eat the hulls, which contain ricin. Chemical experts can purify ricin to produce a potent poison.

However, mechanics earlier in the 20th century had already tried castor oil as a lubricant in engines, and it proved to be problematic, because it gummed up engine parts. Solomon and Dafnis apparently did not do their homework. They believed the friend and decided to grow castor beans. According to Dafnis, Solomon rented big areas of land near Germasogeia—east of Limassol—and hired fifty workers. But they did not have the necessary machinery to remove the seeds and produce the oil. The project failed, and they went further into debt. Solomon's responsibilities for conducting annual audits of the finances of churches in the Limassol area apparently did not transfer to his ability to manage his own finances.

Faced with another debt crisis, they debated what to do. Dafnis said, "We decided to sell the farm to pay off our debt, and with the little money left over, we would buy another farm. So we sold the farm and then we bought this one in 1954." This bleak outcome did not surprise those who were familiar with the family.

Road to Bankruptcy

We interviewed Petrakis, a cousin of Dafnis who lived with the Panagides family for a year while attending high school in Limassol. He got an inside view of how the household functioned, and he became well aware of Dafnis's lack of business sense. To illustrate, the cousin recounted a particular event pertaining to another business Dafnis developed, namely selling imported German tractors. Dafnis had his workshop on the ground floor and his office in a small room upstairs. Dafnis had hired another cousin, Nicos, to be in charge of public relations; and he was adept at conducting business. One day a customer came to get his repaired tractor, and the man asked Nicos how much he owed. When Nicos told the man he owed £50, the customer got angry and began shouting, "I want to see Mr. Dafnis." He refused to pay and insisted that he wanted to see Dafnis. Finally, Nicos pointed to the ladder and said, "Go up there!" The younger cousin told the story as follows:

> He went up to Dafnis, and he began complaining, saying, "Mr. Dafnis, please, I am a poor man. I cannot pay £50 for this work. Please, I want you to make me a discount." "Okay," said Dafnis." And he marked out the £50, and he wrote £25. The man went down to Nicos, showed him the invoice, and paid £25. When the customer left, Nicos went up to Dafnis's office and he told him, "Cousin, how much would you give *me* to come up the ladder to your office? Ten shillings?" Dafnis said, "I don't understand." Nicos said, "This man came once to your office, and you gave him £25. I will accept it if you give me only 10 shillings every time, and I will then go up and down the ladder 100 times."

We laughed at the way he told the story, but the message was clear. Doing business like that is a good way to go bankrupt. People will manipulate you, and if you capitulate to their demands, your business cannot be profitable.

An American at Kakomallis Campground

In 1954, Dafnis played a major role in organizing an international work camp for youth at Kakomallis under the umbrella of the World Council of Churches. Participants came from the Middle East, Holland, America, Germany, and Switzerland. One of the participants, a college student from Kansas named Katy, gave us access to some of the letters that she wrote to her parents in 1954. Katy, an adventurous young woman, spent the academic year of 1954–1955 in Beirut, Lebanon, as part of a Junior-Year-Abroad program established by the Presbyterian Church USA. Part of this study-abroad program included participation in a work camp sponsored by the World Council of Churches. She chose the one in Cyprus directed by Dafnis, mostly because Cyprus is near Lebanon. Another student enrolled in the Beirut program, Nancy, was from Pittsburg; and she and Katy traveled together to Cyprus.

Katy's experiences in the Middle East played a formative role in her life. Dafnis said that she was very brave, "coming to a completely undeveloped place like this forest here—without a road, without electricity, without running water, without proper toilets." I would add that she was also a perceptive young writer whose descriptions create vivid mental images. Here is what she wrote about her arrival in the port of Limassol on 15 August 1954.

> The port is poor and they load passengers and baggage into little motorboats about two miles out and that was a wild, soaking ride. We dripped our way up the 28-step rope ladder… and were parked in the customs office waiting for baggage when up walked the two most wonderful people in the world—to us, anyway: Daphnis Panagides, a local seed grower, son of a priest, director of our camp, and the most fabulous person God ever created—all this wrapped up in a very handsome face and only 25 years, and Bob Bates, whose father used to be a missionary in the far east and is now a professor at Union….

Katy described some of the other participants in the Kakomallis camp, such as Carolina, a mysterious and quiet woman from East Germany, and Marijke, a woman from Holland who "wears typical wooden shoes, is most bossy and at times irritating." Katy was *very* impressed by a tall, handsome, second-year medical student from England named Christopher, who had a great sense of humor and brought much laughter to the other campers.

Regarding cultural norms, Katy explained that the female campers had to be very discrete, because the idea in Cyprus of a mixed camp of young men and young women was shocking. During this time, Dafnis had a pregnant wife, was selling small farm machinery and seeds, trying to stay on good terms with British members of the Department of Agriculture and the Forestry Department, keep things afloat on the family farm, run the international camp for college-age students at Kakomallis, and perhaps was already secretly involved in the beginnings of a resistance movement against the British. One would think that being stretched so thin would frustrate him, but involvement in multiple endeavors pretty much typified his life.

Katy describes the daily rhythm of camp activities at Kakomallis.

> We arise around 5:30,—sleep in tents we put up as the first day's work. Day before yesterday, one of the other camps gave us old iron beds, so we're no longer fighting the gravel under our sleeping bags.... Morning prayers are held around the cement altar at 6:15.... Breakfast at 6:30 consists of our staple—brown sour bread in a round loaf with a crust like iron, canned margarine, jam, and milk, hot Nescafe—that gift of God, on Sunday.

One of their work projects involved widening the path that wound up the hill from Louvaras, the closest village below Kakomallis. Camp participants were turning the path into a road so that they could get supplies to Kakomallis on something other than "our own weary backs or that of the village donkey." The walk from Louvaras took 30 to 35 minutes. Katy's list of daily activities indicates a fairly well developed program: prayers, meals, work details, evening singing and recreation, and "talks in the starlight."

Her description of Solomon is humorous: "We live in an already constructed camp site run by Father Panagides who is a dead ringer for Santa Claus." Although not that old, his health was poor and his hair and beard were grey. Katy wrote that the ecumenical work camp participants shared Kakomallis with Cypriot boys who were there for a work camp. These boys tried to teach the foreigners how to speak Greek. Concerning the facilities they all shared, Katy's description of the toilet is hilarious.

> Plumbing facilities consist of one hole about 6" in diameter in a 4-foot square slab of concrete, covered in lime and fly spray daily and really quite sanitary. You certainly need to adjust your aim and believe me control of speed is the clue. All our water, both drinking and washing, comes from an ice-cold spring. We eat off of enamel plates that are washed with hands full of sand and dirt and then rinsed in cold water, no soap of course. I think it's fabulous that we're all still alive, but we haven't even had a single case of the john-runs in camp.

She mentions that the campers were always busy, and she introduces a note of mystery when she says, "Daphnis takes off on various journeys periodically and reappears, sometimes two or three days later, out of nowhere but always with just what he was sent for."

Katy remarks, "It seems Dafnis knows everyone on the island. He stops about every ten minutes along the road to say 'hello' to someone. What's more, he is to be a father any day." Maroula was very pregnant, yet Dafnis was constantly away from home working on his various projects. Gregarious by nature, he was always quite a talker, and people enjoyed conversing with him. He seldom worried about how much his conversations slowed down his projects.

Meanwhile, the work camp ended, and Katy and Nancy reluctantly left Kakomallis. In a letter dated 2–3 September 1954, Katy indicates they stayed several days with the Panagides family prior to departing for Beirut. Her description is delightful.

> We're staying at Daphnis' plantation—his house is about 300 feet in front of his folks'—and all just a spit away from the sea.... We stay at Daphnis' but eat with the folks. Their house has no doors, just doorways, stone floors, cats and dogs wandering throughout, a bed in every room, with beautiful crotched (sic) coverlets. The entire outside of the house is banked in exotic tropical plants and the heavy, intriguing scent of jasmine prevails overall. There are all sorts of canaries, pigeons and parrots on the porch, and peacocks roaming all over the place, both on the roof and off. Behind is a sort of patio-like place where all the hired help and orphaned god-children hang out; also tractors. No electricity or running water, of course. Down the path lined with bamboo and towering cedars hides the "john" with a real seat! I nearly jumped up and perched on top of it after our single hole for 4 and ½ weeks. Down another path lined with date palms and very tall 12-foot poinsettia plants is Dafnis' house. A bit more modern and surrounded with cactus and carnations. To either side of the road are the orange and lemon orchards with a goat tied to about every other tree. They are used for milk, meat and skin. Their udders get so heavy (just 2 faucets, you know) they are tied off the ground in flannel bags hooked to a contraption up over their poor shoulders. Various seed beds—zinnias, dahlias, roses, etc.—are in between, and wherever nothing else is there are always fig trees loaded now with ripe, sweet and delicious fruit.

Katy did not know that the Panagides family was in serious financial stress and in the process of losing their farm. They evidently remained quiet about their problems and served as gracious hosts for the American students. Katy comments, "Life is so peaceful and wonderful here, and sort of sanctified by the prevailing influence of Father in his beard and robes."

> She told another bittersweet story about the lovely farm and its gracious owners. Our stay there, following the camp time, was in a brand new house in front of the family farm home. It was very up-to-date and was Maroula's wedding dowry. We were told that that was the custom of the bride's family's gift to the groom's family.... [The new house] had an indoor toilet which delighted

> Nancy & me but we were told not to flush it. Late one night I found Dafnis sneaking in and scooping all that junk out and into a bucket. Then we realized it was not hooked up to anything. It was just like a piece of furniture. I was so impressed by Dafnis' humility in serving us in that way.

Always the courteous host, Dafnis went to great measures to make people feel welcome. Katy and Nancy resumed using the family outhouse when they discovered what he was doing. How sad that, because of their bankruptcy, the Panagides clan lost Maroula's dowry, the lovely new house.

Another sad part of the story is that Dafnis's leadership of the Kakomallis work camp partly precipitated the bankruptcy disaster. In an email dated 25 June 2020, Katy explained,

> Dafnis supported the family with his seed-growing business.... There was no certified seed source in Cyprus, so Dafnis started his company. He would start seeds at his farm and then distribute seeds to farmers around the island to grow even more. This required traveling all over the island, which was then not divided. Nancy & I got to go with him on several of those trips to places now on the Turkish side. It was because of this business that he was well known all over the island. He followed it up with the introduction of ... small garden tractors from Germany. During the time we were there, the watering system for his initial seed growing broke. He was up at the camp with us and didn't find out about it until it was a disaster. It was our understanding that that was the cause of the debt and the complete foul-up of the whole seed growing system. We did not know he had to sell the property because when we returned at Christmas (1954) they were still in the original farm home.

The departure of Katy and Nancy from Cyprus in September 1954 involved a tearful farewell to their new friends, but they managed to return toward the end of December to spend a week with the Panagides family. Maroula had given birth to a daughter, Lydia, about ten days after Katy and Nancy had left for Beirut in September, so Dafnis was now a father.

For the two students from America, after experiencing the cluttered chaos of Beirut, the serene, farm setting east of Limassol was rejuvenating—after they finally got there. Dafnis picked up Katy and Nancy at the Nicosia airport in his "dilapidated English Ford." The drive to Limassol was an ordeal that involved "four stops to fix the engine with stones and sticks and genius." Katy complains about the stiff springs of the vehicle and calls it "the Ford kidney smasher." Her description of the drive from Nicosia to Limassol is entertaining.

> The climax of the 60 mile, four hour trip was when a huge brown mule came galloping out of the bush and smashed into the headlights. There was a terrible crash; Daphnes (her spelling) put his hands on his head

> while Nancy grabbed the wheel; I grit my teeth and gripped my Bible, and we all turned expecting to see the sight of four legs sticking upright in the air. Instead, the dark form galloped off into the night, and we retreated from the scene of the crime with heretofore unrealized speed.

The following day they piled into Dafnis's Ford kidney smasher and drove to Limassol to let Katy and Nancy go shopping. In the process, they forgot Papa Solomon in town, and they returned much later to get him. He was pretty perturbed, but "he didn't blow off; we were just four hours late. It seems to be one of Daphne's pet tricks that when he says two minutes he really means two hours."

Katy mentions that Cypriots were so frustrated with the British and U.S. governments preventing freedom efforts that they rioted and beat a number of British and US citizens. She quickly added, however, that Dafnis kept their country of origin a secret and Cypriots treated them very well. They told her they did not hate British or US citizens; they just hated British and US foreign policy that consistently denied their basic, human rights. They were so exasperated with the demeaning way that British rulers treated Cypriots that revolutionary fervor was in the air. Soon after Katy and Nancy left the Middle East, armed conflict erupted on the island. But during Christmas week, the two young ladies basked in the serenity of the Panagides farm.

On Christmas Eve, the Panagides family listened to Christmas carols on a British radio station and encouraged Katy and Nancy to sing along. "Though Nancy can't sing a sour note backwards, we were begged at every meal to sing carols which we cheerfully struggled through." Further contact between the friends occurred a few months later. Katy explained, "Dafnis traveled to Beirut in the spring of 1955 for a conference of young Christian leaders sponsored by the World Council of Churches. He traveled under an assumed name because of political difficulties at home (I believe it was 'Mr. Brown')." Being secretive was by this time a central aspect of Dafnis's life. It kept him out of trouble—for a while.

Katy went on to earn a Ph.D. in Physical Anthropology from the University of Tennessee. Her husband, whom she married in 1959, earned his Ph.D. in New Testament from the University of Chicago. After working in Costa Rica and Mexico for a time, they returned to Kansas and spent years employed at McPherson College. Katy maintained contact with the Panagides family, and she helped them during a time of great need. Years later, Dafnis sent three of his own children to McPherson College so that Katy could keep an eye on them. Katy's daughter, Kathy, spent a year living with Dafnis's family in Limassol in 1978–79 as a foreign exchange student. Some friendships last for life, and we never know when or under what circumstances such friendships will develop.

Dafnis was a lover, not a fighter. Yet even this non-violent man was drawn into a violent rebellion. Among those who came to the farm to visit Solomon and

Dafnis were men who spoke enthusiastically about the need for Cypriot freedom. On that farm would occur momentous events in the history of Cyprus—events that propelled the Panagides family into the vortex of the political storm that was about to unleash its fury. Solomon, Maria, Dafnis, and Maroula would all be swept up into this tempest that had been building for decades. Within two years after Dafnis and Maroula married, the winds of rebellion against British occupation lashed the island. Greek Cypriots had reached the end of their long suffering under foreign occupation; and as the insurgency escalated into guerilla warfare, Dafnis and Maroula were starting their family.

CHAPTER 3
Bloody Rebellion

The Storm Breaks over Cyprus

At 12:30 a.m. on 1 April 1955, bombs rocked Cyprus cities in a coordinated attack on British facilities. The time of preparation was over. The battle commenced. Under the leadership of Colonel Georgios Grivas, a poorly equipped but deeply dedicated group of Greek Cypriots detonated explosives at strategic targets chosen to send a clear message: "We will no longer tolerate your treatment of us as underlings unworthy of self-determination. It is clear that you have no intention of granting our liberty, so we are going to force you to change your mind." Grivas knew he could not defeat the British army, but he was determined to conduct hit-and-run attacks as a means of drawing international attention to the situation in Cyprus and thereby force English leaders to reverse their rejection of the idea of Cyprus joining Greece. He did not command a standing army but directed covert cadres of small groups of rebels who blew up British buildings and police stations. They attacked British forces and then quickly faded away into the countryside, causing chaos for the British rulers.

In 2017, the former rebels we interviewed were elderly men and women. But in 1955, they were young, idealistic, zealous patriots willing to die for their cause. They told us they had waited long enough. For years, Greek Cypriot leaders had

EOKA fighters were mostly young

Colonel Georgios Grivas recruited young men, often in the 14- to 17-year-old range, because youth are daring and will take great risks for a cause. He had schoolboys blowing up police stations and airplanes on airfields (Grivas, *Guerrilla Warfare and EOKA's Struggle: A Politico-Military Study* [London, 1964], pp. 14–15). For detailed studies of the EOKA rebellion, see Andreas Karyos, "EOKA, 1955-1959: A Study of the Military Aspects of the Cyprus Revolt" (Unpublished Ph.D. Dissertation, University of London, 2011); David French, *Fighting EOKA: The British Counter-Insurgency Campaign on Cyprus, 1955-1959* (Oxford University Press, 2015), and Robert Holland, *Britain and the Revolt in Cyprus, 1954-1959* (Clarendon Press, 1998).

petitioned England to grant self-determination, leading to union (*enosis*) with Greece. The large majority of Cypriots were Greeks, and they wanted to be part of Mother Greece—not a British colony. For decades, British officials denied this request. When the bombs exploded on April 1955, neither side knew how bad the end result would be.

Great Britain did not want to lose Cyprus as a colony. They needed the island for its strategic value in the Eastern Mediterranean—near the Suez Canal, where they had vital interests. After two world wars in which millions died in order to preserve freedom for England and other nations, the British denied freedom to people in some of their colonies. And they made life miserable for those who resisted their rule. The aged EOKA survivors told us the British had previously perfected their torture techniques in Africa and employed similar treatment on hundreds of Cypriots. They described sleep deprivation, no food or water, constant beatings, use of drugs, and psychological manipulation. British soldiers even raped one woman (that is documented). Ian Cobain, a British journalist, provides a chilling description of British agents torturing people in Kenya, Cyprus, Northern Ireland, and elsewhere in *Cruel Britannia: A Secret History of Torture* (Portobello Books, 2012). A quick Internet search reveals articles written by journalists in England on the dark side of British policy in dealing with colonials.

Many Turkish Cypriots fanatically opposed EOKA. They were absolutely opposed to the idea of enosis with Greece. They fought alongside British troops and strove to bring about a division of the island into Greek and Turkish zones. Although they comprised only 18% of the population, their numbers in the police force increased dramatically once the rebellion began. Great Britain was skilled in pitting ethnic communities against each other, and they used this tactic effectively in Cyprus. But the Turks were not the only ones who opposed the resistance.

Approximately 30% of Greek Cypriots belonged to the Progressive Workers Party, AKEL (*Anorthotikó Kómma Ergazómenou Laoú*), a communist group initially opposed to the use of violence to attain enosis. They wanted a more gradual transition from being a colony of Great Britain to freedom of self-determination and then *enosis* with Greece. At the beginning of the rebellion, AKEL's leaders vigorously opposed EOKA, but as the rebellion wore on, AKEL softened its rhetoric; and some members worked actively with EOKA.

Colonel Grivas, the leader of EOKA, had fought Communists during the Greek Civil War, and he hated Communism. However, as leader of EOKA, his main objective was to degrade Britain's ability to rule Cyprus, not fight Cypriot communists. He did not want to alienate a major part of the Cypriot population against the EOKA struggle. He did order some AKEL members to be executed as traitors, but these were people whose actions posed a direct threat to the lives of EOKA fighters. British leaders claimed that Grivas was responsible for the deaths of more Greek Cypriots during the EOKA rebellion than were British soldiers; but their assertions were part of a propaganda campaign, and the numbers they declared are open to question. However, the EOKA fight did initially pit left- and right-wing Cypriots against each other—something the British cleverly facilitated. Lynne and I did not interview any former members of AKEL, so we did not hear their side of the story. But one non-Communist, non-EOKA friend of Dafnis told us, "Grivas was a filthy murderer," and he expressed outrage that Dafnis had not openly repudiated the violence of EOKA and repented of his role in the bloodshed—something Dafnis claimed he had already done. To say the situation was complicated is an understatement.

History of Foreign Domination

Cyprus has a long history of foreign domination. In the first century, Rome controlled the island, and most of its inhabitants were Greek polytheists. However, in the middle of the first century, the apostles Barnabas and Paul and other early Christian missionaries brought the message of Jesus to Cyprus. Initially, converts to this new faith formed a tiny minority in Cyprus, but by the late fourth century Orthodox Christianity had become the dominant religion; and that legacy has continued in Cyprus to the present day. Greek Cypriots often fly Greek flags over their houses and churches not because they any longer want to be united with Greece but because the flag declares their ethnic and religious identity. *We are Orthodox Greeks!* Today, even secular Cypriots will tell you, "I am Greek Orthodox. It is my cultural heritage."

In the Edict of Milan, A.D. 313, Emperor Constantine decreed protection for Christians, labeling them as a "tolerated" religious group. In 324, Constantine moved his capitol from Rome to the site of the city of Byzantium; and when he dedicated the newly built city in 330, he renamed it Constantinople (now it is Istanbul). *Polis* in Greek means city, so the name of the new capital meant *Constantine's Polis.* The city was large and wealthy and filled with impressive buildings. Political distance increased between the Roman Empire of the East, with Constantinople as its capital, and the Roman Empire of the West, with its capital at Rome. As the year 400 approached, Roman rulers were giving preferential treatment to Christians; and during the reign of Emperor Theodosius (ruled 527–65), Christianity became the state religion.

Cyprus remained under the jurisdiction of the Roman Empire of the East. In the seventh century, Greek supplanted Latin as the official language in the eastern part of the Roman Empire. Increasingly, distance also developed between the eastern and western parts of the Christian Church. The Roman Empire centered in Constantinople remained intact after the western part of the Empire fell. Called the Byzantine Empire by later historians, the East persisted in its power for centuries; but a war against the Sassanids (602–28), a Persian kingdom in the area today known as Iran, weakened the Roman Empire of the East and left some of its lands vulnerable—including Cyprus. From 645–965, Arab raiders destroyed coastal cities in their campaigns of looting and pillaging. For greater safety, numerous Cypriots moved inland, away from the coast.

Over time, the Byzantine Empire regained much of its strength, and in 965 Emperor Nikephoros II Phokas defeated Arab armies and restored Cyprus to his empire. The island experienced relative calm until 1191, when Richard the Lionheart, King of England, quickly conquered Cyprus with the intent of using it as a staging area and supply base for his crusade to restore the Holy Land to Christian control. In 1192, Richard turned the island over to Guy de Lusignan, a French crusader; and the Lusignan dynasty controlled Cyprus until 1489. During the three centuries the Lusignan leaders ruled the island, they and their clergy tried unsuccessfully to convert Cypriots to Catholicism. The Greek Orthodox Christians of Cyprus steadfastly clung to their Byzantine heritage. Still today, Cypriots use the word *Byzantine* to describe important aspects of their cultural heritage. In 1489, Venice officially assumed control of Cyprus; and these new masters also tried without success to convert the Greek Orthodox to Catholicism. In our conversations with Cypriots, we frequently heard bitter comments about Catholics. But the greatest hostility today is directed toward the Turks.

In 1571, the Ottoman Turks conquered Cyprus and subjected its inhabitants to harsh conditions and high taxation—even worse than what they experienced under the Venetians. Yet the Orthodox Church regained some of its former prestige, because the Turks expelled the Catholics and made Orthodoxy the official Christian presence on the island. Orthodox archbishops repeatedly complained to the Turkish sultans about how Turkish officials mistreated Cypriots. Finally, in 1660, the Ottomans appointed Cypriot Archbishop Nikephoros to be *ethnarch* (ruler) of the Greek Cypriots. They delegated to him responsibility for collecting taxes and representing his people. Over time, the archbishops gained more power until disaster struck. In 1821, the Turkish pasha Küçük Mehmet callously executed Archbishop Kyprianos along with other prominent Cypriots, using false charges that these men were conspiring to rebel against Turkish control of Cyprus. It was a lie, but Mehmet hated wealthy Greek Cypriots—and Europeans, for that matter—and he resorted to murderous tactics to achieve his goal of reining in Christian authority in Cyprus.

But the Ottoman Empire was slowly imploding under the weight of its own incompetence, and following the disastrous results of the Turkish war with Russia (1877–78), the Turks leased Cyprus to Great Britain, whose leaders wanted the island for strategic reasons. In order to have armed forces close to the Suez Canal and thereby strengthen their colonial enterprises, they built two naval bases on the island. In 1914, during WWI, England annexed Cyprus, and in 1925, Great Britain formally made the island one of its colonies.

Chafing under British Rule

When Britain took over Cyprus on 12 July 1878, Orthodox clergy expressed enthusiasm about freedom from the Ottoman Turks. They welcomed the change in government because they believed the British would help Cyprus unite with Mother Greece just as they had helped the Ionian Islands to do so. This expectation did not materialize, and that became a major point of contention.

The British upgraded the primitive conditions that typified much of Cyprus. They improved infrastructure and brought much greater efficiency. But they also introduced the Western concept of separation of church and state—a foreign idea in Cyprus. Church officials expected to regain more authority over the island once their Muslim overlords were gone, but they found their role in government diminishing instead of increasing. And the British had no interest in granting union with Greece.

In 1889, Greek Cypriot leaders sent delegates to London with a formal request for enosis with Greece. In 1895, they organized large protests across Cyprus, where people voiced their desire for enosis. More rallies erupted in 1902. In 1914, after England formally annexed Cyprus as a colony, Great Britain's previous argument that enosis with Greece could not occur because the island technically belonged to Turkey became immaterial.

In 1928, on the fiftieth anniversary of British rule, Archbishop Kyrillos III of Cyprus wrote an official letter complaining that for 50 years Britain had denied their request for self-determination and *enosis*. The British responded that the matter was closed and should no longer be discussed. Cypriots became increasingly frustrated. In 1931 Bishop Mylonas of Kition resigned his position in the legislative council and delivered a fiery speech to a full stadium in Limassol, calling for civil disobedience. Riots broke out all over Cyprus. The governor imposed Marshall Law and abolished many freedoms. The tone deaf, bullying approach used by the British infuriated Greek Cypriots. Civil unrest grew.

Preparation for the Struggle for Freedom

In December 1949, the Church of Cyprus told its members to go to their churches to vote for *enosis* with Greece. In a peaceful plebiscite conducted in January 1950, 95.7% of the Greek Cypriots voted in favor of *enosis*. The bishop of Kyrenia led an embassy to London to submit the results of the plebiscite to the Colonial Secretary, but he refused to meet with them. So the Cypriot delegates flew to New York to present the election results to the United Nations. They requested that the UN intervene on behalf of the Cypriot people, but the UN General Assembly refused to get involved.

When Makarios became archbishop in 1950, he led a national movement for *enosis* with Greece. But the British denied these calls for self-determination, repeating that the matter was closed. In 1951, Georgios Grivas, a Cypriot born soldier with a distinguished military career in the Greek army, began planning an armed resistance for liberation. From 3 October 1952 to 25 February 1953, he conducted detailed reconnaissance of Cyprus. He knew the British would have a much larger, better trained, and better equipped army to quell the rebellion, so he recruited Cypriot youth whose zeal would offset England's advantages. He believed that he held the moral high ground and would ultimately prevail in the conflict by forcing England to grant self-determination.

By this time, Makarios also had decided that armed rebellion was the only way to convince the British to relinquish Cyprus. On 7 March 1953, he convened a committee of twelve men in Athens to plan the liberation struggle. Together, they placed their hands on a Greek New Testament and swore by "the Holy and Consubstantial and Indivisible Trinity" to keep their plans secret, even to the point of enduring torture and sacrificing their lives in order to bring about their goal of *enosis* with Greece. Grivas was one of the twelve, and because of his experience in guerilla warfare, the committee members appointed him to lead the armed struggle.

By 1954, the British were fed up with the *enosis* clamor. They imposed harsh restrictions, including a five-year prison sentence for *any* act they considered to be seditious. Talking about *enosis* became illegal. Undeterred, Makarios used his oratorical skills to inflame the passions of audiences he addressed. As head of the Cypriot Orthodox Church, he had access to extensive finances, and he agreed to fund the rebellion. He arranged for covert acquisition of weapons and explosives, the first of which arrived from Greece in March 1954 aboard the ship *Sirene*. Soon thereafter, Dafnis became an early member of the rebellion.

An American Student in Cyprus

In August 1954, Katy, the nineteen-year-old student from Kansas, participated in the work camp at Kakomallis organized by Dafnis. Regarding Cypriot politics in 1954, Katy wrote in a letter to her parents,

> Cyrus is over-run with nationalistic spirit for union with Greece.... The situation was stimulated by the news... that the 70,000 British troops being moved out of Egypt were to be stationed here—an island with only 450,000 population as is. Cypriots demanded a plebiscite by the UN but British refused and two days before we arrived instituted a new constitution with a majority of a house appointed by the governor and the minority elected. Cyprus says "No"—quite emphatically, and the British

> retaliated last week with laws such as no one is allowed to discuss the matter in public meetings, no firearms, no knives over 2 ½ inches long (we joke much over this) and other really firm measures all punishable by five years in prison.

The British were *not* popular in Cyprus! Katy commented that the Kakomallis work camp was "quite removed from civilization." Then she said something about Dafnis that indicates he had some sort of covert involvement in the resistance even before Grivas came to Cyprus.

> We are one of the main headquarters of the Cypriot underground movement and Dafnis has his finger in everything. However, this is a British forestry department station. We are next week to be planting 200 trees for them, our tents are furnished by the public works department, and we are right in the middle of everything trying to be diplomatic. Pacifism is the by-word, so don't worry about danger. Because of the situation all newspapers and radio have been on strike for two weeks.

Greek Cypriot resentment toward British rulers for rejecting their desire for self-determination had been simmering for decades. Now it was boiling over. What Katy did not realize was that, while she was in Cyprus, Archbishop Makarios and other key figures were actively preparing for an armed rebellion—covertly training young people in guerrilla tactics and sneaking weapons and explosives onto the island. Pacifism was *not* their byword.

Makarios and Grivas begin the Rebellion

Grivas began his propaganda campaign in August 1954 with the clandestine publication and distribution of a newspaper as a recruiting tool. Grivas explained that English chains on Cyprus must be broken in order to end enslavement to Britain. As a result, Greek Cypriots all over Cyprus—particularly youth—became excited about joining the cause. Some Greek Orthodox priests became active members of EOKA, and numerous fighters were deeply religious individuals who believed that their cause was noble for God and country. Some studied Scripture together for spiritual strength before they carried out their missions.

On 10 November 1954, Grivas covertly came to Cyprus and initiated his activities as military commander. He appointed leaders of small groups of fighters around the island and instituted a system whereby his fighters only knew a few others who joined the struggle. That way, if anyone was captured and cracked under torture, he or she would only be able to identify a few others as members of the resistance. In January 1955, he and Makarios officially named their group EOKA (*Ethniki Organosis Kyprion Agoniston* = National Organization of Cypriot Fighters). A lot of his warriors came from the ranks of OXEN (*Orthodoxos*

Figure 12. *Makarios with a group of Cypriot men. Father Solomon stands beside Makarios. Numerous EOKA fighters came from the ranks of those who belonged to Orthodox youth movements started by Solomon.*

Christianiki Enosis Neon), the Orthodox Christian Union started by Father Solomon Panagides. Grivas faced immense obstacles. His zealous youth had no training whatsoever in how to use weapons.

On 29 March, Grivas and Makarios met in Nicosia at *Metochi tou Kykkou*, a branch monastery of the larger Kykkos Monastery located in the mountains west of Nicosia. They decided to begin the active rebellion in the early hours of 1 April, during a dark phase of the moon that would help to conceal their saboteurs. On 30 March, Grivas briefed his leaders on final plans, and at 12:30 a.m. on 1 April, bombs exploded simultaneously, taking the British army and the national police completely off guard. Among the first targets destroyed was the government radio station in Nicosia—silencing the voice of British propaganda. Bombs also exploded in police stations, army barracks, educational offices, and courthouses. Later that day, EOKA members distributed leaflets explaining what was happening. And still the UN refused to bring the Cyprus problem before the general assembly.

Dafnis explained that the original idea was to blow up a few buildings in Cyprus as a means of calling international attention to the problem. Very few Europeans, let alone Americans, knew anything about Cyprus or understood the problems its inhabitants faced. Archbishop Makarios thought that detonating bombs would make international headlines, causing readers to ask, "What is going on in Cyprus?" Unfortunately, the conflict escalated out of control. According to Dafnis, when the EOKA struggle began, Grivas gave strict orders not to kill people,

> but only to blow up military installations and property of the British army and Colonial buildings. And this is what we did for the first several months. I did not blow up anything myself, but I did carry people who detonated bombs and blew up a police station, a military station, and we burned down the poles of the electricity authority.... Later on, when EOKA had the first victims, Grivas said, "Okay, now any member of the security forces is a target—but not civilians."

Grivas sought to disrupt the ability of England to rule Cyprus and to force them to send soldiers to the island—which would be seen as military repression and play well in the foreign press. He was not interested in killing people but in focusing international attention on Cyprus and thereby forcing the British to grant self-determination to the island's residents.

Many high school students joined the resistance, and British leaders closed schools and arrested teachers. Strikes became common. Grade school children created chaos by holding protests and throwing rocks at British soldiers, who found themselves in the embarrassing situation of chasing children around school buildings—which made for marvelous coverage in foreign newspapers. At the beginning of the rebellion, 499 elementary schools were operational in Cyprus. By spring 1956, the British had closed all but 81 of them (see Andreas Karyos, *EOKA*, pp. 117–22 for details). EOKA never had more than 300 armed fighters, but they had a huge amount of support from Greek Cypriots in all levels of society.

Amazingly, Grivas directed the struggle while remaining unseen by the vast majority of his fighters. From carefully constructed hideouts, he gathered intelligence and sent orders

EOKA Oath

(from Varnavas, *EOKA*, pp. 54-55)

I swear the following by the Holy Trinity:

1. I shall struggle with all my powers for the liberation of Cyprus from the English yoke, sacrificing even my life.
2. I shall not abandon the struggle under any pretext, save only when so ordered by the leader of the Organization and after the aim of the struggle has been accomplished.
3. I shall obey absolutely the orders of the Leader of the Organization and only his orders.
4. If arrested, I shall maintain absolute silence both regarding the secrets of the Organization and the names of my comrades-in-arms, even if I am tortured to confess.
5. I shall disclose to no one any order of the Organization or secret which has come to my knowledge, except when so authorized by the Leader of the Organization.
6. My actions shall be guided only by the interest of the struggle and shall be free of any self-interest or party interest.
7. If I forsake my oath I shall be deprived of honor and worthy of any punishment.

to division leaders. Secrecy was paramount. Only a few EOKA members knew his location. British soldiers searching for EOKA fighters did not yet know the identity of the leader—who called himself *Digenis* in flyers (an alias he took from a Greek epic about a Byzantine war hero named *Digenis Akritas* who repelled Muslim invaders). The British spent large sums of money trying to recruit informants to betray EOKA members, and informants became targets of EOKA fighters.

Although Grivas distributed a leaflet in Turkish sectors in July 1955 stating that he had no intentions of harming Turkish Cypriot inhabitants of Cyprus (Grivas, *Memoirs*, p. 52), Turkish militants aggressively armed themselves and joined British soldiers in the hunt. Androula Petrides described for us how a Turkish man broke her arm during a school protest. She said,

> I was not involved with guns. I was only 15 years old. I would write on the walls. I would go every morning, all around the school, and leave leaflets on the desks, and then go to my class... [I would also] go to the churches for memorial services for people who were hung [by the British].... At one of the demonstrations, they got me into a corner. And a member of the Turkish paramilitary put his knee on my belly, and he said, "EOKA, eh?" He had a baton. I tried to resist. He hit me here [pointing to her arm]. Like that. [She demonstrated swinging a baton.] A reporter came and interviewed [me], but nothing was done about the attack.

In spite of the pain, she was proud to fight for her country: "We had enough. We had more than enough. It was time to be free now—like all the other European countries."

Her husband, Petros, a cousin of Dafnis, had been born in England during WW2 but was adopted by an uncle in Famagusta, where he grew up. He also joined EOKA while in high school, and after Cyprus gained independence in 1960, he studied engineering in London. He explained, "I had nothing against the British. For me, I wasn't fighting the British. I was fighting the system. It wasn't fair for anybody in Cyprus to be under the British." During the EOKA rebellion, British soldiers arrested and tortured him. He said he felt proud to be part of the rebellion and he did not break under the harsh interrogation.

Great Britain tries to crush EOKA

On 15 July 1955, the British governor of Cyprus enacted laws that allowed soldiers and police to detain and incarcerate *anyone* suspected of belonging to an illegal organization. They needed no formal charges to hold suspects in custody for as long as officials deemed necessary. They built detention centers, which Greek Cypriots call concentration camps. In May 1956, the British also started hanging captured members of EOKA. They sought to crush the rebellion. But in spite of overwhelming odds, EOKA members continued to conduct their missions.

My goal in this book is not to recount the battles between EOKA and British troops, or to list the names of people killed in battle or by execution or by torture in British camps. Others have already chronicled such information. My goal is to report stories told by Dafnis and his friends who were part of EOKA—to give voice to their memories of the struggle and to reflect on the implications of what they said. Significantly, some of these EOKA members explained that the rebellion was a terrible idea with disastrous consequences. Others remained completely convinced that the insurgency was totally justified.

Dafnis joins EOKA

In 1954, Dafnis and his father faced financial crisis and entered bankruptcy. Sometime that year, they sold their farm by the sea and began the process of purchasing a smaller property closer to Limassol. Dafnis never said exactly when in 1955 they moved their families and their agriculture business to the new location. When I asked him to explain why they moved, he said, "We moved here because I failed in my business. I was under heavy debt, and we had to sell the farm and buy this one here for less money—and so, we survived. This financial problem proved that I was never good in business."

Dafnis did not tell us the exact date he joined EOKA, but he enjoyed telling about how he was recruited.

> Some of the early EOKA members came from [OXEN] the Christian Orthodox Youth Movement [founded by Solomon Panagides]. Two very close friends of mine were key members of the earliest movement. One of them was the Limassol contact for Grivas [Andreas Ioannidis], and the other one was my employee—a mechanic [Christakis Tryfonides]. Both of them ruled me out of joining EOKA because I had many contacts with the Colonial Administration in the Department of Agriculture.... I was a seed grower, and I had frequent visitors from the Agricultural Department.... My friends thought that they should keep me out [of EOKA] because my social network could put Grivas in danger.... So, for many months, I was *out*, although they were working under my nose. On one occasion, I sensed that the behavior of my employee was a little bit different. I talked with him privately, and I said, "Christaki, is something bothering you? Is it something with your family or children, because your behavior has changed recently?" He told me, "Thank you for your interest. I will get back to you in a couple of days."

Things were about to get complicated. Andreas and Christakis worried that Dafnis might unwittingly divulge information about EOKA to someone in the Colonial government, so they were reluctant to recruit him. Only after extended conversation did Christakis approach him.

> A couple of days later, he came with a very good friend of mine—a bookseller in Limassol who was the secretary of the Christian Orthodox Youth Organization. We went out by one of the lemon trees, privately, and they said, "Listen, we are going to disclose to you something that is very serious. You must keep your mouth shut." They explained the dangers of not keeping things secret. They then explained that they had started already this popular uprising, and they said, "The Uncle is here and he is training us." They did not call him Grivas; they called him the Uncle.

Their conversation lasted for hours. When Andreas and Christakis explained things about weapons and ammunition, Dafnis protested.

> I said, "Listen, you know me very well, and you know that I cannot kill even a sparrow, let alone a human being. So, I do not qualify for the violent work you are telling me about." They said, "Once you join the organization, this is none of your business—if you are going to kill a sparrow or some people. This is not yours to decide. You are a member of the organization. There is *strict* obedience." "Okay," I said. "If this is God's will, let it be." And, then I joined. As of that moment, I became a member of the organization… one of the first nine members of the Limassol EOKA group. We were in groups of three—three groups of three. The original idea was to cause physical damage and to stick to this strictly. Some of the targets were public buildings—government buildings—just to stir things up for the international public opinion—to cause them to wonder, "What is happening in Cyprus? We have got to do something about it."

A big problem for this sabotage plan was that EOKA members in Limassol had no knowledge of how to use weapons. Dafnis enjoyed telling a story that illustrated the naïve but brash and patriotic spirit of his young band of militants. They decided to ambush a British military vehicle as it traversed steep turns in the mountains. They had no explosives, so they filled baskets with cactus—which grew abundantly in the area—and were going to dump the cacti down on the jeep when it appeared. Fortunately for them, no British patrol came by that night.

I asked Dafnis who trained them for EOKA missions. He said, "We had people from Greece who trained us in the use of hand grenades and how to make homemade explosives." Evagoras, a trainer from Greece, had much instructing to do; for initially his pupils were clueless when it came to weapons. Dafnis loved to tell another story about two sisters involved in EOKA. They met a British soldier who was impressed by their beauty and visited them in their home. At some point, he offered to sell revolvers to them; so the sisters consulted with other EOKA members on whether or not they should buy the weapons. Dafnis and a few of his friends drove to Nicosia in June 1955 to consult with Archbishop Makarios about the deal. Makarios asked what they knew about revolvers, and they confessed they knew nothing. So, he went to his desk, opened a drawer, pulled out a Colt .38 Special, and told them that, if they could find more like this one, they should purchase all they could get. It was a memorable encounter with the archbishop. Unfortunately, Dafnis did not finish explaining whether or not the two sisters began to purchase more revolvers.

On the Panagides's farm, EOKA members built a cache to hide weapons and explosives. Dafnis explained that, "Basically my main role was to serve as the storekeeper—to bring weapons here and to distribute them to groups on the basis of instructions from Grivas." But they desperately needed more munitions. Grivas directed Dafnis and a few others to meet a man in Nicosia who would supply weapons. Dafnis drove his Ford "kidney smasher," and when they reached the appointed destination, they discovered it was a nightclub. Andreas Ioannides, then leader of EOKA in Limassol, was secretary of OXEN and a man of deep Christian faith. He got so upset when he learned that an immoral place—a nightclub—was used for contact purposes that he resigned as division leader. Evidently, preparing to deceive and kill British soldiers was acceptable for a religious patriot, but not using a nightclub as a place to contact an illegal arms dealer.

Dafnis said he also was troubled when he learned that he must enter the nightclub, but he admitted that he was "very impressed" by the beauty of the women he met there. Grivas accepted the resignation of Andreas Ioannides and appointed Christakis Tryfonides to take the lead in Limassol. Not long after, British soldiers arrested Andreas and took him to the detention center at Kokkinotrimithia, just west of Nicosia.

Avoiding suspicion by British soldiers was paramount, and Grivas kept strict secrecy protocols. Dafnis said, "Our original group was just three, but I knew of more than the three in my group. We were to sabotage one or two things—which we did. Gradually, we increased our activity."

EOKA members at the Limassol port brought guns and bombs to Dafnis's farm. He said, "We hid them in baskets supposedly filled with eggs or planted with flowers so that the bombs were under the roots." EOKA fighters came to the weapons cache to get what they needed for various missions. Consequently, a number of EOKA members knew Dafnis. He added that, when these smugglers came, "usually my mother and my wife treated them to lunch, and then they moved on to various destinations."

The British arrested Dafnis's friend Christakis Tryfonides and sent him to the detention center at Pyla. Dafnis worried that either Christakis or Andreas might succumb to torture and identify him as their fellow member of the EOKA cell in Limassol. But he was committed to the rebellion. He told us, "By the time Christakis was arrested, there were many EOKA groups all over Limassol. We were better organized: in youth groups in the schools and in factories. We had cells everywhere." But with Christakis and Andreas in detention camp, leadership in Limassol was at a crisis point. Dafnis met with the two remaining top EOKA leaders in the Limassol area to discuss what to do next.

> We decided to suggest to Grivas to appoint us as a committee—not to appoint one as responsible but the three of us to act as his representatives in Limassol. He wrote back and said, "Do you think that I came to Cyprus to start a Sunday School? What is this story about three people? I only want one." He appointed Demos [Hadjimiltis], who died last year. Demos and I were very active in the Limassol area. I myself recruited fine, upstanding police officers. I was successful by being courageous, telling some lies, and pushing the right buttons.

One of the more important recruits was Costas Efstathiou, a Cypriot police officer known for his honesty and deep Christian commitment. The man was so rotund that people called him Pachi Costas (Fat Costas). He came secretly to Dafnis and asked him to administer the EOKA oath to his whole family. Dafnis feared it might be a trap, but he and Demos finally decided to take the chance. In his home, Costas brought out icons, and he and his entire family knelt before the icons and took the EOKA oath. Thereafter, he provided valuable information to Dafnis regarding the movement of police patrols and the identity of Greek Cypriot informants.

Beaten with Belt Buckles

The following stories represent different people's memories of the EOKA years, and their accounts overlap with respect to dates. Arranging their stories in chronological order is impossible, so read these vignettes as windows into the experiences of Greek Cypriots during those tumultuous years.

In 1956, British soldiers arrested a 15-year-old EOKA member who later became a friend of Dafnis. He told us that, during police interrogation, they beat him with belt buckles until his whole body was black with bruising. He divulged nothing, so they released him. The beatings strengthened his resolve. Although only a boy, he received orders from Grivas to bomb a supermarket where British citizens purchased their goods. He said, "We decided to show them that we could hit them anywhere. We threw a bomb into the Metropolitan Hotel, but the bomb exploded a few seconds earlier than we calibrated. So, the man who threw the bomb did not have time to come out and get on the motorcycle and leave with the people [waiting for him] there." British soldiers missed when they shot at him, so he escaped. Dafnis's friend said the bombing warned the British: No place was safe for them.

He added that his EOKA section placed bombs at the Akrotiri airport on the British base and destroyed five airplanes. Six months later, they bombed another runway. He said that, although he is not a combative person, during the rebellion against the British, he learned how to make bombs and do things that he would never dream of doing under normal circumstances. In his youthful zeal, he followed orders—no matter the consequences.

He also told us something we heard from other EOKA fighters, including Dafnis: "I am fortunate because I think that I never killed anybody. I gave the bombs to somebody else—to people below me. They were doing the work. I was just giving them instructions and bombs." His wife interrupted him, saying that he was not innocent of the deaths. He looked at her briefly and then said, "But, of course, I have responsibility for what happened."

One thing that disgusted him intensely was the execution of Evagoras Pallikarides, an eighteen-year-old boy who was arrested and sentenced to death for carrying a totally non-functional gun. Cypriots brought the case before Queen Elizabeth, but she refused to change the death penalty to a prison sentence. However, what bothered him even more than the British hanging EOKA fighters was the betrayal he felt from Archbishop Makarios, who broke his promise to bring about *enosis*. During our interview, he also claimed that Makarios had some of his political opponents murdered and that he was also involved in election fraud. He called Makarios a despicable egomaniac. Feelings run deeply in Cyprus, and opinions vary dramatically.

Deeply Conflicted EOKA Officer

As we interviewed George, a frail, old man, we realized that, when he was young, he was a killer. Part of what he said illustrates the brutality of the EOKA conflict as well as the psychological impact of killing other humans. George was one of the earliest members of the revolutionary struggle. He lived in Nicosia and participated with a small group of radicals who in 1952 began agitating for freedom. Although the British were granting freedom to some of their other colonies, they refused to free Cyprus. George and his friends decided to resort to violence.

At first, they met to get drunk and talk philosophy. After numerous conversations, they decided the struggle of the Israelis against Great Britain provided a good model for them. Although the Israeli freedom fighters were few in number, their determination to establish a homeland for Jews worked. George and his drinking buddies agreed: the time for freedom had come. They discussed how the struggle for freedom in India differed from the rebellion in Israel. Gandhi chose non-violent resistance, which George said was probably a better approach, because the Indians did not kill innocent people. On the other hand, India had millions of people, and the population of Cyprus was tiny by comparison—more like Israel. The conspirators concluded that the Indians took too many years to convince England to grant freedom. By contrast, the Israelis actively fought the British from 1945 to 1948 to gain their freedom. George and his friends decided to follow the model of the Israelis instead of that of Gandhi.

George became invisible to the British system. Because he did not graduate from school, his name did not appear in official school documents. He destroyed the few existing photographs of himself, changed his address, and adopted a different name. Later, when the British offered a £5,000 bounty for his arrest, they had no photograph of him to place on the wanted poster. Soldiers actually arrested him once, but because the name on his papers did not match the name of the person the soldiers were seeking, and they had no photograph of him, they let him go.

He enjoyed recounting his youthful escapades, so I asked if he was a bad boy. He laughed and said, "Yes. I was very bad." He did dangerous things, like attending the wedding of a friend, although he knew British soldiers might appear. As he danced during the celebration, soldiers suddenly arrived, took up positions on the streets, and placed snipers on rooftops. In a brash move, George took a tray of sweets and some *Zivania* (a potent Cypriot brandy made from grapes) to a soldier at the gate and asked, "Who is in charge here? Where is the Sergeant?" When the sergeant came, George said to him, "With your permission, I will give some to your soldiers." After distributing sweets to the soldiers, he returned to the wedding party and then slowly began working his way toward the edge of the village to escape.

Suddenly, a soldier shouted, "Halt! Halt!" George ran. He jokingly told us he thought he set a new world record for the 100-meter dash! But the British soldiers caught and arrested him. An informant from the village had alerted authorities that he was at the party—after all, £5,000 was a lot of money (equivalent to £134,565 in June 2021, or $190,465 US, or €156,567). George later discovered that a comrade assigned to watch for British soldiers had gone to sleep at his post and failed to alert him that the British were coming.

George showed his identification papers to the soldiers and protested that they had the wrong man. But they told him they knew who he was and said they were going to pay £5,000 to the man who betrayed him, so he should not waste time denying his identity. They took him to the interrogators. George told us they tortured him for 48 hours, but he lied convincingly under interrogation.

He made up a story about a Greek man in Paphos whom he knew was an informer for the British. He boasted that the soldiers arrested the Cypriot informer in Paphos whom George specified in his fabricated story. He smiled and said, "This was a way of fighting! He was my enemy, and I was his enemy." We knew from Dafnis that Grivas trained his fighters in the art of deception and spreading false information. George bragged about misleading people during the rebellion. He considered it a game. But the harsh interrogation he endured was no laughing matter. He came face-to-face with a British man who was educated at Oxford University in Greek language and history. He asked this man why he was torturing him. The response was, "George, I know that what I do is very bad, but it is necessary."

At times during our interview, George divulged disturbing details. He said that he did not mind killing officers or members of the RAF or British Secret Service, but it did pain him when they ambushed British conscripts who knew nothing about the Cyprus conflict. These young men were drafted and had no choice but to fight, so he bore them no animosity. But he killed them nevertheless. He said they were just boys, and some started to cry for their mothers when he began shooting them. He took no prisoners.

I could not help but remember when I was 18 years old in 1968. The Viet Nam war was raging, and I was dreading the draft. I hardly knew where Viet Nam was on a world map, and I certainly had nothing against the Vietnamese people. But I easily could have been forced to fight in a war that was meaningless to me. And I could have been killed in some nameless rice paddy over a conflict started by others for reasons I did not understand—by a combatant who knew as little about the reasons for the conflict as I did. I was under the constant cloud of being drafted and sent to Viet Nam, and I wanted no part of that conflict. I was more like the British conscripts sent to fight rebels in Cyprus than I was like the young Cypriot men and women who fought the British. But because of a basketball scholarship, I got a student deferment and did not go to Viet Nam.

Killing other humans leaves permanent mental scars. According to Dafnis, George was the most psychologically damaged member of EOKA we interviewed. George said he became a member of EOKA in Athens in March 1954, where he met Papa Stavros, a priest from Nicosia who was working under the authority of Archbishop Makarios. When the priest discovered that George was looking for a job, he said, "If you like to fight, you should go back to Cyprus now. Already the first load of guns and ammunition is in Cyprus." The priest got a Bible and had George swear an oath of allegiance.

George was employed at the Nicosia airport when Grivas got to Cyprus in November 1954. He and his friends had already been conducting reconnaissance, calculating distances for launching mortars at the airport, and planning attacks. They were enthusiastic young men with no training in warfare, so they were eager to receive instruction from Grivas.

After the rebellion had been underway for a while, police arrested 15 EOKA members in Nicosia. George's team planned to retaliate. Another rebel leader, Gregoris Afxentiou, was waiting in the Kyrenia area with machine guns, poised to conduct an ambush. But George found himself caught between Archbishop Makarios and Colonel Grivas (Grivas was promoted to General following the EOKA rebellion, and most EOKA veterans referred to him as "the General").

> At the beginning, Grivas was very keen to do it. [But] when Makarios heard we were planning this ambush, he called me to the archbishopric and said, "No, George, don't do it." I said, "It is the order of General

> Grivas." "George. Don't do it. It is wrong. It is too much." I said, "But ... the other is the chief." [Makarios said,] "Don't do it!"

George pondered his options. Reluctantly, he sent a message to Grivas suggesting they postpone the mission. Grivas asked him if he was afraid. George responded that he feared he and his team would be killed, but if Grivas ordered the raid, they would do it. As their discussion continued, George complained that he felt caught in the middle. Makarios had told him *not* to conduct the ambush; it was too dangerous and too many British would be killed. But George said Grivas did not care who got killed. So, George requested that the two leaders discuss the matter and come to an agreement before giving orders to the fighters.

Then another complication arose. The British freed *one* of the 15 arrested EOKA members. Grivas concluded that this man must be a traitor and ordered his execution, but George refused to kill the man until he examined the matter. If the fellow was a traitor, then they would kill him; but George did not want to kill an innocent man. After investigating, he concluded that the man was indeed a traitor, so he tasked Marios, the man's nephew, to do the hit.

Marios took a handgun and went to his uncle's house. But his aunt asked Marios to kill her first; because if he killed her husband, she would be left alone to raise four boys. Marios could not bring himself to shoot his uncle. He returned to George and said, "Kill me instead but do not leave my cousins without parents." George was reluctant to kill Marios. He added that, when he explained his decision to Grivas, the commander commended his actions. He told the story to illustrate that Grivas could be merciful, but he did not divulge what ultimately happened to the traitor. Typically, Grivas did not flinch from ordering executions.

George bragged that Field Marshall Harding was embarrassed that with 40,000 troops he could not crush EOKA. He added that only after Harding realized his goal was impossible did he seek another solution to the conflict. George said the British wasted an immense amount of money and manpower seeking to crush the rebellion, with very poor results. Finally, Harding decided to listen to the EOKA members.

After the fighting ceased, George had poor relations with Makarios. At this point in the interview, he pointed to my recorder and said, "And I will tell you something that I don't want you to write." He wanted to recount something that he promised Makarios he would never divulge, so I stopped the recorder. Although he disliked Makarios, and he often lied during the EOKA years to deceive the British, for some reason he felt a need to honor his promise to the now dead archbishop. He would tell me, but he did not want me to publish the story. I have honored his wish.

George grew somber when he told us about going to speak with a monk at Stavrovouni Monastery (located south of Nicosia). He confessed that he had killed people during the fight with the British. After listening, the monk said, "My dear brother George, no paradise for you." Later, as he spoke with Dafnis, he said, "Dafni, for me no paradise. What about you?" He seemed troubled as he told this story. George was a killer. At times boasting about his actions. But deep inside the memories tormented him. Believing that he was on the right side of the war helped his conscience somewhat, but ambushing and killing British conscripts haunted him.

Dafnis explained that George was "the right hand of Grivas, and he was very much involved in acts of violence"—which affected him deeply. Dafnis said George's wife confided in him that her husband was a tormented soul. She complained that Dafnis and other EOKA fighters seemed to cope better with life and not be so plagued by the past. He told her that killing people had damaged George deeply, and she would just have to be patient with him. Dafnis said, "All of us who went through these years of the uprising, we are not normal people. You have to accept our abnormalities." She answered, "Yes, I realize that. But of all the ones I know, you have the least abnormalities. My husband and some others," she said, "have the most abnormalities." Dafnis later told us, "I believe that at a certain point violence really changes one's thinking and personality." He said, "Father Gennadios divides people into two categories: those who took part in actual acts of violence and in killings and bloodshed; and those who were playing a supportive role but were not directly involved in such things, in which category he puts me."

Bankrupted by Generosity

Koralia, Dafnis's cousin from Kalo Chorio, lived for a time in Limassol with the family of Father Solomon Panagides so that she could attend high school. She said the Panagides home was always full. When we interviewed her at Dafnis's house, she explained, "Dafnis lived here with his wife and two children. Maroula never said, 'This is my house and my husband.' She said, 'This [house] is for us all.' At one time, there were 17 people living here, including, of course, Dafnis's parents, and my grandfather, Socrates." She added that every room had beds, and "everyone slept just fine."

Regarding the influence of the Panagides family, Koralia emphasized "the sincerity, the spirit of companionship," and the fact that the "people who went through this house acquired life values." She said, "People from high standing, big names, down to paupers would find a place here and also food. This was a very poor neighborhood. When I moved here, it was considered the slums of Limassol." She observed Maroula helping poor people in ways that protected their dignity: telling a woman to meet her out back, "because she did not want the others to see her give the woman charity." Koralia and the other girls in the house knew

Figure 13. Maroula, Lydia, Louisa, and Dafnis after the EOKA rebellion ended.

"everybody would find love here and assistance and help."

Dafnis was translating for Koralia, and at this point he decided to illustrate Maroula's hospitality. He explained that she kept a diary detailing the number of people who came for lunch or for dinner. After her death, he checked her records and discovered that in one year 1,112 guests ate in their home. He said that customers came from all around Cyprus to purchase tillers from him or to have them repaired. For some clients the trip to Limassol took two days. Of course, Dafnis invited them to eat dinner and stay overnight. "Until today," he said, "when I go to Paphos, they say they remember what kind of food Maroula cooked for them.... By the way, this was always a strong criticism I had from Maroula. She would say, 'Why don't you tell me that we are having guests?'"

Dafnis seemed totally clueless about such practical matters. He spontaneously invited people for meals and simply expected Maroula to prepare food for his guests. I am amazed that, as generous as she was, she did not take more drastic measures to educate him. But perhaps in this regard he was not open to education.

The EOKA struggle put the Panagides family in danger. Cousin Koralia secretly joined the youth section of EOKA and distributed propaganda leaflets in the schools. One day, after circulating flyers, she brought some home and hid them under her bed. Maria, Dafnis's mother, discovered the EOKA leaflets, and she was horrified. She knew that Koralia was an innocent teenage girl who brought the materials to Solomon's house without knowing about other, far more important things happening at the house. To reduce the danger, Maria sternly said to Koralia: "We have nothing to do with EOKA. Don't get us involved with EOKA. Please. Don't touch these leaflets."

Lynne asked Koralia if she had any idea that the Panagides family was involved in EOKA. She replied that she suspected they were part of the cause, because two men hid at the farm for a while. She suspected the two were part of EOKA, and later she found out each man had a bounty of £5,000 for his capture.

Smuggling weapons into Cyprus

Petros Avgusti was only nineteen when he agreed to take charge of smuggling through the Limassol port. Early in the rebellion, Archbishop Makarios saw him as a valuable asset because he worked in customs, examining baggage and cargo. Makarios recruited him through a man at the port who took Petros into a dark room and there administered the oath. Petros told us he really had no choice in the matter. It was too late and too dangerous to step back. After he took the oath, he discovered that EOKA fighters did not yet have any pistols, so he arranged to purchase one for £12. He did not have that much money, so four EOKA members each contributed £3 in order to make the purchase.

An Orthodox priest was first to smuggle a pistol through customs, and a Turkish customs official prepared to inspect the priest's baggage. Petros saw the priest's face grow pale with fear, so he stepped in and told the Turkish inspector that he would take care of the man, because he also was an Orthodox Christian. As he took the priest's passport and pretended to look through it, he noticed color returning to the priest's face. After that initial success, another priest brought five pistols through customs.

Revolvers and Pistols

The Cypriots we interviewed used the term *pistol* to refer to both revolvers and pistols. Revolvers typically hold six bullets in a revolving cylinder. Pistols are semi-automatic handguns that, when fired, automatically eject the spent brass and load another bullet into the chamber. Different models hold varying numbers of bullets stacked in magazines, usually in the pistol's grips (handle). I do not attempt to decipher whether Petros and others meant *revolver* when they said *pistol*.

Petros devised a system whereby they marked particular luggage with chalk, changing the colors of chalk each day to avoid others noticing a pattern. The conspirators took marked luggage outside to the street. Someone else drove up and collected the bags and transported the concealed cargo of weapons to a hidden stash. Others went to the stash to get munitions and deliver them to EOKA groups around the island for particular missions. Petros avoided placing his signature on baggage claim forms for luggage that contained weapons—just in case trouble arose. Initially the system worked well, but as more weapons made their way to EOKA fighters, officials at the port began watching baggage more closely. Once, when Petros told a Turkish baggage inspector to let him take care of a particular bag, the man got suspicious and followed him. Things were getting tense.

Petros developed a scheme to bring big crates of guns to Cyprus for EOKA. Problems arose when informants in Greece reported a suspicious shipment. Four big boxes containing books—and weapons hidden among the books—left Athens on a ship that first made a stop in Alexandria. Suddenly, the port in Alexandria swarmed with soldiers inspecting cargo. They did not discover the guns, but they were on high alert. When the books arrived in Limassol, Petros and several other accomplices went to the port at 11:00 p.m., got the book boxes, and took them to the big bookstore in Limassol. Unfortunately, British soldiers soon came to the store, searched the boxes, found the guns, and arrested the bookstore owner.

An EOKA leader named Demos later told Petros if it had not been for the weapons he helped smuggle into the mountains, Grivas would certainly have been killed. A few months later, Petros found himself out of the smuggling loop for a time. In February 1956, following the increased passenger traffic from Greece to Limassol during the Christmas season, the official in charge of customs transferred Petros to the smaller port at Paphos, promising he would be in Paphos for only six months. Petros had to inspect everything, especially cigarettes and alcohol, to reduce the level of smuggling. The smuggler had to catch smugglers!

Although Petros reluctantly moved to Paphos, his attitude changed when he met a lovely young woman there. Soon he did not want to go back to Limassol. But on 1 December 1956, the Limassol port manager ordered him to return. On 13 December 1956, he reported back to Limassol, and on 14 December, he was arrested. A woman broke under British interrogation and revealed that Petros was involved in smuggling. Now it was his turn to endure British torture. Petros added that the British sent some EOKA captives to Turkey where they endured unspeakable suffering. He said when two men he knew finally returned from Turkey, they were so emaciated he did not even recognize them. He shuddered with the memory and said he was amazed these men could bear so much without dying.

Forgiving a comrade who divulges your identity to the enemy is difficult—especially if the result is weeks of torture. Petros said Dafnis forgave those who cracked under torture and revealed that he was part of EOKA, but not all detainees were so forgiving. The happy part of the story for Petros was that, after the EOKA rebellion ended, he returned to his sweetheart in Paphos, and they got married. Not all fighters were so fortunate.

CHAPTER 4
Eye of the Storm

Hiding in Plain Sight

EOKA involvement changed dramatically for Dafnis in June 1956 when his farm became the center of operations. His free-spirited lifestyle was about to collide with the ultra-disciplined demands of Colonel Grivas, who required a new hideout. British troops had almost captured Grivas in the mountains north of Limassol, and he needed desperately to relocate. After protracted discussion, he decided to move down from the mountains to the more populated area of Limassol. Demos, the head of EOKA in Limassol, came one day to tell Dafnis that Grivas was in grave danger. As a temporary measure, they quickly constructed a hideout underneath the detached garage Dafnis used for his agricultural business. Grivas had no idea of the number of people who came to that garage, or he never would have agreed to move there. When he asked Demos how many people knew Dafnis was part of EOKA, Demos lied: "Two or three." When Grivas learned the truth, he was *not* happy.

To sneak Grivas to Dafnis's farm, Demos tasked Pachi Costas to drive him in his police car. Costas did not know the identity of his mysterious passenger. He was told only that the man was a trainer—and that he was not to turn his head around to look at his passenger. Dafnis and Maroula nervously awaited the arrival of Grivas. By this time "the Uncle" was a legend. What would it be like to have him at their farm? The plan was to

The Oral and the Written

When he died, Dafnis had almost finished writing ΠΙΚΡΟΔΑΦΝΕΣ (*Bitter Leaves of Laurel*), a book about his experiences in EOKA and parliament. His family arranged to have the book published posthumously. In 2021, Dafnis's brother, Stahis, published an English translation of the book: *Cyprus: Island in the Storm: An Individual Encircled by Violence becomes a voice for Reconciliation and Peace*. Predictably, much overlap exists between what Dafnis wrote in his book and what he told us orally. I found his written accounts to be no more consistent than the impromptu oral versions he delivered to us. Dafnis was a great storyteller–not a fact-checking historian. I draw mostly from his oral versions to construct the following narrative.

house him temporarily while a more appropriate hideout was constructed. Dafnis and Maroula met Grivas for the first time when he arrived just before 1:00 a.m. on 19 June 1956. The drop off went smoothly, and soon Pachi Costas drove away.

When Dafnis told us the story, I got the impression that only he and Maroula greeted Grivas. His description made it sound like just the two of them stood there speaking with Grivas in the darkness of the night. However, about 15 people lived on the farm: Dafnis, Maroula, Solomon, Maria, Chloe, Stahis, Socrates (grandfather), Iphigenia (grandmother), Despinou (Solomon's assistant), Pollys (a farm worker), Hellmut Zaoyer (a German technician for their tillers), and various cousins from Kalo Chorio who were in Limassol to attend high school. I do not know who all in the Panagides household knew of the presence of the "Uncle."

Constructing the hideout in complete secrecy from the other household members would have been difficult, as would hiding Grivas in the midst of a bustling farming center and place for the sale and repair of agricultural equipment. I intended to ask Dafnis in 2019 how many members of his household knew Grivas was hiding right next to their house. Sadly, I did not get that opportunity to ask for clarification. But in his book, *Bitter Leaves of Laurel,* additional details supplement his oral accounts. He wrote that a small group of EOKA members worked together to move Grivas to the farm. Because they feared a military roadblock, they used two cars for added security. Andreas Papadopoulos drove the lead vehicle, and with him were Stahis Panagides and his fiancée, plus another young woman named Elizabeth Nicolaou. Pachi Costas followed in his police car, and with him were his wife, Agni, Adonis Georgiadis, Demos Hadjimiltis, Nina Drousiotis, and, of course, Grivas. Thus, nine people were involved in transporting Grivas. Who in the little caravan knew that Grivas was in the second car is not clear. According to Dafnis, Pachi Costas did not know the identity of his passenger until after the EOKA rebellion was over. However, Dafnis quotes Demos Hadjimiltis's book, *The Brave Ones of 1955*, stating that Stahis was part of the original discussion of moving Grivas to the Panagides farm—and on the night when Grivas arrived at their farm, he helped Dafnis and Maroula get the Uncle settled into his new hideout.

Dafnis told us that he and Maroula were intimidated when Pachi Costas's car disappeared into the darkness. He said,

> *General* Grivas was a very imposing personality with his *moustache* and his sharp eyes. And my wife asked what kind of food he would like for us to provide for him. She was a vegetarian and was very interested in food. He said, "Bring me lemonade from fresh lemon juice. And, from now on, I want a lot of vegetables. And every day I want garlic."

Maroula provided the food and drink Grivas requested, and over time he came to trust her completely. Dafnis, however, was a different story. Grivas soon learned that he was foolish to believe what Dafnis told him—particularly pertaining to the security of the hideout.

> Grivas asked me how many people knew I was a member of EOKA. I had to lie, of course, and said, "Two or three." *Not 300!* And he said, "Okay, up to three, we are safe. Jesus and his mother saved us, but neither Jesus nor his mother will save crazy people. If more than three people know you are part of EOKA, and I stay here, then we are crazy, and nobody will save us." Very soon, however, he began to realize that we had lied to him; and he wanted to move out as soon as possible. He stayed three months here [i.e., 19 June to 14 September 1956], and then we moved him *there*.

Dafnis pointed a short distance west of his house toward the Museum of Griva Digenis, which preserves the hideout the colonel used after he left the room under Dafnis's garage.

Dafnis described Grivas as a courageous and disciplined patriot, totally devoted to his cause. He inspired people. Grivas was mostly a vegetarian who did not smoke or drink alcohol. He was meticulous about shaving daily. And he was *very* particular with the way he groomed his large moustache. He was thoughtful and at times lighthearted and humorous. He could be ruthless in executing people, yet he could also be magnanimous. Once, when his men captured a young British soldier and wanted to execute the man, Grivas said, "No! He has a mother just like you do. He is a prisoner of war." Dafnis did not explain what EOKA did with a prisoner of war. Perhaps most telling is the fact that thousands of British troops on a relatively small island could not capture Grivas or defeat his poorly supplied EOKA fighters. Still today, instructors in war colleges have their students study his tactics—including professors at the British Royal Military Academy!

The Fine Art of Deception

Grivas needed to teach his fighters much more than how to use weapons and how to build and deploy explosives. He trained them to deceive their captors. Dafnis was a natural at learning how to mislead people, and he employed this skill for the rest of his life. In 2017, he kept us guessing constantly as to whether he was telling us the truth. During one interview, he said,

> I learned three very important rules—which I apply in your case also. Number one: never disclose the source of your information. If you ask me, "How do you know? Who told you?" I will say, "Sorry." Number two—and this applies to you, Michael: the more credible the person you talk to appears to you, the more you suspect him or her. Number three: never volunteer information. For example, there is no reason for me to tell you what I did this morning. If I tell you, "This morning, I went to the farm," once I open my mouth, you can respond, "Oh, you went to the

> farm! Who was there? Who went with you? What did you do when you were there?" So, I apply these rules to everyday life, and I find them very useful.

As he spoke, he was enjoying himself immensely. He went on to incorporate us into his lecture on deceiving others.

> If, as I suspect, you're CIA spooks, you will know one of the tactics we used during the EOKA years: to mislead—to give wrong information. For example, the question might be, "Do you have any idea where Grivas is hiding?" Of course, I knew where Grivas was hiding, but I would say, "You know, the latest I heard was that he was hiding near Polis in the Akamas area." And the next day, thousands of British troops would be there searching for Grivas. And, so, we would achieve two things. We would take their attention away from where Grivas was hiding, and the troops would be doing something that wasted their time and took them elsewhere.

He deviously added: "I may use these same tactics also with you. You will have to scrutinize all this information that I tell you and put it under strict scrutiny."

We bantered back and forth, and then I said, "We plan to listen to what you say and then just make it all up anyway." Dafnis was delighted and replied, "This is the only way that we can get the book so that someone will buy it—if you make up the stories." "No problem," I replied. "The more we learn from you how to lead people astray, the better we will be able to fabricate all sorts of things and not feel guilty about passing them off as the truth."

As we tried to scrutinize wizened old Dafnis, we realized he was too crafty for us. He could with complete sincerity tell us the most unreliable information. And he liked misleading us. Grivas taught him well, and he could bluff his way through virtually any situation, using half-truths and misdirection as a means of making falsehoods sound plausible. Sometimes it was funny—when we knew what he was doing. But sometimes it was frustrating, because we were trying to track down the truth of a serious matter. How many times did he go to sleep at night with a smug smile, remembering how he had skillfully manipulated us that day? We do not know. I smile when I realize that Grivas faced the same problem of sorting truth from falsehood as he listened to Dafnis—except the stakes were *much* higher for the Colonel.

The Unwitting Newlyweds

One of Dafnis's favorite stories was about transporting a newly married couple to their honeymoon site at the height of tensions between EOKA and the British.

> I want to tell you the story of when I drove my niece and her new husband on their honeymoon. The wedding was in Famagusta, and I drove to

> Famagusta for the wedding because she was my first cousin. There were very few cars in those days, and I was one of the few to own a car. After the wedding, I drove the newlyweds to Larnaca for their honeymoon. They had booked a small apartment there. I drove them from Famagusta to Larnaca because I was going to Limassol and it was on my way. The wedding was in 1956, during the peak of the emergency, and lots of troops were everywhere. At a checkpoint, British soldiers stopped us to search the car. They asked me, "Do you carry any weapons or bombs?" I said, "Yes, sir, I have a lot of them in the trunk, because what shall we do? We have these terrorists around. We must protect ourselves. So we need to have some guns." The soldier smiled and said, "Oh, really?" Then he waved and said, "Okay, you may go."
>
> Later on, my cousin and her husband realized that while I was taking them on their honeymoon, the boot of my car *was* full of bombs and weapons. And we went through this checkpoint without being searched. If the soldiers had searched my car, of course, there would never have been a honeymoon. All of us would have been arrested.

He laughed and said, "It pays to tell the truth." Then he continued,

> In such situations, it is important not to panic. If you panic, you are done. You are finished. You have to keep your cool.... Nobody in his right mind would dare say, "Yes." But it worked. I have more such stories, but this one was with the newlyweds. They knew nothing. They had no idea. If they did, they would not have come with me in my car.

I pointedly asked, "How would you have explained that to their parents if the British had found all that stuff?" Dafnis smirked and said, "I did not have to explain." The young husband later became a member of EOKA. If Dafnis's story was true, perhaps he and the groom later laughed about the near disaster if the soldiers had searched the car. I never could see the humor of brazenly putting a happy young couple in a potentially horrific situation on their honeymoon. I also could never understand why they would not have insisted on putting some luggage into the trunk of the car.

Fleeing Cyprus to the USA

Dafnis's younger brother, Stahis, became the leader of EOKA youth at his high school in Limassol. During one anti-British demonstration at the school, a student threw a bomb at some British soldiers, killing one of them. Consequently, British authorities closed the school. However, quick maneuvering by Cypriot educators allowed the *Athenaidium* Gymnasium for Girls in Limassol to grant diplomas to Stahis and the other graduating seniors of his class.

During the summer of 1956, Katy from Kansas "received a frantic letter from Dafnis stating that the situation had become dangerous and he was deeply concerned to get Stahis out of Cyprus before he [Stahis] got in trouble with the British government." Katy took swift action: "I wrote to the president of the College of Emporia asking if he could find scholarship funds and legal papers necessary to get Stahis into this country ASAP. He agreed to do so." Her connections no doubt facilitated the process of enrolling Stahis. Katy's father, who graduated from the College of Emporia in 1926, pastored a Presbyterian Church closely associated with the college. But the British Colonial government suspected the Panagides family of EOKA involvement, so Stahis experienced a delay before receiving permission to fly to the United States. By facilitating the process of enrolling Stahis in college and getting him out of Cyprus, Katy probably saved him from being arrested and tortured. Stahis put it more poignantly: "I owe my escape from the likely British Colonial gallows to her."

His account of the trip to Kansas is bittersweet. On 2 September 1956, he boarded a British Airways flight at the Nicosia airport. His mother, Maria, sewed money inside the lining of his jacket and bid farewell to her son. First, he flew to Athens—where the plane was delayed due to mechanical problems—then to Rome, then to Paris—where he stayed overnight in a hotel and thought that he had missed his flight because he did not know the difference between A.M. and P.M.—then to Shannon, Ireland, where he connected to a 14-hour flight to Newfoundland. From there he flew to Bangor, Maine, then to Idlewild Airport (later renamed JFK) in New York City, then to Pittsburgh, then to Indianapolis, then to Saint Louis, and finally to Kansas City.

At the train station in Kansas City, while waiting to board the train to Emporia, Kansas, an exhausted Stahis encountered his first drinking fountain. Thirsty, he watched people go to this shiny steel column and drink water from it, but he did not know how to make it work. He tried and failed to get a drink, and at that moment he broke down and cried. Finally, he noticed that people would put a foot on the pedal at the bottom of the drinking fountain and the water came out of the spout. Triumph at last! He got a drink of water. After he boarded a train to Emporia, he met friendly people and had pleasant conversations, in spite of his limited English. Finally, his long and arduous journey over, he arrived at his destination on 4 September 1956.

Because he arrived in Emporia late in the evening, he spent the first night in a hotel. The next morning, a hotel employee called the college to say Stahis had arrived. A driver came to the hotel and took Stahis to the Dean's office, where things got weird. The dean was expecting a girl and had arranged for Stahis to stay in a girls' dorm. The confusion resulted from Stahis's high school diploma being issued by a girl's school in Limassol. Administrators at the College of Emporia had no idea of the curious chain of events that led to the mix-up.

Stahis was reassigned to a male dorm. His fellow students made him feel welcome, but he struggled with homesickness. He missed his family. He missed his fiancée, who was studying in Italy. He missed Cyprus. But he adapted, and during his second year at the college, he was elected to Student Council. His English skills improved dramatically. He transferred to Kansas State University, where he finished his B.S. and M.A. At KSU, he met and married Joy. When he finished his Master's degree, he and Joy moved to Ames, Iowa, where he earned a Ph.D. in economics at Iowa State University. Because Katy and Dafnis got him out of Cyprus, Stahis had a long and distinguished career. He and Joy live in Bethesda, with children and grandchildren nearby.

"Get those prostitutes out of here!"

For the most part, Dafnis worked amicably with Grivas, but on a few occasions, Grivas became furious with him. Too many people were coming and going at Dafnis's farm, and Grivas insisted he needed to move immediately. So they rented the farm just to the west of Dafnis's house in order to construct a suitable hideout for Grivas and his two closest associates. Dafnis explained to the landowner, Hambis Demetriou, that an uncle returning to Cyprus from Africa wanted to plant clover. Hambis believed the lie and agreed to rent his farm. The problem was that "three beautiful sisters" who were prostitutes with prosperous clients from Limassol —including high-ranking civil servants and Turks—lived in that farmhouse. These women did not want to change their place of business, and they refused to move.

Grivas ordered Dafnis to solve this situation. Time was of the essence. But Dafnis failed to get the job done. Grivas could be volatile when people did not follow his orders precisely, and he became increasingly frustrated with excuses and delays. He grew so angry when Dafnis reported that the three sisters still had not moved from the house that he slapped Dafnis twice across the face, kicked him in the backside, and ordered him out of his presence. Dafnis said, "For a few weeks I did not dare to go and see him."

Figure 14. *Elli Christodoulidou showing the secret entrance to the underground hideout of Colonel Grivas.*

Finally, Dafnis convinced the sisters to move to another location, and then construction of the hideout began. Only the most devoted EOKA fighters were chosen to participate in the project, and they conducted their work at night. Dafnis said he devised the pretext of digging a new septic system in case anyone should ask questions. In early September, they finished the hideout, and Grivas prepared to move. But an unexpected problem arose.

They had created a secret entrance to the underground hideout inside the sink cabinet in the kitchen. The wooden bottom of the cabinet was really a trap door so that Grivas and his assistant could squeeze through a small opening to the hideout below. But the trap door did not fit exactly because moisture from the newly poured cement expanded the wood and made the door too large. This delay angered Grivas, but they had to fix the problem. British soldiers had started pouring water on people's floors in order to detect hidden hideout entrances, so the trap door had to fit flawlessly in place to avoid detection. Not until 14 September 1956 could Grivas relocate to his new hideout, but the deception worked. He remained there until the end of the conflict in February 1959.

Entertaining Grivas with Stories

During the construction phase of the new hideout, Dafnis feared going near Grivas. "I was here in my house," said Dafnis, "and he was in the hideout under my garage. My wife would take him food and things, but I would never go to him until they convinced me that I was safe to go." However, when Grivas was on good terms with Dafnis, the two had lengthy talks.

Grivas grew to appreciate Dafnis's humorous stories. The Colonel, under constant stress from leading the rebellion, needed humor to maintain his equilibrium. Dafnis explained that Grivas "carried two guns: one to kill whoever he could and the other to kill himself. He was hiding continuously, under the threat of being arrested.... The man needed some company." Dafnis added that Grivas could be a lot of fun when he was not angry. I asked if he had a good sense of humor, and Dafnis said, "Yes. And he used to laugh. But when he got bad news—somebody was killed or some ambush or something failed—he would not eat. He was very disciplined in his exercising every day, morning and evening. Taking walks around in the night, and eating healthy food."

To keep Grivas in a good mood, Dafnis made up stories to amuse him. Dafnis said Grivas ordered him to go around town and listen to what people were saying about EOKA. Then he was to return home in the evening and report what he heard. Dafnis began to spin stories.

> On one occasion I told him, "You are not telling us the truth. You are lying to us." He said, "Am I?" I said, "Yes." He said, "*Why* do you say this?" "Because," I said, "I went to have coffee in a small café in Limassol, and at a nearby table two people were talking to each other over coffee; and then I heard one say, "George, did you hear what Grivas did yesterday?"

> "What?" "He dressed himself as a British army officer, and he inspected a contingent of British soldiers on the RAF base in Akrotiri." "Really?" And of course, he would burst into laughter.

With a degree of pride, Dafnis said that he made up many such stories to entertain Grivas.

Sacrificing Family for EOKA

When the new hideout was finally finished, a couple needed to pose as legitimate renters before Grivas moved there. The choice was very sensitive. Dafnis discussed with Manolis, a good friend from the Christian Youth Movement, who would be a reliable person. Manolis suggested Marios Christodoulides, who managed a branch of the London-based Barclay's Bank [in his book, Dafnis said it was the Ottoman Bank, which is puzzling] and had credentials to enter the British military base near Episkopi. The British would not suspect him as being a collaborator. After much discussion, Grivas agreed to this choice.

Manolis went to the home of Marios and his wife, Elli, in the nearby village of Polemidia and he asked if they would occasionally host EOKA fighters. He told them to discuss the matter and let him know their answer the next day. They agreed, but they did not know the full scope of their task. When Manolis said they would be hiding Grivas, they were stunned.

The couple hastily prepared to move from Polemidia to Limassol. Marios rode his motorcycle to see the house where they would live, and he did not get home until 1:30 a.m. The next day, Elli's mother asked her, "Why did your husband come home at 1:30? I heard his motorcycle at 1:30 in the morning." The next night, Marios did not get home until 2:30 a.m. Elli's mother asked, "What is wrong with your husband?" Elli lied and said that Marios had a gambling problem.

Grivas needed to relocate to his new hideout, but Marios and Elli had a four-year-old daughter. Grivas said the girl posed a security risk, so she could

EOKA Network

Some EOKA operatives were fighters who carried out raids. Others were tasked as couriers. Others, like Dafnis, were primarily involved with information gathering. Because of his agricultural business, he could legitimately travel around the island without raising suspicion. While on business trips, he did reconnaissance work for Grivas. By the end of the resistance, EOKA had operatives in virtually every part of society, feeding information via couriers to Grivas regarding plans of the Colonial Government and operational details about troop deployment. Grivas had an inside track on many of the British government's plans and could adjust his orders to his fighters accordingly. His spy network was extensive.

not come to the farm with them. They had to con Elli's mother into asking to keep their daughter. Dafnis explained:

> In front of Elli, Marios says [to his mother-in-law], "Listen… I don't want to see you any more. I rented a house in Limassol. I am leaving with my wife, and I don't want you in my house." Her mother had a heart problem, and when she heard this, she fainted. They called Emergency, and the doctor came. When she recovered, she said, "Okay, you have my blessing, but I have a special request. Please, leave your oldest daughter with me."

Marios and Elli pretended to begrudgingly agree to leave their daughter with her grandmother. They took their baby and moved to Limassol on 10 September 1956, and a few days later Grivas and his assistant, Adonis Georgiadis, relocated from Dafnis's farm to the new hideout.

Clandestine Correspondence

While Grivas was hiding on the Panagides farm, Nina Drousiotis delivered messages to him from EOKA fighters all over Cyprus, and she transported letters from Grivas to couriers who took them to the fighters. Because the Colonel directed operations via written messages, he spent much of his time writing letters—as many as 20 per day. Obviously, having a secure network for delivering orders and receiving reports was extremely important, and EOKA members developed a sophisticated network for such mail.

When Grivas moved to his new hideout, he modified his courier setup. Nina no longer knew his location, but she continued to deliver messages. Grivas set up a system whereby Nina brought correspondence from EOKA fighters to Maroula at a set time and place, and Maroula returned home with these letters. Meanwhile, Grivas handed letters for his fighters to Elli, and she hid them under her clothes and walked the short distance to Maroula's home. In a specific room inside the Panagides house, the two women exchanged letters to and from Grivas. Maroula took Grivas's letters to Nina, who delivered them to others. During the entire time they used this system, Elli never saw Nina or knew she was the courier. Nina did not know Elli, because that would have been a security risk for Grivas if Nina were captured and broke under interrogation. Grivas knew that British troops were far less likely to frisk women than men, so women played a vital role in delivering his messages.

The security protocols Grivas had in place were so tight that Elli did not know who else was part of EOKA until after the rebellion was over. Grivas trusted her abilities enough that on three occasions he sent her on secret missions to deliver messages to the king of Greece. She smuggled letters to and from the king by hiding them in her clothing. Cool under pressure, she confidently navigated through security checks to complete her missions.

On one occasion, Maroula told Elli, "Today, together with the mail, you will take two hand grenades and a pistol to Grivas." So, Elli put the hand grenades in her pocket and the pistol under her clothes. Carrying her eight-month-old baby and holding the hand of her two-and-a-half year-old child, she started walking the short distance home. Trees obscured her view of the house where she and Marios lived and hid Grivas. Suddenly, as she neared her house, she saw English soldiers searching the basket of a woman. She wondered, "What shall I do now? If I go back, the soldiers will suspect me and they will follow me." So she cut oranges from a nearby tree and gave a few to her toddler. When she approached the soldiers, her toddler offered the oranges to them. The soldiers assumed that she had other oranges in her pockets, so they let her go without searching her. Shortly thereafter, Grivas told her, "Congratulations, you handled this very well. But as of today, you are not allowed to carry anything except mail. If there are other things, Dafnis should bring them in the evening."

The Role of Garlic in the EOKA Underground

Elli devised clever methods of protecting Grivas. British soldiers used dogs to discover hideouts. The dogs could smell the EOKA fighters in their underground lairs and were trained to alert their British masters to the presence of the hideaways. Men living underground needed oxygen, so they had to construct air ducts. Elli knew that dogs do not like the smell of garlic, so every day she would place fresh garlic cloves by each of the air inlets to the underground hideout of Grivas. Consequently, the dogs avoided sniffing at these places and alerting the British soldiers. Her simple but ingenious scheme worked.

On another occasion, soldiers came at midnight and encircled the house where Marios and Elli lived. Grivas said, "We are surrounded. Leave this to God." At 8:00 a.m., the soldiers knocked at the door, and they began searching the house. One found a picture of Queen Elizabeth in a drawer, and he said, "Why do you keep this in the drawer and not on the wall?" Marios replied, "I work on the bases. I have many friends who are English. One gave me this picture, and I would like to hang it on the wall. But what if Grivas knows about it? I don't want to risk my life." Quick thinking produced a believable lie. The soldiers left.

A Narrow Escape

Hiding Grivas and two of his close associates sometimes required split second decision-making. One morning, soldiers came to their door at the very time Grivas's assistant was taking a shower. The man sprinted to the secret entrance to the hideout under the sink. The soldiers kept knocking at the door, and the situation rapidly became dangerous. Elli considered how she could justify the water on the floor. Quickly, she took off some of her clothes, put her hair under the shower, put a towel over her hair, opened the door a slit, and said, "I am sorry I delayed opening to you. I was taking a shower." The soldier said, "Sorry, Madame," and he left. Elli smiled at us and added, "By the way, the water was very cold."

On another occasion, Grivas needed Elli to deliver an urgent message to Maroula. She put her baby to sleep and hurried to Maroula. But no sooner had she left her house than the priest of St. Nicholas Church, Papa Georgios, came and knocked on the door. The baby awakened and began to cry. Obviously, no one was home, and the priest grew agitated and decided to call the police. As he walked away, he met Dafnis, and he said, "Who is this woman who left her baby unattended." Dafnis deceived the priest. "Father," he said, "I will tell you something very confidential. Please don't mention it to anybody. This woman is from a village, and she has been fooling around with men. To save her marriage, we brought her here. She is under our supervision. Please don't do anything. Keep it among ourselves." The priest accepted this explanation. Chuckling, Dafnis added, "Now Elli complains that I ruined her reputation."

Lynne asked Elli, "What did your mother think when she found out the truth?" Elli explained that every Sunday she would go to her mother's house to see her daughter. After three years of these visits, the girl was seven years old. Once, her daughter said, "Why don't you take me with you? Don't you like me [as you do] my other two sisters? Every night I pray, and I say, 'Jesus, if my mother does not love me, please take me to you.'" Elli's sister said, "What kind of mother are you. You are so cruel." Elli replied, "I am going to sacrifice my daughter, but not my country." Suddenly, her mother realized what was happening, and she said, "Oh, my God, you must be in EOKA." Elli responded, "Mother, I am not going to tell you what a serious role I am playing in EOKA. But eventually, you will be proud of your daughter." When the EOKA rebellion ended, Elli brought her mother and sister to the house in Limassol and showed them where Grivas hid. At this point, her mother said, "Now we know, and you have my blessing."

Sorting through Confusing Narratives

Dafnis said that, while he was on an EOKA mission in Lysi, a village NE of Limassol in what today is Turkish occupied northern Cyprus, he received a phone call from Thanos Ellinas, a neighbor in Limassol. Thanos told him that up to 300 British soldiers and Turkish auxiliary police were searching his property. Dafnis said he wondered if someone had tipped off the authorities on the location of Grivas's hideout. If they found Grivas, the rebellion was over.

Today, most people have mobile phones, so such a call seems normal. But how could that call have happened in Cyprus in 1956? Elli said the Panagides family was unusual in that they had a telephone in their home, so neighbors would come to their house to make phone calls. Thus, Thanos could have used this phone to call Dafnis by dialing the village phone in Lysi. Whoever answered the phone could step out of the phone box and yell, "Dafni! Telephone!" But why would anyone in Lysi know that Dafnis was there if he was on an EOKA mission? Grivas was extremely strict about secrecy and security, so it is not like Dafnis would tell Thanos, "I am going to Lysi today to plant a few bombs. I will be back by dinner." Perhaps Dafnis traveled to Lysi to conduct agricultural business—which would make more sense. His movements would not be secretive. He might have been doing his normal business work and also gathering intelligence for Grivas.

According to Dafnis, after receiving the call in Lysi, he was terrified and made his way to Lefkara, where he called Thanos—I assume at the Panagides's house—and learned that the search of their farm was still under way. Dafnis told us he thought his phone was being tapped, so he said, "They won't find anything, and they will be disappointed. I have nothing to do with EOKA." As it turned out, the British had no idea that Grivas was in a hideout not far from Dafnis's house. They had learned from interrogating EOKA members that firearms and explosives were hidden on the farm, so they came to search for weapons. But they found nothing, because EOKA fighters had already moved the cache to another location.

Dafnis claimed that, toward the end of the day of searching his farm, a Turkish policeman found the electrical wire that led to Grivas's underground hideout. The man did not know the purpose of the wire, but he began pulling it out of the ground, unknowingly following it toward the hideout. Inside the house, Solomon, Maria, and Maroula watched horrified through the kitchen window. As the man approached the hideout, Dafnis's mother, Maria, swiftly left the kitchen, grabbed the policeman by the arm, and said, "For goodness sake my child, you will be electrocuted with this thing. God bless you." Startled, he dropped the wire, and at that very moment, the officer in charge loudly announced, "The search is over." Upon this order, all the men left.

Dafnis admired how calmly his mother reacted during this crisis moment. He said she was a woman of strong faith and courage, and her quick thinking saved the EOKA rebellion. The problem with the story, however, is that Grivas was no longer hiding underneath Dafnis's garage when soldiers raided the farm. Elli clearly told us that, when the soldiers searched the Panagides farm, Grivas was in his new hideout under the house where she and her husband were living. Consequently, Dafnis's dramatic account of his mother preventing the discovery of Grivas is problematic. Indeed, his stories about when Grivas relocated to the new hideout varied in detail. In one interview, Dafnis said that, *after* the soldiers and policeman left the farm and he returned home, he and the other EOKA members felt great urgency to build a new hideout for Grivas. He probably had a memory lapse, which was not unusual—especially for incidents that happened

61 years earlier. The story about his mother may well contain dramatic embellishment. He loved to tell it.

Dafnis's normal version of the story was that, after the soldiers searched his farm, he knew they were looking for him. Sometimes he said that, while he was off on a trip to Paphos, a few soldiers came to his house and told Maroula that, when he returned home, he was to present himself to their headquarters. Consistently, however, Dafnis said that, when he discussed with Grivas the problem of soldiers looking for him, Grivas thought it unwise for Dafnis to go underground to evade capture. The British would place him on their wanted list and offer a reward for his capture. The colonel observed that he did not believe Dafnis was made of the right stuff to go join a guerrilla group, setting bombs and organizing ambushes; because, he said, "Dafnis did not want to kill a bird, let alone a human" [In his book, Dafnis has Grivas say, "He would not kill even an *ant*."]

Dafnis claimed that Grivas told him to give himself up, because if he joined the list of the wanted terrorists, it would put the colonel at very high risk. Such a directive would indicate that Grivas did not believe Dafnis would crack under interrogation and divulge the location of the hideout—a calculated risk to be sure. British torturers were relentless and skilled at extracting information from people. Dafnis claimed Grivas told him to present himself to Douglas Williamson, who headed the Security Services at Platres. But the details he gave about his arrest varied enough to raise questions in my mind.

When was Dafnis arrested?

Dafnis told us he obeyed Grivas and went to the Red House, the headquarters of the British Security Forces, where he presented himself as a law-abiding citizen. He tried unsuccessfully to talk his way out of being under suspicion. In the most developed version of this story, Williamson said to him,

> "You know, Dafnis, there is a movie going on, and when we watch this movie, all of a sudden, we see you in this movie as one of the actors." And I told him, "Mr. Williamson, I suspect the light was not good enough, and you definitely mistook me for somebody else." He said, "Well, this only the interrogators will find out." And he sent me to the interrogators for 43 [days], and they… got enough evidence. So, I could not fool Mr. Williamson. I fooled others for a long time, but not him.

Dafnis described exhausting, all-day and all-night tortures directed by a man named George Pereira, who was fluent in Greek and cunning in manipulating people to divulge information.

Dafnis ascertained that Pereira had extracted evidence from others that weapons and ammunition were hidden on the Panagides farm, but the agent had no idea that Grivas was hiding in the area. He said Pereira also had information from a document found on a wrecked bus near the village of Spylia that implicated Stahis and Dafnis. According to Dafnis, the leader of EOKA in Limassol, code name Nemesis [Demos Hadjimiltis], had written a report to Grivas in which he said, "I entrusted this mission to Adonis, whose brother was remarkable as the head of the youth of his high school, but who, unfortunately, left last week for the US to study." Once the British found the report from Nemesis, they determined the identity of the few students who had left Cyprus recently for the USA. On that basis they deciphered that Adonis was Dafnis's code name. They had their man—according to this version of the story.

Defaming the BBC

Dafnis claimed his friends later told him that the night after he surrendered to Williamson, a BBC radio reporter proclaimed, "The security forces had great success today in Limassol, Cyprus. They arrested Dafnis Panagides, one of the most dangerous terrorists on the island, and they dismantled his group." Dafnis snorted and said, "My group! I had no group! But this is how they described me." He added, "This was the first time I was described as a dangerous terrorist. I never considered myself as being such a dangerous person." He chuckled and added, "Maybe some of my friends think I am." I have not found any such news report, but it does make the BBC look bad and at the same time makes for a better story.

Stahis left Cyprus on 2 September 1956 to attend college in the United States, so that would mean that Demos wrote his report to Grivas a week later. But Dafnis was not arrested in September. Did he surrender willingly as he said, or did British troops simply arrest him? I always had to keep in mind how Dafnis smiled when he told us, "I have a tendency… to exaggerate, to add some dressing on the salad…. But would you like your salad without dressing?" He enjoyed embellishing his accounts, and he always kept us guessing as to which story elements were factual.

The claim that British soldiers found the report by Nemesis on a bus near Spylia is puzzling. This village is 50 kilometers north of Limassol in the mountains. On paved roads today, the drive from Limassol to Spylia takes more than one hour. In the 1950s, a journey over the roads, such as they were, would have taken much longer. Why would a report from Nemesis, the Limassol director of EOKA, be on a bus up in the mountains north of Limassol? And why would he send a report to Grivas explaining a mission of Dafnis and complimenting Stahis when Grivas was in close contact with the Panagides brothers? Would he not know what Stahis was doing? When Stahis left for America, Grivas was still living in the hideout underneath Dafnis's garage. He moved to his new hideout on 14 September 1956.

In *Bitter Leaves of Laurel,* Dafnis wrote that in *early October* a group of British soldiers and Turkish auxiliary came to his farm looking for him while he was away in Paphos—*after* Grivas had moved to the new hideout. They told Maroula to have him contact officials at the Red House—the headquarters of the Special Branch of the Security Forces—when he returned to Limassol. He wrote that he reported to the director, Douglas Williamson, a high-ranking official in the Intelligence Services during the EOKA years. Dafnis added that later, on *6 November 1956,* Williamson met a horrible death when he opened a package that turned out to be a mail bomb sent by EOKA. Dafnis should have been more careful to verify these dates.

Robert Holland wrote in his book on the EOKA rebellion that Williamson died from a mail bomb during the *14–15 November 1956* EOKA offensive (*Britain and the Revolt in Cyprus: 1954–1959* [Oxford University Press, 1998], 158). Holland reports that EOKA fighters killed 33 people during the first three weeks of November—the largest casualty rate during the entire conflict. He also points out that, during early November, the British were focused on their brief war with Egypt, not Cyprus. They were using the airport at Akrotiri to launch massive attacks against the Egyptian armed forces at the Suez Canal. Thousands of British troops were redeployed from Cyprus to Egypt for the battle, and Grivas exploited the situation. While the British were distracted with their war in Egypt, EOKA soldiers bombed British targets in Cyprus. Williamson was the highest-ranking officer assassinated by EOKA—but not on the date Dafnis specified.

Dafnis also gave different dates for his arrest. He claimed in his book that he was arrested in early October and mistakenly said Williamson was killed on 6 November 1956. But during one interview with us, he asserted that he voluntarily went to Williamson on *11 November 1956*. Fortunately, I was able to correct these memory lapses. I contacted Renos Lyssiotis (Ρένος Λυσιώτης), who was arrested shortly after Dafnis. Renos kept meticulous, written records of his own experiences and those of other detainees; and his incarceration overlapped that of Dafnis. Renos published his own experiences based on his diary: To *ημερολογια του D.P.743: 1956–1959* [*The Memoirs of D.P.743: 1956–1959*] (Nicosia, 2012).

Renos was born in 1931 to well educated and affluent parents: the lyric poet Xanthos Lyssiotis and his wife, Maria Aloneftis. Renos attended law school in London, earned his degree in 1955, and returned home to Cyprus to practice law. Soon, he began to witness the unlawful way the British treated Cypriots, and he started defending EOKA detainees *pro bono*. Young and brash, he used aggressive defense techniques, thereby angering the British. Renos's girlfriend joined EOKA, and then he joined EOKA; and the British rightly suspected him.

In an email from Renos to me dated 23 March 2021, he explained that British soldiers arrested him at his law office on the morning of 5 November 1956. They searched his office and his home for evidence, and then they took him for interrogation to their Omorfita station. After his first interrogation session by a Major

Sanford, they took him to Cell Number 2, where he met Dafnis and a man nicknamed Tsoukas (Renos explained that the man's name was Nicos Vanezis, and the British paid him to spy on the others). When Tsoukas asked Renos why he was arrested, Renos noticed Dafnis wink at him, indicating that he should be cautious of the man.

Later, after a Turkish guard let Tsoukas out of the cell, Dafnis explained that this spy circulated around Omorphita, gathering information. He encouraged Renos to be brave and he could endure the 18 days the British might interrogate him. He and Dafnis supported each other and became good friends. Renos said, "On the floor near the place that Tsoukas slept I saw a stump of a pencil. I took it and on a small piece of paper I was writing daily all happenings and main points of my interrogation." He added, "On the 8th November, following my interrogation, I was sent down to my cell. Tsoukas was there. He told me 'Dafnis sends you his regards. He was taken to detention camp.' Later Tsoukas admitted to me that he betrayed [his country] and was paid by the British £30 and promised to be sent to England. He told me that he regretted what he did and advised me not to admit anything."

In Dafnis's own account of the transfer from Omorfita to Pyla, he said,

> After 43 days of interrogation at the notorious Omorfita Interrogation Station in Nicosia, I was sent to the Pyla Detention Camp. The emergency regulations imposed by the government of Cyprus at that time gave power to the government to detain people without trial—a violation of basic human rights. And because they found nothing—they did not secure enough evidence to take me to the court for some criminal or terrorist action—on the basis of the Detention of Person Law, they sent me to the Pyla Detention Camp, and I was given a number. We had no names there; we only had numbers—DP, Detained Person number so-and-so. I was Detained Person/DP 722.

His claim of 43 days of torture is problematic. Renos explained, "I knew as a lawyer that one could be held for interrogation not more than 18 days and thereafter, he should be set free, or taken for trial, or sent to a detention camp."

After 18 days at Omorfita, Renos was taken to the Pyla Detention Camp, where Grivas soon tasked him with keeping a record of the tortures endured by detainees. Renos interviewed detainees, wrote down their stories, and smuggled these accounts out of Pyla in a secret compartment built into a food delivery truck. Others outside Pyla retrieved these documents and sent them secretly to the Greek Consulate in Nicosia, and an official there forwarded them to the United Nations and the European Council in Strasbourg.

When I asked Renos about the date of Dafnis's arrest, he investigated the matter and reported back to me.

> Myron Christofides, a journalist, kept meticulously daily notes of happenings as reported in the local newspapers, which later author Leonidas Leonidou found them and edited them in a two-volume book named *Χρονολόγιον Αγώνος 1954–1955* [*Chronology of the Fight: 1954–1959*]. I have this book and in the entry of **Thursday, 25 October 1956**, amongst many other happenings, it says "Dafnis Panagides, a merchant of Limassol, was arrested for interrogation." Thus, **Dafnis was arrested and sent to Omorfita for interrogation on the 25th October**… and was taken to Pyla Detention Camp on the 8th November 1956. (emphasis by Renos)

The British only kept Dafnis at Omorfita for *15 days* before sending him to Pyla. Renos said in an email dated 24 March 2021: "I do not believe that he exaggerated the number of the days of his stay in Omorfita purposely. I know that every day there seemed an eternity and this is the reason that in the cells the walls were scratched by the persons who were held there—one scratch for each day to remember when their suffering would be over." Point taken, but there is a 28-day difference between 15 days and 43 days, and Dafnis knew the limit for interrogation was 18 days.

In summary, Dafnis was arrested on 25 October 1956, interrogated at Omorfita for 15 days, transferred to Pyla on 8 November 1956, held there until late in 1958,

Figure 15. *Former detainees posing by a Nissen Hut at a detention camp.*

was moved to Kokkinotrimithia, near Nicosia, where he was released on or before 23 February 1959—the day when Hugh Foot released all EOKA detainees. Dafnis was detained a maximum of 28 months—five months less than the 33 he repeatedly specified. A five-month difference might possibly be the result of a memory lapse, but a similar explanation for the 28-day difference for his time spent at Omorfita is extremely unlikely. Perhaps the larger numbers simply made for a better story.

Covert Communications

At Pyla, detainees slept in Nissen huts, which are similar to Quonset huts and accommodated about 25 men. In summer, these corrugated steel buildings were extremely hot, and men were locked inside at night. The camp was divided into sections consisting of four Nissen huts per cluster, so men could potentially visit with 100 other prisoners in their part of the camp. Grivas and select EOKA detainees devised clandestine systems to get messages in and out. He assigned one or two men in each section of the camp to receive instructions, and he used different means for getting letters to and from each of the sections. Renos explained that each week an EOKA member or sympathizer drove into camp the food truck with a secret compartment for letters. One driver even smuggled a camera into the camp, and Renos began taking pictures of the detainees. Some of his photos are now on display in the Museum of the National Struggle in Nicosia.

Grivas appointed Dafnis to be his contact person in the section of the Pyla camp where he lived. Messages circulated around the entire camp through the cooks, who distributed food to the various sections. Although Dafnis told few stories about life in British detention camps, he repeatedly told us about Maroula's chocolate box.

> I arrived just a few days before Christmas of 1956.... [Actually, it was 8 November!] There was compound A, B, C, D, and so on. I was in Compound B.... And in the camp, on the basis of this law, people who had no connection whatsoever with EOKA were also detained, simply on suspicion. But once they came to the camp, of course, they became fanatic supporters of EOKA.
>
> Now, in the camp—because my wife Maroula had direct contact with General Grivas—a few days after I was put in this camp, I received a written message through this chocolate box telling me that I am appointed as his personal EOKA representative to keep him informed of what was happening, to give him information about the relationships among the detainees, and also to handle more serious cases, like escapes from the camp, which we had occasionally....

At this point, Dafnis picked up the chocolate box and explained how the system worked.

We were allowed one visit per week, unless we were under punishment when something happened, like some people escaped. Then we were prohibited of having any visitors for a month or even more. Or if there were some demonstrations in the camp for some reason, then the privileges of sending letters and receiving visitors were revoked.

To schedule these visits, we had to send an invitation letter. It was a card with the person's name, and it said, "You are invited to visit Detainee Number 722 once a week." I think our visits were every Friday. And Maroula would come with the children, one at a time; and other relatives would come, and we could talk through the barbed wires. The corridors were about two meters wide, and we could only see people from the outside while under the supervision of the guards.

Now the correspondence was brought in this candy box, which most probably was British made. [He had a broad smile when he said this.] We were allowed to have cakes and candies—which of course went through strict inspection. The visitors left [these sweets] at the gate and after the guards inspected the boxes, they delivered them to us the next day. And this box was one that went through several inspections. And so one week I would receive this box, and the next week I would give it back to the guards to return it to Maroula.

It was just an innocent candy box. But, you know, people who appear innocent are not always innocent; and this box is not as innocent as it looks, because the cover slides open and inside we could put a number of letters.

To illustrate how it worked, Dafnis slid open the secret lid and retrieved a piece of paper on which Maroula had written in Greek, "This is the box in which I carried the secret messages by General Grivas and I received also the messages from Dafnis to the General." Then he demonstrated how to insert the letter in the lid and close the slide so that it could be handed to the security officers. Dafnis smiled deviously and said, "The security officers checked the chocolates; maybe they helped themselves also; I'm not sure; and then they handed it to me."

Figure 16. Dafnis holding the chocolate box.

Dafnis had to be cautious when opening the lid. He could not risk anyone, including other detainees, seeing him retrieving messages. He waited until after sunset when the men were all locked in the barracks. When he was sure that there was nobody who could see, he secretly took the chocolate box into the toilet. He said, "I would sort out the correspondence to other secret EOKA members, and I would send the correspondence to the recipients in other compounds. And I would receive also the correspondence from other compounds." He placed letters into the lid of the box and the next week he would hand it to the guards along with a note to Maroula thanking her for bringing the chocolates. The British guards never discovered the deception.

I asked Dafnis what would have happened if the British had discovered that the chocolate box contained secret messages. He grew very somber and said, "If they found the box… they could trace Grivas through the correspondence…. So the consequences would be catastrophic." We wondered what it was like for both Dafnis and Maroula every week when she brought messages from Grivas and returned messages to Grivas. She was obviously very brave.

According to Dafnis, Grivas used this chocolate box to send permission for four detainees to escape in a secret compartment built under the food truck. We saw this truck in an EOKA museum in the village of Sotira. An elderly priest

Figure 17. *EOKA museum in Sotira. A priest and Dafnis stand in front of the food truck used to smuggle four prisoners out of the Pyla Detention Camp.*

who met Dafnis when they were both inmates at the Pyla camp is the caretaker of the museum. Dafnis translated for the priest, who showed the truck to us and explained how the men crammed themselves into the tiny space underneath it.

One of the four detainees who escaped was Andreas Karyos from the village of Avgorou. Dafnis said the man told him he was happy that Grivas consented for him to escape. Dafnis also said that Andreas had no idea that he (Dafnis) had delivered the approval from Grivas. More likely, the permission actually came via Renos Lyssiotis. In his book, *My Marshall, I Surrender!* (Nicosia, 2016), Renos states that Grivas "informed me that he had approved the escape of four of my fellow detainees: Fotis Pittas, Christakis Tryfonides, Andreas Kayros, and Frixos Dimitriades, and he asked me to inform them, and to help them with whatever they might need" (p. 59).

Dafnis told us that, before the escape, Andreas spoke privately to him, saying he hoped he would survive, but he was willing to die for his country. If he died, he wanted Dafnis to go to Avgorou and tell his wife and children that they should be proud of him and uphold the honor of his name. He handed Dafnis a piece of paper with a detailed list of his debts. He wanted Dafnis to tell his wife to pay his debts and not spend money on a memorial service for him. Dafnis said he and Andreas knelt, prayed together, and said "Goodbye." They never saw each other again. Andreas escaped from Pyla on 13 March 1958, but British soldiers killed him on 2 September 1958 in the village of Liopetri, which is less than five miles (7.8 km) from Avgorou. Dafnis said he kept his promise and delivered the letter to Andreas's widow shortly after he was released from the detention camp.

Problems abound with Dafnis's story. Some details are anachronistic. For example, he quotes Andreas as talking about his children, but the man had only a son when he was in the Pyla camp. *In Bitter Leaves of Laurel*, Dafnis also quotes Andreas saying,

> "I give you," he told me, "this list of my debts, and if it is God's will to sacrifice my life for the Fatherland, please give this list to my wife and tell her that it is my wish that instead of another memorial service, to pay my debts, to the last penny!"

Andreas Kayros was the commander of EOKA operations in the Avgorou area. During the six months between his escape from Pyla and his death, Andreas spent time with his wife, *Théspina (Δέσποινα)*. Indeed, she became pregnant during those six months, and she gave birth to their daughter six months after his death. He would have had plenty of occasions to tell her about paying his debts by not having a memorial service. The truth is, the amount of debt he owed vastly overshadowed the paltry amount a memorial service would cost. Today one would pay a priest only €10 to do a brief liturgy at the gravesite. Andreas was up to his eyeballs in debt.

I have had lengthy conversations with Andreas Karyos, named after his grandfather Andreas (Dafnis's friend). The grandson Andreas earned his Ph.D. in history at the University of London and wrote his 2011 doctoral dissertation on EOKA ("EOKA, 1955–1959: A Study of the Military Aspects of the Cyprus Revolt"). Consequently he brings an academic rigor to his historical work that differs dramatically from Dafnis's memoirs in *Bitter Leaves of Laurel*. When I explained to Andreas the things about Dafnis's story that puzzled me, I learned that there were more problems than I imagined. Andreas told me that his family does, in fact, have the document in which his grandfather listed his debts. But Dafnis delayed delivering this list of debts to the widow of Andreas until about two years before she died in June 2017.

Andreas explained that in 2015 he drove to Avgorou to visit his grandmother. She was happy when he arrived and said, "Oh, you missed what happened today. Dafnis Panagides visited me and gave me this paper that lists the debts of your grandfather. Dafnis believed this paper must be returned to our family. So you and your father may have it now."

Dafnis told me multiple times he drove to Avgorou soon after he got out of British detention and delivered the list of Andreas to his widow in 1959. He gave the same account in his memoirs:

> One of my first acts following my release was to go to Avgorou to fulfill the promise I had given to Andreas Karyos when he left the camp.... I arrived in Avgorou, where I met the late fallen patriot's wife and his minor children. I shared details about our lives together as prisoners in the Detention Center in a climate of heavy emotion. I communicated his last wishes to pay his debts and honor his legacy.

Dafnis even included a scan of this document in his memoirs—a scan that he apparently made sometime around 2015. Obviously, he would not have been able to scan the text in 1959! He waited nearly 60 years before taking Andreas's list to his widow. When he finally decided to keep his promise, he evidently made it look like he was being magnanimous in delivering the document to the widow—without mentioning the fact that for decades he had been telling a story about taking the list to her back in 1959.

When I examined the list of his Andreas's debts, I was stunned at the magnitude. He owed a total of £4,768 in 1958. Using a monetary conversion program, I calculated that the equivalent amount in 2021 is £94,433.62 British Sterling—the equivalent of €109,847 or $133,485 U.S. Andreas (the grandson) told me the sad story of how his grandfather incurred so much debt. Andreas explained that creditors came to the Pyla Detention Camp and demanded payment from his grandfather, who promised to repay the loans; but there was little he could do while in detention.

Andreas asked Grivas for permission to escape from Pyla, and Grivas finally consented. Andreas, the grandson, told me his grandfather's father-in-law visited him at Pyla, and (grandfather) Andreas hinted that he might escape. His father-in-law was furious, because his daughter was having a hard time already, and things would only get worse if she became a widow. *Théspina* had to take care of their fields on her own, and she had creditors after her to pay loans. Her father asked, "Where are you going to go if you escape? Why are you putting yourself in this danger? You have a son!" *Théspina* agreed with her father and complained to her husband about his EOKA involvement. Andreas, the grandson, believes his grandfather gave the list of his debts to Dafnis, because he knew his wife would strongly object if he told her of his escape plan.

Andreas (the grandson) explained that his grandmother, *Théspina*, visited her husband at Pyla, and he let me see a few of the letters she wrote to her husband while he was in detention—and a few of the letters her husband wrote to her. The letters reveal a great deal of love between the couple. They frequently wrote love poems. Andreas's letters apologize for the hardships *Théspina* had to endure because he was at Pyla. Her life was very difficult, but Andreas escaped anyway and resumed his leadership activities in EOKA. *Théspina* was about 22 years old when Andreas was killed in Liopetri. She never remarried, because she believed she needed to respect the memory of her husband. She suffered alone, a bereaved widow with two small children. But Andreas (the grandson) is proud of the way his grandmother became a model for how widows of Greek Cypriot heroes should behave. She died at age 86.

I will never know why Dafnis fabricated his story about going to Avgorou soon after he was released from detention. Did he not consider the consequences of repeating this claim in his memoirs? Did he never think that someone might check the validity of his account? And why would he include in his book the scan of Andreas's list of debts? He did not ask the family for permission, and anyone who reads the list and considers the sums would immediately realize the cost of not having a memorial service for Andreas would cover only a fraction of his debts. Nevertheless, Dafnis loved to tell his story of going to Avgorou. More puzzling still is why he included in his fictitious account a description of an encounter with a literate shepherd that changed him from a terrorist to a pacifist. That imaginary encounter, which I will describe later, took on immense significance for Dafnis's life—and influenced many of his listeners. But first, there is more to tell about that chocolate box and spy work in the Pyla Detention Camp.

The Deadly Wreck

Using the chocolate box to deliver messages to and from Grivas worked well—until one terrible evening after Maroula and her daughter Louisa had departed following a visit. Dafnis explained,

> I was called over the public broadcasting system: "Detainee DP722, please come to the office." I was scared, of course. When the commandant wanted to see a detainee, it was something serious. I appeared in the office of the commandant and he told me, "I want to inform you that your wife and child were in a wreck on the way back home in a small private car. But don't worry, they are safe."
>
> I did not believe that this report was correct. All night I worried about what might have happened. On the following day, we had visitors from Limassol, and Maroula sent me a message that she was safe and the baby was safe.... On her way back, the car overturned and they were thrown out of the car. And a Turkish policeman with a British officer in charge of the checkpoint at Kofinou went to help. The driver of the car died a few days later. But Maroula and the others—the baby and the other girl who was in the car and came to see her father—they survived. But Maroula was saying, "The box, the box, where is the box?" and the British officer said, "What is this woman saying?" The Turkish policeman said, "Sir, she suffered a nervous shock because of the accident, and instead of looking for her baby, she wants the chocolate box."

Dafnis told us he was going to donate the chocolate box to a museum, but he never got around to making the arrangements. His children, however, met with Andreas Karyos, Director of The National Struggle Museum in Nicosia, in 2021 and agreed to donate the box and some other Grivas memorabilia to the museum. Museum visitors will be able to see this interesting relic.

Love Letters during Detention

In the summer of 2021, Dafnis's daughter Lydia discovered a collection of letters written by Dafnis and Maroula while he was in detention. Although Dafnis deeply loved his family, he told few stories about them. Consequently, the correspondence from the 1950s that Lydia found in Dafnis's office opened up new dimensions in our understanding of his relationship with Maroula. These letters illuminate the love they had for each other. They also seem to illustrate the old saying, "Absence makes the heart grow fonder." The letters reveal the pain of separation and the difficulties of life in the detention camp. Lydia's brother, Thales, translated these letters into English.

In a letter dated 7 January 1957, Dafnis wrote to Maroula that years earlier his father, Solomon, asked kids in a Sunday School class to state what was the happiest day of their lives. Dafnis explains that he had difficulty deciding at that time, but not now.

> If they asked me the same question today, ... without a doubt, I would say it was the moment I decided to bind my life with you. Perhaps, still young

> at the time, I didn't realize the importance of having a good companion, as you are, my dear Maroula. But now, after being married to you for a few years, especially in these difficult times our family is experiencing, I feel God's greatest gift to me is my wife.

Hesitations he had in the past were gone. In a letter dated 28 January 1957, Maroula tells Dafnis how much she loves getting letters from him; and she admits to being a little embarrassed by how complimentary he is in praising her. She adds, however, "I accept them and thank you. For a woman to be considered a good wife, it also depends on her husband. Since you are so good to me, how can I not follow and be good to you? You write to me that you are very happy that we are together. And I am also happy...." In a letter dated 16 February 1957, she tells him how happy she was when she received an invitation from him to come and visit him in the camp. She adds,

> How I miss those lovely years under the grapevines, the carob trees and so many more. I remember you would tell us so many jokes and the nights would pass pleasantly. Do you remember how the sound of bees would put us to sleep and how I looked forward to helping you collect honey? It's impossible to forget. Fifteen days have passed since I last saw you but it seems like 15 years have gone by.

In a letter dated 21 March 1957, she says,

> *Dafni mou,*[1] I'm doing my duty as a good wife, and as for you, it is God's will for you to be away. It is with great pleasure that I do as much as I possibly can for your work, the family and home. I thank God that you are well even though the house is without its protector. God willing, when you are free again everything will be all right. You write that everyone loves you at the camp. But of course you are such a respectful and loving person my dear Dafni. Those who have the good fortune to meet you are magnetized by your kindness and love. It is impossible for them to forget you.

On 14 May 1957, Dafnis wrote,

> My dearest Maroula,... You know how happy I am when I receive your letters.... The dull life in prison is very difficult. Only the ones who live here can understand. We often need to rest psychologically and of course the best rest is receiving letters from loved ones. Many days may pass before we meet again. We will have many things to talk about when you come. I am anxious to hear about the children, especially Louisa. You wrote about her illness. Really Maroula, she was born in troubled times.

---

[1] A term of endearment: "My Dafnis."

> Remember last summer after her baptism, I was in a dark cell room of the prison.

Maroula wrote on 6 July 1957,

> My dearest Dafni, Your mother enjoys it when I read your letters over and over to her. Thank you for your kind words which show your love for me. Really Dafni, our love continues to blossom for each other. I feel so much love for you as never before.... May God reunite us to live lovingly together for the rest of our life.

On 12 November 1958, close to the day of Dafnis's release, she wrote,

> My dearest Dafni, I received your two letters, which are full of anticipation and express your love towards me and our children. Your letters move me every time I read them. I feel your love for me is blossoming as my love is for you too. I also received a nice letter from Chloe, who said that you wrote how happy you were to have me as your wife and she had no doubt about that. I'm so grateful that God granted me a special life partner.

Interestingly, in a letter to his father, Solomon, dated 14 August 1958, Dafnis wrote, "I'm so glad you're happy with Maroula. This justifies your decision, because she was your choice. I also feel happy because now I see more clearly her beautiful character and virtues." Arranged marriages can be happy marriages.

British soldiers read all of the letters going in and out of their detention camps, so Dafnis and Maroula needed to be cautious in what they wrote and did not write. Expressions of love were acceptable, and the pain of separation is apparent in their letters. But Dafnis was not merely rotting away in the detention camp. He was assigned important work there.

Spy work in the Detention Camp

Ioannis, or John, another friend of Dafnis from the Pyla camp, said Grivas appointed Dafnis to examine new detainees. The British sometimes pretended to arrest certain men and placed them in the camps as spies. Consequently, the detainees developed an elaborate system of identifying spies. John said, "They would receive information [from an outside source] saying things like, 'Pavlos has arrived. Don't trust him. We believe that he is a traitor.'" Only a few, trusted individuals knew that Dafnis was a contact person. The rest thought he was just another detainee. John said Dafnis sent reports detailing what he determined the British knew about EOKA activities by gluing them into boxes that contained dirty clothes that the men were allowed to send out of the camp. He never mentioned the chocolate box.

John praised Dafnis's gifts in diplomacy, such as an instance in which two detainees got into a fight, and the guards were considering punitive measures.

Dafnis persuaded the men to stop fighting each other, because they all needed to be together and support each other. John and Dafnis became life-long friends, and they learned to accept each other's eccentricities. Dafnis endured John's lengthy lectures about the Bible being an esoteric code full of symbolism, his theories about prophecy, and his belief that electromagnetism controls the universe. Twice, devious Dafnis set me up so that I had to listen to John's theories. I think he enjoyed watching me squirm. Both times Dafnis conveniently left the room, saying that he had something he needed to accomplish.

I finally managed to refocus John on Dafnis. He said Grivas got frustrated with Dafnis but he trusted him to relay information in and out of the Pyla camp. John praised Dafnis's respect for others and for his helpfulness. However, he added that Dafnis was an immature child when it came to finances. He shook his head, laughed, and said, "If a matter had to do with finances, forget it!"

Meaningless Promises

Elli, who hid Grivas and served as his courier, became a dear friend of Dafnis and Maroula during EOKA days. However, she candidly told us Dafnis was unreliable and said she believed *maybe* 50% of what he said. Elli complained that, time after time, he failed to keep his promises. She said Grivas grew exasperated with Dafnis's deceptions and always questioned him and did not trust him. Maroula, however, was steady and reliable. Grivas trusted her.

I asked Elli why Grivas made Dafnis his contact person in the detention camp if he did not trust him. She responded, "Because, of the people who were arrested, Dafnis was the only person who knew that the General was here." Perhaps there were other reasons. Grivas trusted Maroula. She was an experienced courier, and she had a legitimate reason to visit her husband at Pyla. The British would expect her to come. Also, Dafnis endured interrogation and did not crack. If Grivas entrusted to him responsibility for getting confidential messages in and out of the camp, he must have seen the necessary skills in Dafnis to accomplish these tasks. A lot was at stake. Dafnis knew the location of Grivas, and that knowledge would have been priceless for the British.

Marios and Elli worked closely with Grivas for nearly two and a half years while he hid under their house, and Elli was fearless in following his commands. They knew Grivas. They knew Dafnis. Over time, she increasingly saw Dafnis as undependable. On the day we interviewed her, she was very frustrated with him. She gave recent examples of how he made meaningless promises to her that he did not keep. "Why are you still friends?" I asked. She replied, "You have to accept people the way they are.... I am not perfect. He is not perfect."

Was it worth it?

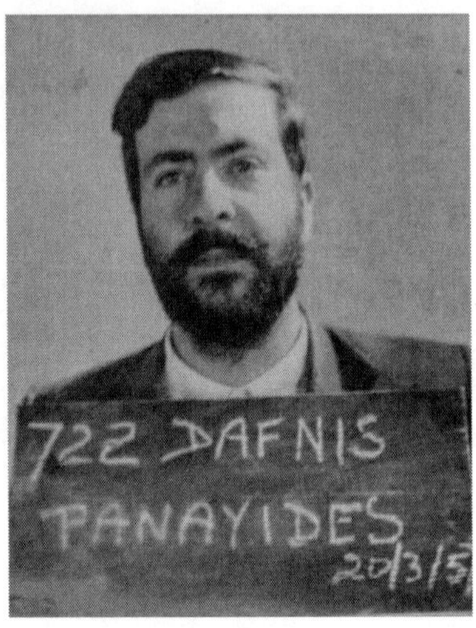

Figure 18. Detained Person #722.

As the EOKA struggle neared completion, three months before the British signed the final agreement for granting freedom, Dafnis and other detainees were moved to the Kokkinotrimithia Detention Camp near Nicosia. Later, Cypriot patriots partially restored this camp and opened it for visitors—as a means of keeping alive the memories of those who suffered there. Dafnis did not make the yearly pilgrimage to this camp in October, as do numerous elderly EOKA members, who want their children and grandchildren to see the camp and learn what happened there. Dafnis felt conflicted about the matter.

During a trip to Nicosia in 2017 to interview friends and relatives of Dafnis, we had several hours between appointments. Dafnis asked if we wanted to see the detention camp, and we readily accepted. As we drove toward the memorial, Dafnis grew increasingly contemplative. Our stroll through the camp was somber, and I could see agitation on his face as he explained features of the facility. In one of the buildings is a large display of photographs of EOKA detainees arranged according to their Detained Person numbers. I found the picture of a much younger, bearded Dafnis. Across the bottom of the photo is handwritten, "722 Dafnis Panagides."

Following our visit to the camp, Dafnis was more pensive than I had ever seen him. Finally, I asked him to explain how he was processing our tour of the camp. He replied, "I am wondering if it was all worth it." His statement hung in the air unanswered. He could not decide. Was all the suffering and bloodshed worth it? Was there a better way to gain freedom? What would Cyprus look like today if EOKA had never happened? Would the Republic of Cyprus be intact with Greek Cypriots and Turkish Cypriots living together in peace? We will never know. Some of Dafnis's friends assert that the EOKA rebellion was an absolute disaster. One man who joined EOKA while a high school student said emphatically, "As far as I am concerned, EOKA was definitely not worth it; and it was definitely immoral!" Others, however, fundamentally disagree with his assessment.

Destroying the Social Fabric of Cyprus

Although Dafnis was totally committed to EOKA in the 1950s, he admitted in 2017 that EOKA tragically destroyed the social fabric of Cyprus "by legitimizing violence in an otherwise peaceful society." He added that previously there were "crimes of honor, crimes because somebody cut [off] the water.... There were crimes, but the *legitimization* of crime destroyed the social fabric."

Before the EOKA struggle, Cyprus had a relatively peaceful social contract; but murders became common during the rebellion. Even after independence, political leaders continued to kill opponents. Dafnis said that an acquaintance of his came to his office one afternoon and said,

> "I received instructions to kill somebody." He told me who. I said, "But why are you going to kill him? Do you know that killing is a very serious thing? Thou shall not kill." He said, "But I have instructions." "Who gave you instructions?" He told me the name ___, who I knew very well. I was alarmed. I said, "What is this? ___ gave you these instructions?" "Yes. He came to Limassol and he said, 'You must [kill him]'." And he did. I was in Nicosia when I heard on the radio that the minister was killed. And I knew who killed him.

Dafnis explained that, in war, it is easy to adopt the philosophy "The end justifies the means." Tragically, the same became true during times of peace.

Figure 19. *Col. Grivas stands in the middle of the front row, wearing a white suit. Dafnis stands at the far left in the front row beside Glafkos Clerides, who later became president of Cyprus.*

After Cyprus gained independence, Dafnis grew increasingly disenchanted with the philosophy and methods of Grivas. He still admired the man's dogged commitment and respected his military genius. From his perspective, Grivas simply did not understand his own historical context. He wanted to split Turkey away from NATO and create an AXIS with Yugoslavia, Egypt, and Greece. Dafnis said,

> He was corresponding back and forth with the Greek government, but the Greek government would not agree with him, because for them NATO was more important than Cyprus. And the alliance with the Americans and the British had priority over Cyprus. For Grivas, Cyprus was the real issue. Sometimes Grivas would get a letter from the minister or the king… and would get very angry and say, "These people just do not understand."

In 1955, Dafnis agreed with the tactics of Grivas. However, when the elderly Dafnis pondered the past, he judged the use of violence to be counterproductive.

> They pursued a policy that was self-defeating in terms of achieving their goals. They chose violence when we came out of the war [WW 2], and people were tired of violence. They wanted a new climate of diplomacy and discussions. As Gandhi showed, passive resistance could bring more positive results than could violence. In other words, they used tactics that were popular in past ages. In my opinion, they misread the developing new political situation in the Middle East.

As an old man analyzing the events of the 1950s, he saw things much differently than he had as a younger man who had sworn allegiance to EOKA.

Dafnis contemplated the larger political environment and offered the following insights.

> Four major things were happening in the Middle East. Number one, the establishment of the state of Israel in 1948. Number two, the Middle East becoming *the* major energy source and economic source for sustaining Europe—primarily the western countries. Number three, the Suez Canal with Nasser there nationalizing the canal and driving the British out. And, number four, the increasing role of the Soviet Union in Eastern Europe.

Then he offered his critique:

> So, here we are opening up a new chapter ignoring these *major* factors—and believing that people would care about this small island with 600,000 people. We missed the major economic, military, and political interests of the super powers.

From his perspective, the EOKA leaders made fatal mistakes because they misread the international scene and were blinded by their own nationalistic interests.

After the EOKA struggle for freedom, Dafnis watched Cyprus devolve into warring factions; and he came to despise the way rival leaders ruthlessly maneuvered for power. He said,

> So, yes, I am angry with Makarios. Less with Grivas, who was an honest person. He was used by people around him.... They exploited his nationalistic and anti-communist feelings.... But Makarios, as a church leader, should have created a City of God, which he promised in his speech. But he never did. He did exactly the opposite. He laid the wrong foundations. Instead of establishing the state on morality and good government and the rule of law, he did exactly the opposite.

Dafnis criticized Orthodox Church leaders, especially Archbishop Makarios, for playing partisan politics instead of seeking to establish an ethical government that considered the needs of *all* citizens—both Greek Cypriots and Turkish Cypriots. They stooped to manipulation and murder to implement their political agendas. Instead of doing what was right, they did what enhanced their own power. The result was disaster.

CHAPTER 5
From Parliamentarian to College Freshman

Setting the Captives Free

As the EOKA rebellion dragged on with no resolution in sight, the British grew weary of their conflict with Cypriot rebels. The mounting expense and death toll finally caused the British to acquiesce. But they granted independence to Cyprus, not *enosis* with Greece as EOKA wanted. Also, they did not let the Greek Cypriot majority compose their own constitution and form their own government. British statesmen made independence contingent on Great Britain, Greece, and Turkey *all* agreeing on specific conditions. In other words, they forced a compromised constitution on Cyprus that the Cypriots did not want. Archbishop Makarios finally agreed to the constitution, but only because everyone was weary of fighting. He intended to alter it later.

When Great Britain signed the agreement in February 1959 granting quasi independence to Cyprus, the deal included granting amnesty to *all* EOKA detainees. Grivas absolutely insisted on amnesty as a condition for ceasing hostilities. The day of their release brought jubilation for the captives set free. Dafnis boarded a bus, left the camp in Nicosia, and headed for Limassol. When he arrived, he experienced his father's poignant gesture of opening the door to the birdcage and allowing all his captive birds to fly free. What a sweet homecoming!

When we first met Dafnis in 2011, his birdcage was the same size as it was when Solomon was alive. Dafnis loved to listen to the birds, and he always found it amusing when my wife, Lynne, would "talk" with the birds by imitating their sounds and listening to their responses to her. When we returned to Limassol in 2017, we found a much-enlarged birdcage. We told Dafnis the major increase in space now qualified it to be called an aviary. He sheepishly admitted he recently had troubles with a snake that kept returning to eat his birds. Dafnis twice removed the snake to another location, but he finally killed the reptile. He expressed sadness at killing the predator, but he could not make it leave his birds alone. And I, because of my propensity to joke around, asked if this act jeopardized his commitment to pacifism. He flashed his Dafnis smile and changed the subject.

Dafnis loved animals, and he wanted his captive birds to have enough room to fly short distances. He took good care of them, but they were captives. He denied their freedom, because he enjoyed watching and listening to them. Certainly, their incarceration did not mimic Dafnis's experiences in the British camps. But he pondered the fact that the birds were not free. In a fitting tribute, during the three-month memorial following Dafnis's death, his children set all his birds free.

Quasi Independence for Cyprus

Cyprus did not experience sudden freedom like Solomon's captive birds. They received a quasi freedom based on the dictates of the three Guarantor Powers. Because Greek Cypriots comprised 77% of the population of the island, election of a Greek Cypriot president was a foregone conclusion. So the Guarantor Powers insisted that the vice president be a Turkish Cypriot with veto power over laws passed by the elected majority. Although Turkish Cypriots comprised only 18% of the population (4.7% of the population was listed as "others"), the externally coerced constitution gave to them 30% of the parliamentary seats. It was a formula for gridlock and frustration that ultimately resulted in the disastrous Turkish invasion of the island in 1974.

If Great Britain, Greece, and Turkey had allowed Cypriots to figure out their own future, perhaps the tragedies that followed would have been averted. Politicians in these three "guarantor" countries cared mostly about what they considered to be best for their own countries—not what was best for Cyprus. To be sure, freedom would have been messy, but the price paid for external meddling was disaster. These three countries signed agreements in London and Zürich in February 1959—agreements ratified by Archbishop Makarios, elected president of the Republic of Cyprus, and Fazıl Küçük, elected vice president by the Turkish Cypriots.

On 16 August 1960, Cyprus officially became a dysfunctional, independent republic. The cobbled constitution guaranteed failure of the new nation. To call the document *odd* is a serious understatement. Intense problems began almost immediately. By 1963, the government went into meltdown. Greek Cypriots wanted what was best for Greek Cypriots. Turkish Cypriots wanted what was best for Turkish Cypriots. Neither group made their priority what was best for *all* citizens of Cyprus. Nationalistic bickering increased and eventually led to bloodshed. And Dafnis Panagides was plunged into the stormy waters of the new government—an unwilling conscript into the melee.

Just War and Pacifism

Dafnis became a pacifist at some point after the EOKA rebellion concluded. What caused this radical shift in philosophy? He claimed that, during the EOKA years, he had accepted the Catholic concept of Just War, whose origins largely trace back to St. Augustine (born AD 354, died 430). We knew that, before EOKA, he joined a peace movement; so I asked how he justified joining EOKA and fighting against the British. He said Catholic theology led him astray. I found his comment puzzling in light of numerous examples of the Orthodox Church promoting wars. Numerous frescos and icons on the walls of Orthodox churches depict warrior saints with their weapons. But Dafnis traced the problem to the more theologically precise philosophy formulated by Catholic scholars. Of course, philosophy and theology emerge from historical contexts.

Figure 20. *Many such depictions of warrior saints may be seen in Orthodox churches in Cyprus.*

St. Augustine converted to Christianity in AD 386, a time when the Roman Empire had moved toward establishing Christianity as its national religion. Combining Christian faith with political power brought a dramatic elevation of the status of the church, and church leaders had to adapt to this new political reality. What would followers of Jesus of Nazareth, who said to love your enemy, say about wars conducted by the Roman Empire? Augustine believed that Christians should be peaceful *unless* they are wronged in such a way that violence is necessary to resolve the injustice; but he did not list principles for such defensive actions.

Centuries later, St. Thomas Aquinas (AD 1225–1274) built on the works of Augustine and formulated criteria necessary for a war to be just: (1) War cannot be inspired by desire to acquire wealth or power; (2) War needs to be under the legitimate authority of the state; (3) For war to be legitimate, peace must be the primary reason for the use of violence. Going to war must be an appropriate response to conditions so heinous that *not* going to war would be less moral than going to war. For example, many Christians today argue that for the United States to declare war against Germany and Japan during WW2 was *more* moral than not going to war and thereby allowing Germany and Japan to slaughter people and take over their lands. They argue that, as terrible as the war was, the alternative would have been even worse. In other words, the Allied war against aggression met the criteria of being a *Just War.* Mennonites and members of other Christian peace movements reject this reasoning.

In 1955, Dafnis became part of EOKA. He said he believed "violence could be justified for just causes." He thought, "You have to fight for justice, for equality, for freedom." In retrospect, he concluded he had been wrong in believing violence against the British was justified. He claimed his change of philosophy traced back to an encounter with a shepherd during a mission to deliver a list of debts from his dead EOKA friend, Andreas Karyos, to the man's wife, *Théspina*, instructing her not to have a memorial for him but to use the money to pay his debts. We heard this story so frequently that we realized it had reached the level of a legendary quest for truth—legitimizing Dafnis's move to pacifism. He had been telling the story to others for decades.

As I explained earlier, Dafnis did not in fact journey to Avgorou in 1959 to keep his promise to a fallen comrade. It was not until 2015 that Dafnis took this list of debts to *Théspina*. However, part of Dafnis's fictitious account of the 1959 trip involved a momentous encounter with a shepherd—which he claimed was a watershed event in the development of his thinking about just war and pacifism. According to his narration, he became lost while trying to locate the small village of Avgorou, because in 1959 roads were few and directional signs were rare. Suddenly, he saw a shepherd sitting on a rock; and oddly enough, the man was reading a book. Dafnis explained this unusual scene.

> I never heard of a shepherd reading a book. I never saw one in my life. This was the only one I ever met, and the book he was the reading was the New Testament.... I asked him first if he could show me the way to Avgorou village. It was a completely undeveloped area. No paved roads. And he said, "Yes, I will show you, my young man."... And he said, "You seem to be an educated man coming from town, and I have a question for you. If the president of Cyprus was Jesus himself, rather than our archbishop [Makarios], would he take a gun to drive the British out?"

Sometimes when telling the story, he expanded the shepherd's words: "If our Lord Jesus Christ were the Archbishop of Cyprus, would he be using machine guns and land mines, killing the English and shedding blood to gain the freedom of Cyprus?"

Literate Shepherds were rare

According to Andreas Karyos, the historian grandson of Andreas Karyos, shepherds in eastern Cyprus in the 1950s were flute players who maintained oral traditions as folklore poets. Very few could read and write. Andreas's great grandfather on his mother's side, a shepherd and a singer of folklore tales, died at the age of 103. Andreas's grandfather, a farmer who did not attend high school, read a lot; so he had a higher level of education than most men in his area—which enhanced his leadership capability for EOKA.

Dafnis claimed that the shepherd's question caused him to enter into a time of deep reflection about justice and just-war theory. He said,

> Even before EOKA, I was a member of World Resistance International, but I never thought that fighting for freedom or human rights would involve violence. And now I believe that violence *cannot* be justified. Even fighting for justice. You fight with love. You don't fight with bullets.
>
> So eventually, I decided that violence was not compatible with the principle of Christian love, and that is when I added this dimension to my religious beliefs. I was already a pacifist, but more in a narrow sense of "no more war." And I participated in anti-war demonstrations and other anti-war activities. But after EOKA, I decided that *any* form of violence was wrong. About that time, I met an Indian who was a follower of Gandhi, and we talked extensively on the Indian word *Satyagraha*. It means passive resistance, and this was the principle of Gandhi—how he was able to liberate India, practicing *Satyagraha*.

As he spoke to us in 2017, Dafnis stroked his goatee in a reflective manner, choosing his words carefully. He explained that he never could decide whether he had talked to a literate shepherd—a very remote possibility at the time—or whether the shepherd was actually an angel sent from God. Given the fact that he did *not* deliver the list of Andreas Karyos's debts to his friend's widow in Avgorou until 2015, the immense significance Dafnis placed on his fictional narrative is puzzling. He told the story frequently, tracing his commitment to pacifism to imaginary events that occurred during a trip that never happened. The story provided divine initiative to his conversion. His precise reasons for becoming a pacifist remain a mystery, but the transformation probably occurred slowly.

Reluctant Representative

In August 1960, Dafnis was weary of conflict. Beaten down by his captivity, he simply wanted to be with his family and reestablish his farming business. Cyprus was now a quasi-independent republic, and Cypriot leaders switched from battling the British to fighting with each other for power. Dafnis wanted nothing to do with such political feuds. He said,

> I decided not to get involved in any public activities and definitely not in politics. I had a family. My business suffered during my imprisonment. So I said, "I must concentrate on my family and on my children." And so I left Cyprus and I traveled to Germany and England and then the elections took place in my absence.... By the time I came back in September, Makarios formed his first cabinet, and one of the elected representatives of Parliament from Limassol was selected to become the first Minister of Public Works and Communications. So there was a vacancy for Limassol, and it was necessary by election to fill this vacancy in the Parliament.

Figure 21. *From the left: Choe and her husband, Andonis. In front of them are their children Pavlos, Thyrsos and Christina. Their son Soli (Solomon) sits on Grandmother Maria's lap. From the right: Maroula holding Dora, Louisa, Dafnis, and Lydia.*

At this early stage of the Republic, the most organized group in the Limassol area was the Communist Party. According to Dafnis, all the centrist and far right organizations existed under the umbrella of Makarios—a group called the Patriotic Front, which included ex-EOKA members.

Makarios offered to Dafnis the position of Secretary of the Patriotic Front for Limassol; but he declined the offer, and Makarios took the refusal personally. Dafnis said Makarios appropriated a scriptural statement: "'Whoever is not with you is against you.' So when I declined, he immediately concluded that I was anti-Makarios. Because who would decline a prestigious position offered by the President? As of that time, Makarios always thought of me with some suspicion."

Meanwhile, people in the Limassol district began to approach Dafnis about running for the vacant seat in parliament. According to Dafnis, two ladies paid him a visit.

> One was a high school teacher from Greece who worked in Cyprus, and she was a member of a very powerful Orthodox religious fraternity in Greece, *Zoe*, which means life. *Zoe* is a brotherhood of lay people, and she was a member of this, and I knew her from the Christian movement. And together with the young lady who was the only contact with my wife when she served as a courier of Grivas's correspondence.... These two women said, "We came to tell you that you need to run for the Parliament." I said, "No! No way! I decided to look after my business and my family, and I have no intention to go into politics." But they said, "But we have pressure and the bishop of Limassol asked us to come and try to convince you." And I said, "No way!" Then the bishop called me, and he said, "Dafnis, you need to accept this [position] because I have pressure from the credit unions and the farmers unions and from the villages. You are very popular, and they want you." I said, "No. I cannot."

Dafnis claimed that the bishop did not convince him, but a childhood friend from Kalo Chorio did. The man called and said, "You have to accept—for one reason. You played a role in the EOKA struggle, and we ended up with this republic. The job is not finished. Will you abandon this unfinished job? Don't you think you have responsibility to help build this republic which we created?" Dafnis said this argument convinced him, and he agreed to run for office.

Soon the name Dafnis Panagides was on the ballot. But Archbishop Makarios had someone else in mind for parliament, and he wanted Dafnis to withdraw. But Dafnis's supporters said, "No! We want Dafnis. We are under pressure mostly from the rural areas and the farmers' organizations and the labor unions. They want Dafnis."

To the chagrin of Makarios, Dafnis received 80% of the vote and became a Member of Parliament. Dafnis told us, "For me it was a blessing because I was elected without the support of Makarios. So, I did not feel any obligation to do what Makarios said. On many occasions, I disagreed with Makarios's proposals."

For example, Makarios wanted to create a National Guard. Dafnis argued instead for creating something like the Peace Corp that John F. Kennedy instituted in the USA. Dafnis saw great value in organizing Cypriots to serve their country. In his version of a Peace Corp, youth could do reforestation and other civil works in their communities instead of serving in the army. Makarios responded, "Listen, Dafnis. I like your proposal. But what can we do with all the people who come to me every day and ask for a job? I want to create this National Guard and put people on a government salary."

I asked Dafnis what kinds of initiatives he tried to get through Parliament. He said,

> I was seen as representing the rural people, and I was more accessible than the others were, who were doctors and lawyers in town. Anybody could come to my home, knock at the door early in the morning, and he would be received.... I always brought to the Parliament things that were of interest to farmers and members of labor unions.

He and a friend from Larnaca tried to pass a law requiring people running for public office to declare their financial worth, but the other legislators would not let it come to a vote. With this law on the books, reporters could say to elected officials, "You were penniless when you came into Parliament. Now you have accounts in Switzerland and in the Bahamas. Where did this money come from?" Dafnis added, "Not until two weeks ago, under public pressure and after many scandals, members of Parliament passed a law [about officials declaring financial worth] that was watered down completely, but at least it is something."

While serving as an elected representative, Dafnis learned more about the art of wheeling and dealing. Villagers in Arakapas and Kellaki wanted the road between their villages paved. So Dafnis went to the Director of the Ministry of Public Works with their request. The man, a good friend of his from the EOKA years, said, "But there are only four cars per day using this road." They discussed their options, and finally the man said, "Listen, Dafnis. Keep it between the two of

Figure 22. *Cypriot government officials. Dafnis is the first one on the right in the first row.*

us. We will fix a particular day, and I shall install a traffic counter. And on that day, you tell the drivers in Arakapas and Kellaki to drive back and forth, back and forth over the counter." Consequently, the number of vehicles on the road jumped from four to 35 cars a day. Dafnis gave a conspiratorial smile and said, "And so, the next year, it was on the budget." He paused and asked, "Is this cheating? I don't want to be God, because he would have difficulty deciding."

Laughing about Prostitution

As a Member of Parliament, Dafnis sometimes dealt with issues that required bending the rules—as if that were a problem in Cyprus! One day, he got a call from the district commissioner, who told him, "The owner of the Rose Hotel quarreled with the police because the police wanted to enter the hotel, and he refused to let them in. He insulted them and they quarreled. Please, he is your friend. You talk to him." Dafnis explained:

> We spoke privately, and he said to me, "The police wanted to come in because they suspected that I was involved in prostitution." This was in a neighborhood of nightclubs. And of course, so-called *artists* used to go to this hotel after the performances. And he said, "No way would I let the police enter, because one of your colleagues [in the parliament] was in one of my rooms. And I love Makarios, and I love his government. And what if they came and they found one of the members of his parliament in my room?"

Dafnis told the story in an amusing way to elicit laughter, but I thought the Member of Parliament should have been exposed. What is humorous about a married man having sex with prostitutes? However, we noticed in Dafnis and some of his friends the opinion that, if married men have relations with other women, that is their own business.

Systemic Corruption

Petros, the EOKA member who had directed smuggling of weapons through the port of Limassol, admired Dafnis for the ways he helped anyone in need regardless of the person's race, nationality, occupation, or religion. He admitted, however, that Dafnis could be infuriating because "he is *never* punctual" and is terrible about keeping his appointments. Petros laughed and added, "We cannot change Dafnis." Truly! Dafnis was a free spirit who conformed to no one's expectations but his own. He took pride in his spontaneity, even when it inconvenienced others.

Unlike Dafnis, Petros was a successful businessman, but he made his way to the top by virtue of his ability to focus. Raised in extremely impoverished circumstances, he worked hard to gain positions of responsibility. At the end of the EOKA rebellion, he was assured that he could return to his old job at the Limassol port, but the promise of that position proved to be hollow. Following Cypriot independence, Petros had to face new rules that emerged under the constitution forced on the Republic of Cyprus. The requirements imposed on Cyprus stipulated that the workforce needed to be 70% Greek and 30% Turkish. Because of this quota system, he lost his position at the port. Refusing to give up, he succeeded in getting a job in the newly established department that handled movement of ships. Over time, he advanced until he finally became manager of the Port of Limassol, which employed over 2,000 workers. He sadly added, "I can tell you without reservation that 1,990 [of these] people were thieving. I could not trust 1,990 people." Port employees, to keep from being caught in their shady dealings, warned each other every time Petros made his rounds of the port. "So much corruption," he said. "So much corruption!"

Petros said that Archbishop Makarios gave jobs to people because they were loyal to him—not because they were competent in their positions. Petros added that when the archbishop was president, he considered those who crossed him to be blasphemers; and those who resisted his policies could face grave danger. Petros believed that he and Dafnis were under constant suspicion because they did not back all of Makarios's positions.

Promises, Promises

Dafnis loved being the life of the party with an audience hanging on his every word. One of his friends told us that when Dafnis was a parliamentarian he would find some object to stand on in order to elevate himself above a crowd gathered on a street. Then he would hold forth on some topic. The friend said that Dafnis was always promising things to the crowds, but he hardly ever kept his promises. "Typical of politicians," he said, "always promising but seldom delivering."

Another friend said he once took Dafnis to see a movie called *A Thief is Wanted*, because, "The movie plot is about a parliamentarian who promises, promises, promises—and no action. I thought it was perfect for Dafnis to see it because that is what he was doing. He was promising, promising, promising, but not delivering actions."

This friend said the house of Dafnis and Maroula was always full of people asking something from Dafnis the parliamentarian, but Dafnis never delivered anything (Mediterranean overstatement). Nicos, a cousin of Maroula who went into business with Dafnis, also told us about Dafnis making promises he never meant to keep. With Dafnis sitting right beside him, he said,

> We started Agria at his house because the only place we had when we started the company was his house. He was still a member of the parliament, so he had another, temporary office. A woman came by one day,

Figure 23. Dafnis driving one of his various Agria machines.

> and I heard her say, "Mr. Dafnis, please try to get my son out of the lunatic asylum." He said, "Okay, I will do it." A while later, a man came, and he went inside, and I heard him say, "Mr. Dafnis, I know that my wife came here and asked you to get my son out of the lunatic asylum. Please don't do that, because he is crazy. If you get him out, he will kill us." And Dafnis said, "Okay." When they finished talking, I asked, "How are you going to satisfy both the one who wants him out and the one who wants him in?" He says, "You are right. I will do nothing." But he did not say to anybody that he would not do it. He wanted everybody to be happy.

Dafnis smiled and said, "That is very true."

Nicos was very candid. Concerning Dafnis's business dealings, he said people continually asked him for special considerations, and Dafnis had difficulty saying "No."

> So many times such requests were against his interest, and this was the problem he had accumulated over the years. Many customers took advantage of him. A lot of people owed him money, and he could not collect anything. After he left for America, I took a lot of these people to court. That was the only way they would pay. They did not believe we would go to court. Some of them could pay, but they did not pay, because Dafnis was here. And some of them would tell me, "If Mr. Dafnis was here, he would not demand his money." That was their excuse always. But, I collected, and it helped Dafnis in those days.

> Dafnis does not want people thinking that he does not agree with them. And this in my opinion is a weak point. You cannot agree with everybody. There are people with whom you disagree. If you agree with everybody, then what is the use?

Dafnis nodded and admitted, "He is right." Nicos described Dafnis as being like water—which takes on the shape of its container. He adapts himself to the situation so as not to make others uncomfortable. He tries to be friendly even when he opposes somebody. A lot of the customers Nicos took to court for not paying their bills told him they respected Dafnis, because he was kind to everybody—even when being kind caused him personal problems. In response, Dafnis shrugged and said again, "Nicos is right."

Nicos added that at first, when *Agria* was not well known, they were the first business to run advertisements on TV in the Cypriot dialect. "We were the first," he said, "but now you hear it everywhere." They hired actors who used the Cypriot dialect to recommend the harvesters and the cultivators, and these advertisements made a big impression on people in the villages. The strategy worked so well that other businessmen began to follow their lead.

Then Nicos decided to tell one last story to illustrate a tactic that Dafnis used. He said,

> At the beginning of our corporation, Dafnis told the agents we had in Morphou and Famagusta that he had ordered the machines and was expecting them to arrive any day. We were not actually placing any orders yet, but Dafnis assured our customers that we had. Our agent in Morphou phoned to ask, "When are the machines coming? We have customers waiting." Dafnis said, "Next week, they are coming." They were not coming, but he said, "Next week." So the customer said, "Okay, next week I will come to get what I need." When the next week came, Dafnis left Cyprus and went to Greece, so he was not here when the customer came. The man said, "Where is Dafnis? Where are the Agria machines?" I said, "They have not come yet." He said, "But Dafnis told me to come because they will be ready." I said, "I am sorry, but Dafnis is not here. He is in Greece." The man was furious.

Nicos paused and then added, "Dafnis went away because he thought that was the only way to avoid trouble. We were having a difficult time economically at the beginning, and this event happened before we were able to import the machines that we needed." Dafnis simply got out of town to avoid having to deal with the man's wrath. He was a master of deflecting and cajoling and smoothing things over.

Youth Conference in Moscow

While a member of parliament, Dafnis served as the Secretary of the National Youth Council of Cyprus. The Secretary of the Communist Youth of Cyprus, a

Figure 24. *International Communist Youth Forum in Moscow, 16–23 September 1964.*

Turkish Labor Leader who was later assassinated, invited Dafnis to attend the World Forum of Solidarity of Youth in Moscow (16–23 September 1964)—a conference attended by Communist youth from all over the world during the Cold War, a time of escalated tension between East and West. The Soviet Ambassador in Nicosia asked Dafnis what he wished to see during his time in the Soviet Union. Dafnis told him he wanted to visit a Soviet school, a collective farm, a Soviet family, and a Russian Orthodox Church. The ambassador agreed to organize all four of these visits.

Dafnis and the Turkish Labor Leader became good friends. They shared a hotel room with a window overlooking Red Square, where they saw huge portraits of Marx, Lennon, and Khrushchev. Early in the conference, Dafnis met Khrushchev, shook hands with him, and presented to the premier an ancient artifact from Cyprus as a gift. He said of Khrushchev, "In general he was a very friendly and likable person. He mixed easily with the young people. I think that he was a good man." He added that, during the conference, Khrushchev was deposed; and overnight all pictures of him and all books written by him were *gone.* [Khrushchev was actually removed quietly on 14 October 1964.]

Because of his interest in communal agriculture, Dafnis was pleased to tour a collective farm in Russia; but his most memorable experience came when visiting a high school. He said,

> They welcomed me. And then a girl sitting in the front asked me a question, "Did I ever meet a capitalist?" And I said, "Yes, I am a capitalist. I come

Figure 25. *Dafnis is fourth from the right in the third row in the Cyprus contingent of the Communist Youth Forum.*

> from a capitalist country." And she was embarrassed and seemed very afraid. I said, "But why are you afraid?" She said, "Sir, capitalists eat people."

Dafnis was deeply disappointed by such brainwashing of Russian children, but he said he had a good visit at a Russian Orthodox Church and an enjoyable evening with a Soviet family in their condominium.

He left the conference early to attend a memorial for his father, 40 days after Solomon's death. On his return trip to Cyprus, Dafnis met Toby Belcher, the American Ambassador to Cyprus, on a connecting flight. Belcher wanted to know what happened at the Communist Youth Conference, so Dafnis said,

> "Listen, my very good friend, Toby. You are losing not [just] the war. You are losing the battle and the war." He said, "In what sense." I said, "You. The Americans." He said, "Why do you say this?" "Because the slogan of this conference [in Moscow] was friendship and peace. What do the people in Africa want? What do the people in Asia want? They want food, friendship, cooperation, and peace. And what do you do yourself?"

Dafnis said they had a candid discussion on the failures of American foreign policy. But their conversation evidently made no impact on decision makers in Washington, D. C.

Later, in a similar discussion with a British citizen, Dafnis criticized Britain's inconsistent foreign policy. Concerning the Commonwealth of Nations, he said,

> You cannot have two measures in your foreign policy. You have to have one principle, and you must be consistent in this policy. You cannot apply

> one principle to one country and completely opposite to another country. But this is what you are doing. If you are for peace and justice and freedom, you have to apply it equally. If you believe in democracy, you have to be democratic. If you believe in justice, you have to be just.

The man agreed with Dafnis, but their conversation never exerted any influence on the decision makers in London.

Friendship Road

In 1964, the same year as the Communist Youth Conference, Dafnis organized an international work camp and invited volunteers from various nationalities, including Turkish Cypriots, to restore a three-kilometer road connecting the Greek village of Dali and the Turkish village of Lourougina. He called it Friendship Road—an attempt to overcome the racial hatred between Greeks and Turks.

Dafnis announced the project at a meeting of the Cypriot National Youth Council, and news media gave the story wide publicity. But the project failed. "Unfortunately," he said, "a climate of insecurity prevails until now [i.e., 2017] and is the cornerstone of the problem. The Greeks do not feel secure with Turks, and the Turks do not feel secure with Greeks." Tragically, Turkish nationalists in 1964 derailed the effort by ambushing a car carrying two of the Friendship Road leaders, one a Greek Cypriot and the other a Turkish Cypriot—whom they shot dead. The murderers were never brought to justice, and their violent act doomed the project. A few brave souls, however, did not flee the violence.

Roy Calvocoressi read about Friendship Road in the *London Times* and decided to participate in the effort. He traveled to Cyprus in spite of the danger and came searching for Dafnis Panagides, whose name was on the advertisement as the contact person. He went to the Parliament building and asked where he could find Mr. Panagides. Dafnis said,

> I was having a Nescafé in a café in Nicosia, near the office of the Youth Council. And a thin guy with a rather big nose and blue eyes approached me. And he asked me, "Good morning, Sir. Do you speak English?" I said, "I understand some." And he handed me a piece of paper, and he said, "Do you by any chance know this guy?" And the name on the paper was *Dafnis Panagides*. I looked at the name and then I took a serious look and I told him, "Yes. I have heard of him. He is a member of the Parliament." And he said, "Do you know where I can find him?" I said, "Go to the Parliament, ask the receptionist, and she will tell you." He said, "I just came from her, and she told me she saw him this morning but he left. I think he is in the office of the Youth Council, which is in this area."
>
> I told him I just came from the Youth Council office myself, and he was not there. So, I said, "Do you really want to see him? Why do you

want to see him?" "I want to see him because I read in the *London Times* that he is organizing with the Youth Council a mixed camp in the village of Dali, and I am very much interested in peacemaking. I want to ask him if I can join this project." I said, "But why are you interested in peace activities?" He said, "My great, great grandfather came from the island of Chios. During the 1821 massacres by the Turks, they killed thousands of inhabitants of Chios. But my great grandparents managed to escape, and they went to London. I am baptized an Orthodox Christian. I have a Greek origin from Chios, and I am a lawyer by profession. My father made money with the Indian Tea Company, and after I heard the story of the massacres, I decided to work for peacemaking and for reconciling the Greeks with the Turks."

I listened attentively to this man, and I tried to determine his motives. His motives, I concluded, were Christian motives, because he started telling me about peace and the Bible and how violence was against Christian principles. But of course I did not forget that, coming from England, he *might* be an agent of the Intelligence Service. And I took all these things with a grain of salt, but I told him, "Listen, do you *really* want to see this guy?" "Yes," he said, "I want to talk to him." So I said, "I'm going to Limassol. He lives in Limassol, so I invite you to join me in my car. Pretty soon we shall leave, and I will be happy to take you and you shall find him there."

So, innocently he accepted my invitation. We got in the car. At that time there was no highway—not the motorway of today, just roads—and there were very few cars around. And while driving, I realized he started feeling uncomfortable because he thought probably a terrorist had kidnapped him. I deliberately threw in some words that made him more suspicious, just to see his reaction. We talked about EOKA, and we talked about his being strongly against violence. He told me that he donated all his wealth to setting up an international peace organization called CHIPS (Christian International Peace Service).

So, we continued driving and talking. And then we reached the house here in Limassol, and my father was sitting *there* [he points]. And I said, "Mr. Roy, I want to introduce you to my father and family. And we will have something to drink, to eat, and then we'll try to find this Mr. Dafnis you want." And he was very happy that eventually he would meet Mr. Dafnis. And then I introduced him to my father and I said, "This is Solomon Panagides, my father, the father of Dafnis Panagides." And then he understood.

"So, how long did the Friendship Road project last?" I asked. "Just one month. We had no funding, and the assassination of the two men in the car pretty much ended the effort." People became so frightened of being murdered that they ceased work on the road. Roy, however, was not inclined to retreat to a safe place back in England. He insisted on living between hostile factions and not taking sides in the conflict. As a result, neither side trusted him. The Turks thought he was working for the Greeks, and the Greeks thought he was on the side of the Turks.

Roy started his first CHIPS project in Cyprus. He assembled a team of about 20 international volunteers and set up a small Christian community in the Turkish village of Kidasi. The Turks had abandoned their orchards and moved to the north. And, of course, Greek Cypriots were driven from their orchards in the north. Roy's team took care of the abandoned orchards, cultivating and watering fields belonging to both Greeks and Turks.

Reflecting on the CHIPS work, Dafnis gave a Cypriot saying, "Be careful when you feed the chickens, because they will bite your hand." Both Greeks and Turks viewed Roy with suspicion, and eventually he was deported from Cyprus as a possible secret agent. He had to abandon the project. In spite of all their hard work, Roy and his CHIPS team ultimately had little effect on reducing hostilities in Cyprus. The murderous actions of the nationalists stymied the efforts of those who wanted peace and reconciliation. Hostility and hatred prevailed. However, Roy's focus on Christian peacemaking made a profound influence on Dafnis. The two became lifelong friends. Years later, Roy's wife, Elfrida, asked Dafnis to deliver a eulogy at Roy's funeral, and Dafnis gave an eloquent tribute to Roy's commitment to making peace in war-torn countries.

Figure 26. *Old friends: Roy Calvocoressi and Dafnis at the Kakomallis Campground.*

Fulbright Tour of the United States

While in the Cyprus parliament, Dafnis witnessed increasing corruption. Their government sank deeper into chaos. Dafnis wanted out. As the end of his first term in parliament approached, Dafnis asked Maroula if she thought he should run for re-election. She said, "If you ever do, I shall immediately go to the bishop to ask for a divorce!" She was exhausted. People were coming and going so much at their house it was like a beehive, morning and night. Citizens made such demands on Dafnis's time that he neglected his family and his business.

Fortuitously, the Fulbright Commission extended an invitation for him to participate in a new program involving exchange of political leaders. He said,

> The idea was for persons active in politics to be given the opportunity to get to know the United States. And so, they invited me without my even applying. The ambassador called me one day and he said, "Dafnis, you are selected to go on this program." I said, "Yes, I would be delighted."

He soon learned about the history of the Fulbright Commission.

In 1945, in the aftermath of WW2, Senator J. William Fulbright proposed a new program to promote peaceful relationships between the USA and other nations. The program was to be funded by selling surplus war materials, and Fulbright envisioned educators from the United States going to teach in other countries and educators from other countries spending time in the USA. He believed the resulting cultural exchange would promote greater understanding and therefore more peaceful relationships between nations. In 1946, President Harry Truman signed Fulbright's bill into law, thus creating the Fulbright Program. Over time it expanded to include student exchange and to sponsor scholars to travel abroad to conduct research. As a matter of fact, we met Dafnis because I was awarded a Fulbright Fellowship to journey to Cyprus in order to conduct research on the development of traditions about the Apostle Barnabas down through the history of Christianity. In 1966, the Fulbright Program provided a lifeline for Dafnis and brought about a major shift in his life focus. As a guest of the United States, he did not pay for the trip.

The Fulbright program allowed Dafnis to choose specific places to visit. He considered the invitation to be a wonderful opportunity to go to a developed country and learn farming techniques from agricultural experts. He envisioned learning new methods and returning to Cyprus where he could help his homeland with his newly gained knowledge. He also thought that he would benefit from observing a functional democracy. Finally, given the lack in Cyprus of institutions of higher education, Dafnis was eager to see how an American university operated.

He was excited to see his brother, Stahis, in Ames, Iowa, home of Iowa State University, where professors were on the cutting edge of agricultural innovation. Dafnis did not know why the Fulbright Commission offered the opportunity to him. He assumed that the American ambassador to Cyprus made a recommendation based on what he had seen of Dafnis's work in parliament. Regardless of the reasons, Dafnis jumped at the chance to plan with members of the Fulbright Commission an itinerary of places in America he would visit.

But first, he had to resign his position in parliament. Dafnis nervously approached President Makarios to explain that he was leaving for the United States. Makarios pointed out that Dafnis was popular among voters and therefore resignation was not a good idea. Dafnis politely replied, "Your Beatitude, I want to leave because I am dissatisfied with the situation." He explained his frustration with the political rivalry between Makarios and Grivas and having to choose a side in the vicious dispute. [Grivas was extremely angry that Makarios abandoned *enosis* with Greece, which was the rallying philosophy of the EOKA rebellion. The dispute between these two leaders became exceeding bitter after independence in 1960.] Dafnis said to Makarios, "I took an oath to the Cyprus constitution, not to you or Grivas.... I don't want to be a part of any military or political organization. I want to leave." Makarios was not impressed.

Dafnis gestured with his hands and added, "I realized during these years in parliament that I needed to have some authority. My name was not enough. I needed to support what I was saying with evidence." He concluded that, to be taken seriously, he had to become an expert in something so people would listen to him because of his credentials. At the time, he had a mortgage with the Bank of Cyprus, and he was almost bankrupt. The chairman of the board of the Bank of Cyprus was also a parliamentarian and the chairman of the Cyprus Federation of Trade and Industry. He called Dafnis and said, "On Friday I want you to support my bill in the parliament. Your vote is very important." But the man's bill was against the trade unions and the farmers—people with whom Dafnis identified. He did not know what to do, so he left for Athens and later told the man, "I am very sorry. Unexpectedly, I had to fly to Athens on important business." He was weary of navigating such political problems.

Dafnis wanted to get away—to become an expert in a field so that people would not challenge his opinions and condemn what he was saying as nonsense. He was also aware that political dissenters in Cyprus faced mortal danger. Increasingly, paramilitary organizations ravaged Cyprus. Members had guns and behaved as if they were the law.

Makarios reluctantly accepted Dafnis's resignation, and Dafnis prepared for his big adventure in the USA. He left his wife and young children and journeyed west to experience a different culture—an experience that fundamentally changed his life. He had no notion at the time that his two-month trip would become an eight-year educational odyssey.

In 1966, Dafnis finally got his wish to attend college and immerse himself in academic work. The experience transformed him. Although he was 37 when he started as a freshman, he thrived in an academic setting. Away from the turmoil of political battles in his homeland, he basked in the opportunity to explore the life of the mind. His classes expanded his worldview, and he became an academic able to draw from a wide range of disciplines. The knowledge he gained served him well for the rest of his life, and he owed his positive experiences to the Fulbright Program and to his brother, Stahis.

Comical Encounters with Americans

Dafnis was naïve regarding American culture, and he met interesting characters on his journeys. On a flight into Lexington, Kentucky, he sat next to a portly fellow dressed in a white suit, sporting a full head of white hair, a white goatee, and spectacles. Dafnis said,

> As we took off, he gave me his hand and introduced himself to me. I was too shy to take such an initiative myself. "I am Colonel Sanders," he said. "Oh," I responded, "You work for the Pentagon." "No, no," he said, "I am retired from the Army. I am the founder of the Kentucky Fried Chicken chain." "Oh, I understand. You are a chicken farmer. A friend of mine in the chicken business just opened the first restaurant in Limassol, selling roasted chicken."

By that time, Colonel Sanders seemed embarrassed to meet someone who had no idea of what Kentucky Fried Chicken was. Dafnis said the Colonel told the story of how, "many years ago, he met an old lady in the Appalachian Mountains who gave him a secret recipe of how to fry chicken. Using her recipe, he developed the KFC Empire."

The confusion went both ways. Colonel Sanders did not understand where Cyprus was on a world map. Dafnis said, "He was keen to know if people in Cyprus ate chicken meat and if they lived in houses or huts made of banana leaves." Dafnis smiled broadly and added, "Ever since, when I see his face on the KFC advertisements, I remember this experience. Needless to say, his business is doing well in Cyprus; and despite the health warnings, I am one of his customers."

"We landed at Lexington," Dafnis continued, "and a good friend of mine met me as I walked out of the arrival lounge with Colonel Sanders next to me." The friend asked, "Was Colonel Sanders on your flight?" So Dafnis told him the whole, humorous story. Indeed, he loved that story. We heard it multiple times.

Dafnis found some things about the USA to be perplexing. He said, for example, "Two things I could not find explained in the English/Greek dictionary: Bible Belt and Corn Belt." He loved to travel, and he had a grand adventure. To witness American government in action, he went to Washington, D.C., to attend a congressional committee hearing. Then he flew to Chicago to experience the Chicago Commodities Exchange. Someone arranged for him to shadow a broker, and Dafnis felt completely lost as he observed events in the Commodities Exchange. The broker said, "We just lost three million dollars." Dafnis was totally mystified. "The man told me he lost $3 million speculating on coffee! He was actually smiling as he said he lost $3 million on coffee futures! And later on, by the end of the day, he made up $6 million by speculating on something else!" It was a different world.

Dafnis received from Fulbright an itinerary and a stipend—he pronounced the word *stĭpend*, with a short i. They gave him tickets to his various destinations and money to pay for meals and lodging. When he traveled to Washington State to observe agriculture sites, his hotel room puzzled him: "It was a very luxurious suite [he pronounced it suit] without a bed." Reluctantly, he called the desk and asked where he was supposed to sleep. "A man from the reception desk came to the room, pushed a button on the wall, and the bed sprang out." Dafnis laughed at himself and added, "It could be embarrassing sometimes—coming from an underdeveloped, Third-World Country."

Long Layover in Ames

Dafnis relished his journeys, but the most significant stop was Ames, Iowa. He asked to go to Iowa for two reasons. First, Ames is located in a major agricultural area of the United States, and he wanted to see the latest agricultural technology and tour Iowa State University, an institution known for research in international agricultural development. He wanted to meet some of their agriculture professors. By 1966, Stahis was pursuing his Ph.D. in econometrics at Iowa State University, and Dafnis planned to stay with him for a while. He smiled at us and said, "And that is how I was trapped. The two months became ten years in the States." Actually, it was eight years.

Stahis suggested that Dafnis observe a class to get an idea of what was available at Iowa State University. Dafnis had never attended college, and he was intimidated. Unfortunately, Stahis overestimated his brother's knowledge base and arranged for him to attend a graduate level course in Advanced Econometrics. Dafnis was totally out of his league. He said, "I sat there and this guy had a huge black board filled with all kinds equations. Way too advanced for me." He got depressed and concluded, "This is not for me. This *junk* is for academics—it has nothing to do with me." He complained, "Stahis, is *this* what you came here to study? These useless numbers? What do these numbers have to do with us?" Stahis realized that Dafnis needed to observe a much lower-level class, so he said, "I'll put you with Professor Timmons."

Dafnis described Timmons as a lovely person, a devoted Catholic with a Ph.D. in Land Economics. Timmons's research interested Dafnis immensely. He worked in Peru as a consultant for rural development, and he supervised projects in Asian countries. Dafnis got permission to sit in on his land economics course, and he enjoyed seeing how excited Timmons was about his subject matter. Dafnis asked him, "Is there any way I can continue sitting in some of the courses?" Timmons said, "Yes. We have a classification called Special Student. You enroll as a special student, not as a degree candidate." Always one to make impetuous decisions, Dafnis immediately enrolled as a special student and dropped out of the Fulbright program. He did not stop to consider how that decision affected his standing as a visitor to the United States.

Dafnis did not confer with Maroula. He simply made his decision and wrote to his wife and explained what he had done. Dafnis told us repeatedly that he was *spontaneous*, and he took pride in this trait. Indeed! Friends and family simply had to cope with his spontaneity and deal with the consequences. In this case, Dafnis had to contact the Fulbright folks and tell them he was dropping out of their program early. So, there was the issue of having a visa to stay in the United States. He assumed that he could talk his way around the situation as he would in Cyprus, and in this case he actually did so—mostly because he was a friend of Charles McCaskill, an American diplomat who had worked closely with Ambassador Belcher in Cyprus from 1960 to 1964. McCaskill had recently been transferred from Nicosia to Washington, D.C., and was in charge of the Cyprus desk at the Department of State from 1965 to 1967. Dafnis called McCaskill and said, "Charlie, I am going to drop out of the Fulbright program and I shall prolong my stay in the United States. Is that okay?" McCaskill said, "It's okay."

Dafnis lived with Stahis and Joy, and Maroula came to Iowa between two and four months after he became a student (his memory was vague on this detail). She left their two older daughters, Lydia and Louisa, in the care of Chloe and Andonis—Dafnis's sister and brother-in-law—and Dafnis's mother, Maria (Solomon died in 1964); but she brought their three-year-old daughter, Dora, with her to Ames. Dafnis explained that Maroula got pregnant shortly before he left Cyprus, but they kept her pregnancy a secret. She gave birth to their son, Thales, in October in Mary Greely Hospital in Ames.

Maroula's education and English skills were limited. She found herself thousands of miles from her extended family and the social network that gave her life meaning. She did not understand how to take care of a house in the United States. She had to learn how to use modern appliances. She had to learn American standards of hygiene. She became depressed and wanted to return home to Cyprus. Dafnis said,

> In the beginning, Maroula did not like life in America. She did not speak English. She was isolated in the academic environment. It was a very big change for her. One day Maroula wrote a letter to her father. And she gave me the letter to mail. But I [had] studied how to open letters by putting

> them over steam from boiling water, and then you can open the glue. In this letter, Maroula told her father that she was suffering in this inhospitable country. "I have no friends. I feel very lonely. I miss you so much." As a good husband, I destroyed the letter, and I never mailed it. Many years later, after she spoke fluent English, she learned how to drive a car, thanks to Stahis, and she became involved with the university women, and she attended various craft things and learned how to make many things. She liked it. Then I told her I destroyed her letter. She told me, "It was a good thing you did."

Dafnis added, "Stahis played a significant role in teaching Maroula English. When she was able to communicate, then she made many friends. And she was also active in the foreign student wives club. They organized an international food fair... [and] they published a cookbook with international recipes. She became quite popular in America."

While in Ames, Maroula became better educated, more confident, and more independent. But she had her cultural limits. An American friend encouraged her to color her hair, but Maroula refused. Another woman said, "You have to dress more fashionable, because your husband was a Member of Parliament." She answered, "If I dress differently, I shall not be the same Maroula." One of her friends was a Russian Orthodox woman, the wife of a Greek nuclear engineer who taught at ISU. Maroula had long hair, and Dafnis liked it that way. But Marsha told Maroula, "You must follow the fashions here. When Dafnis is gone, I am going to cut your hair short." Dafnis said, "One day, I had to go somewhere, and when I returned, Maroula had short hair. I was very upset, but there was nothing I could do." He shook his head. His wife was out of control. Lynne and I looked at each other and laughed. Maroula became her own person while living in Iowa.

Daughters adjust to a New Culture

Dafnis's oldest daughter, Lydia, told us that when her father left for the United States, she believed that he would return home soon. She had no thought of moving to America. All that changed because of a conversation in Kalo Chorio. She said,

> We went to the village one time with my grandmother and all the aunts and uncles and everybody. And one lady at the village said to my sister and me, "Oh, welcome to the orphans." I didn't think about it. But an American man who was there—a friend of Dad—heard what this lady said, and he told my father. Right away it was arranged for us to go to the States. We didn't want to go. But then it was arranged, and we left our school and everything. We didn't know the language. We didn't know anything. We didn't want to go. But Mom and Dad decided we should go.

Figure 27. *Lydia, Dora, Thales, and Louisa Panagides in Ames, Iowa.*

Neither Dafnis nor Maroula flew to Cyprus to get their girls. Several of Dafnis's friends were moving to the States, and he arranged for them to bring his daughters. When Lydia and Louisa arrived at the airport terminal, they had their first encounter with an escalator, which frightened them. *Everything* was different, and Lydia said of the trip to Iowa, "It was horrible!" She was about twelve years old at the time, and Louisa was about ten.

When they went to school in Ames, people were friendly, but the girls could not speak English, which made them feel stupid and excluded. Dafnis arranged for a tutor to come to their home to help the girls, and their English skills improved. Gradually, they made friends, and over time they became happy in America. "But at the beginning," Lydia said, "I didn't want to clean the house or wash the dishes. I thought we were leaving, so we didn't need to do these things." They grew more comfortable, however, and when Dafnis and Maroula returned to Cyprus, Lydia and Louisa remained in the United States to finish their college education.

Financing an American Education

By the end of spring semester in 1966, Dafnis's experiences at ISU were so positive that he decided to enroll as a regular student. True to form, he then needed to figure out how he would finance his education—not to mention dealing with Immigration regulations. To finance his studies, he got a part time job at Metal Products Company in Ames. Housing help came from a professor at Iowa State University, Dr. Jeffrey Shepherd, and his wife, Eleanor. Shepherd, an agricultural specialist in marketing at Iowa State, was active in international agricultural programs with USAID. Because he was stationed in Peru, the Shepherds allowed

Stahis and Joy and Dafnis and Maroula to live in their house, which turned out to be a fantastic environment for them.

Dafnis had experience in agriculture, had been a member of EOKA, and had served in the Cyprus parliament, so he was not like the average 18-year-old college freshman. He was more of a peer to some of his professors. Because of his experiences in government, he took a political science class from a professor who happened to be writing about the failures of America's AID programs in Africa and other countries. As he and Dafnis drank coffee in the student union one day, Dafnis told him, "If you are writing about food and food production, say 'We fed them promises, promises, promises.'" The professor laughed and said, "What a fantastic title! *We fed them promises.*"

Dafnis enjoyed telling the story of how he met the head of the philosophy department. The professor saw him sitting on the steps of the administration building and he asked, "Who are you? And what are you doing here with these young kids from the farms of Iowa?" Dafnis replied, "I am here to study." "Study? *What* do you want to study?" "Learning," I told him. "Learning? You want to study learning? You need to come to my office." A non-traditional, international student who wanted to study *learning* intrigued the philosopher. The two men became friends, and Dafnis ended up taking philosophy courses—which added to the well-rounded education he received at ISU.

Dafnis thrived in the academic environment, and he earned a grade point average in excess of 3.5. In the 1960s, before the ravages of grade inflation at American colleges and universities, a GPA in excess of 3.5 was an accomplishment. In those days, a grade of C meant "average"—unlike today when "average" means B+ or A–. I remember the provost of a college where I taught lamenting to faculty members that, with the way things were going with grade inflation on our campus, within 10 years the *average* GPA of our students would be 4.0. However, later that same year my dean called me to his office and told me that the grades I assigned to my students were too low. I was too rigorous, and I needed to give higher grades so that students would not complain. He saw grade inflation as a means of keeping students content and paying tuition to take courses in the Humanities. Perhaps Stahis could have authored a study on the economics of grade inflation.

Because of Dafnis's academic achievements, he was invited to participate in a newly initiated program of Honors Students at ISU. He was also among a small group of students who received a teaching and research assistantship, which included a stipend that helped his financial situation. Maroula got a part-time job at the Holiday Inn, which added more income, but they still struggled financially.

After some months, the immigration service notified Dafnis that his visa had expired. He was now an illegal immigrant, and he would need to leave the country right away. True to form, he called his friend Charlie McCaskill at the State

Department, who somehow fixed the problem and enabled Dafnis to stay in Iowa on a student visa.

Big Fish eat Smaller Fish

In addition to the stipend from his assistantship, Dafnis received money from his agricultural machinery business in Cyprus—which became more financially successful *after* he left for America. Before he left Cyprus in 1966, more Cypriots wanted to mechanize their farms, but Dafnis was poor at managing the financial aspects of his business. As usual, he was heavily in debt. However, Maroula's cousin Nicos, a successful car salesman in Tanzania, Africa, moved to Cyprus shortly before native Africans in Tanzania began confiscating the property of lighter skinned people and expelling them from Africa.

Nicos was married to a woman from Greece, and her father had a thriving cinema business in Athens. The couple pondered whether to settle in Greece or Cyprus. In the process, Nicos discussed with Dafnis his agricultural machinery business and realized that it had considerable potential. He had capital from selling his car business in Tanzania, so he went into business with Dafnis. When telling this story, Dafnis got a smirk on his face and said,

> Usually the big fish eats the smaller one, so [I] was absorbed by the one who had capital. I was given 17% of the shares of the company and the others had the majority. But this was good for me, because it helped me pay off my debts. And so I left for the States, and I was able to pursue my studies free of debt and at the same time receive some money from the company. They were making a lot of money; it was a very profitable business—this little machine there, outside.

Dafnis pointed to the small, tractor/cultivator prototype (*Agria*) that he had developed with German engineers. He kept it under a green tarp outside his back door. He repeated his observation that "until now, when you go to the villages, they know Dafnis not from politics or EOKA but from *Agria*. I hear things like, 'Oh, Dafnis, my father bought the first *Agria* in the village!' Our *Agria* machine business was a great success."

Figure 28. *Agria prototype in Dafnis's backyard.*

Pouring Dressing on the Salad

When Dafnis was a graduate student at ISU, he taught a few undergraduate classes. From what he told us in 2017, his course evaluations indicated that students liked him. Although he was 88 years old when he told us about it, he still needed to talk about young women being attracted to him. Regarding his course evaluations, he said, "I had some interesting comments. Somebody would say, 'I would love if he was available, I would love to propose marriage.'" He laughed proudly. Inwardly, I rolled my eyes. I have photos of Dafnis at Ames, and I doubted that any of his students would be pining over their overweight, middle-aged instructor who sported a comb-over on his balding head. I later found out, however, that a few indeed had amorous feelings for him. Evidently, some young women were drawn to his charismatic personality, and he did not discourage them.

Dafnis said his favorite professor and mentor, John Timmons, "challenged my way of thinking…. He would ask me a question and I would answer. Then he would say, 'What is the probability that the answer will be what you're saying?'" We frequently witnessed Dafnis overstating things he told us, so we found it interesting when he laughed and continued,

> I have a tendency—*they tell me*—to exaggerate, to add some dressing on the salad. *They* say. I don't say this. But would you like your salad without dressing? So, I used to tell Timmons these things with some salad dressing, and of course he would challenge me with this question: "Okay, Dafnis. But what is the probability." I learned to quantify things. So, he influenced my mode of thinking and made me more methodological.

Timmons brought more discipline to Dafnis's thinking, but I guarantee that he did not remove Mediterranean speech patterns from him. Dafnis learned Western academic rigor, but he continued to tell stories peppered with hyperbole—or should I say, "covered with salad dressing"? At Ames, he was immersed in American

Mediterranean Hospitality in Ames

Particularly while Dafnis was a Member of Parliament in Cyprus, the Panagides family hosted a large number of guests. That habit of hospitality continued while they were in Ames, albeit on a reduced scale. Thales told me, "I remember that we constantly had guests over. Dad took numerous pictures, and they show dozens and dozens of guests in our house." He added that he often went to sleep while parties among the adults continued into the night. He remembered that Dafnis and Maroula were active with foreign exchange students. He recalled awaking one morning and seeing exchange students sleeping in various places in their house, including outside on the veranda. Sometimes he wondered, "Why are these people here? What are they doing in my house?"

research methods, but he never completely assimilated a Western mindset. He became more sophisticated due to his experiences at Iowa State University, but he remained at heart a Cypriot village male.

Intellectual Growth at Iowa State University

Dafnis earned his bachelor's degree at ISU and then finished a master's degree in rural development and irrigation engineering. During this time, his mother, Maria, became gravely ill with cancer. Dafnis and Stahis brought her to America for better medical treatment, but she died in Ames on 22 March 1969, at age 63. The brothers dealt with their sadness and moved forward with their careers. Stahis had taken a position with the Institute of Social and Economic Research (IPEA) in Rio de Janeiro, Brazil, functioning from 1967 to 1969 as a Technical Advisor to the Brazilian Ministry of Planning—a job funded by USAID. Meanwhile, Dafnis decided to pursue a Ph.D. in agricultural economics. He did not focus on what he *ideally* wanted to study. He decided, because of funding possibilities, to research contract farming, which involves people not owning their own land but doing a sort of sharecropping, working on a contract basis for the landowner.

Part of his research involved interviewing 168 Iowa farmers. He had them complete a questionnaire and then conducted a statistical analysis of the data he gathered. He wrote several research papers on how, historically, the owners of small farms lost their property and ended up owning shares in a company that somebody else managed.

This system differed dramatically from the history of property ownership in the USA. Dafnis analyzed the concept of owners as stewards of their land and the environment. What happens when the land is viewed as a revenue stream instead of an inheritance that you cherish and protect and pass on to your children? Lynne and I could not help but remember the abandoned farmhouses we had seen while driving through the Midwest in the 1990s. Increasingly, fewer farmers owned more and more of the land and hired workers to plant and harvest crops with large machines on thousands of acres. Deteriorating and collapsing farmhouses dotted the rural landscape. Silent sentinels of a lost era.

Dafnis studied at ISU during the early years of the environmental movement in America, so books like Rachel Carson's *Silent Spring* (Houghton Mifflin, 1962) were beginning to influence thinking about the dangers of pesticides. His later environmental efforts in Cyprus owed their origins to reading such books and interacting with researchers at ISU. Dafnis's academic work in Iowa converted him into a well-rounded intellectual who could quote the works of philosophers as well as interact with scientific approaches applied to farming methods. His time at Ames, Iowa, became an eight-year odyssey during which he matured as a man who could dialog with complex issues by drawing from a wealth of interdisciplinary perspectives.

The Bougainvillea Factor

In spring 1974, Dafnis received a call from the Cyprus ambassador in Washington, D.C. By this time, Stahis was working with the World Bank and living in Bethesda. The ambassador asked, "Dafnis, are you about to finish your studies?" "Yes," he said. "I am writing my dissertation." "Okay," the man said. "We have a job for you. Can you become the manager of The Phassouri Plantations?" Dafnis knew that, in 1933, Palestinian Jews established The Cyprus Palestine Plantations Co. Ltd. and launched a successful effort to convert the marshy area around the salty Lake Akrotiri into a large farm for growing citrus fruits. The plantations, comprising approximately 1,273 acres, came under Cypriot ownership in 1974 with the name The Cyprus Phassouri Plantations Co. Ltd. Today, their citrus fruits are marketed under the name Red Seal.

The possibility of managing Phassouri excited Dafnis, and soon he found himself flying to Cyprus for an interview. He told us that when he returned to his homeland in March 1974, he arranged to see both Grivas and Makarios while he was there. He said that when he met Grivas, the former head of EOKA noticed he had gained weight in America. Grivas sneered, "What is this? You went to America and you became like a pig." Dafnis laughed and continued his account, "A few days later I saw Makarios, and he said, 'Ah, what a nice time you have in the States. You really seem to be doing very well.'" Dafnis said these divergent comments illustrate the difference between the military language of Grivas and the diplomatic language of Makarios. Dafnis added that Grivas warned him to stay in America because Cyprus "is going to be destroyed." The problem with his account, however, is that Grivas died on 27 January 1974, prior to Dafnis's trip to Cyprus in March 1974 to interview for the job.

The folks at Phassouri interviewed Dafnis, and because of his graduate work in horticulture, they offered him the job of managing the plantation. The CEO spoke with Dafnis for hours, but he never mentioned a salary figure. He only explained all he wanted him to do on the plantation. Finally Dafnis said, "Okay, but what salary are you going to give me?" Dafnis said the CEO replied, "We don't care about the salary. We will give you whatever you want. You decide and you tell us. Under one condition: what the company gives you, you must give back, plus a little profit." The Phassouri board agreed to let him go back to Iowa to finish his Ph.D. dissertation at Iowa State; and then he was to return later that year to assume his duties.

When Dafnis told Stahis he had accepted the offer, Stahis asked him if he took the position because of the generous salary. "No," Dafnis said, "It was the Bougainvillea Factor." Stahis was taken aback by the comment, so Dafnis explained: "They said, 'This is the house where you and your family will live.' There was a bougainvillea in full bloom, and I was so excited. I thought to myself, 'I don't care about the salary. I am going to come and live in this place because of this bougainvillea.'" When Stahis later recounted the incident, he shook his head and said with a chuckle that his theory of economics flew right out of the window, and he had to add another variable in his equation called The Bougainvillea Factor.

Dafnis returned to Ames and immersed himself in his dissertation research, not knowing that he would never finish it. The situation in Cyprus was about to devolve into a humanitarian crisis that would draw him back to his homeland before he finished his Ph.D.

CHAPTER 6
Fall of the Republic of Cyprus

1974 Turkish Invasion

After Cyprus gained independence in 1960, an increasingly large rift had developed between Grivas and Makarios. Over time, Makarios either suspended or gave up his plans for *enosis* with Greece, which had been the rallying cry during the entire EOKA rebellion. Grivas believed Makarios had betrayed the cause, and he secretly returned to Cyprus on 31 August 1971 to found EOKA B in an attempt to overthrow Makarios by armed rebellion. Warring factions among the Greek Cypriots led to an increasing number of murderous atrocities. It was basically a civil war. In March 1974, while in Cyprus to interview for the Phassouri position, Dafnis spoke with people who were organizing a coup against Makarios. He said everyone knew what was happening, including Makarios.

The American Ambassador to Cyprus asked Dafnis for an assessment of the political situation. Dafnis told him, "My impression is that Makarios will be overthrown before Easter." The ambassador called Makarios in the middle of the night and told him, "I have reliable information that you will *not taste the Easter cake*" (a reference to the Cypriot custom of making a special Easter cheesecake). Makarios refused to take the warning seriously. His attitude was, "I am the Archbishop and the president of Cyprus. They would not depose me." He was so wrong!

On 15 July, Dafnis received an urgent call from the Iowa State campus TV station: "Dafnis, did you hear the news that there has been a coup in Cyprus?" Dafnis learned that Greek soldiers and the Cypriot National Guard, working with members of EOKA B, had stormed the presidential palace in Nicosia. He also learned that Makarios was now in exile.

Makarios had earlier infuriated Demitrios Ioannidis, the military dictator of Greece, by demanding the removal of 550 Greek military officers from Cyprus. Then, on 27 January 1974, Grivas died of a heart attack. Following his death, the leaders of EOKA B secretly signed an agreement with Ioannidis, whose agenda included eliminating Makarios. Foolishly, Ioannidis instigated a coup d'état in Cyprus on 15 July 1974. Makarios barely escaped and fled the island. Military commanders from Greece established a junta to rule Cyprus. But this brash move resulted in the Turks invading Cyprus on 20 July 1974, and taking over a wedge of land that extended from the north shore city of Kyrenia to the capital city of Nicosia. Shortly thereafter, the junta of Ioannidis collapsed, and later that year parliamentary democracy was restored in Greece. Problems in Cyprus only got worse.

Makarios ended up in the United States, and he asked Dafnis to intervene on his behalf with the Department of State to help him return to Cyprus. But by that time, Makarios had burned all his bridges with the USA. Government officials felt no good will toward him because he had aligned himself with Russia and distanced himself from America. As far as they were concerned, he was on his own.

Dafnis on the primitive nature of people

In a 1972 letter to a friend, Dafnis included a quotation as part of his reflection on the conflict in Cyprus: "Man, who today can split the atom and even fuse new atoms, has never learned to govern his emotions or to control his actions by reason.... After five thousand years of what we call civilization, he lives no more harmoniously with his fellow men than did his ancestors of the Stone Age."

Dafnis and Maroula discussed the chaotic situation with their children. He told them he could not stay in Ames while his relatives in Cyprus were experiencing the war. Then the Cyprus Ambassador to the United States called and begged Dafnis to return home to help with the crisis in food production. Dafnis purchased a ticket to London and left his family in Ames. From London, he boarded a flight to Athens, but no planes were flying to Cyprus, and Turkish submarines were blocking ships from entry. Finally, the United Nations assured a Greek company that they could send a ship to Cyprus. Dafnis bought a ticket for this ship. A British lady at the port asked Dafnis where he was going. When he said, "Cyprus," she exclaimed, "You're going to *Cyprus?!* You must be either brave or crazy." Dafnis replied, "I think I am both." He boarded the ship at the Greek port of Pyrgos and headed for Limassol—hoping that a Turkish submarine would not sink them. He reached Limassol before the second invasion.

On 14 August 1974, Turkey launched a second wave of attacks and violently took over the northern third of Cyprus. They displaced a third of the Greek Cypriots on the island, about 150,000 people, forcing them to flee for their lives to the south before the advancing Turkish army. Many escaped with little more than the clothes they were wearing, producing a refugee crisis. Dafnis helped coordinate aid for desperate people who had to abandon all their possessions in the north. Thousands of families needed food and shelter. Huddled in fear and confusion, they contemplated how to rebuild their lives. The abject failure of the Cypriot government and the merciless conquest by the Turks produced a humanitarian disaster.

Petros Petrides, Dafnis's cousin who lived in Famagusta in 1974, told us, "We lost in Famagusta 100% of what we had. We lost *everything*! When we left Famagusta, I had five pounds in my pocket." His wife, Androula, added, "We left at 5:00 in the morning with two children and my father from the hospital, and my mother-in-law, in one car. We squeezed into a Ford Capris. We left with the clothes on our back. And that was it. No money. *Nothing! Nothing!*" Then she added bitterly, "And we had the British guarantors who saw Cypriots as their *dependents*. They did *nothing!*"

Petros reflected on the disaster for a moment and then said,

> In a strange way, it made us succeed afterwards. It made us so resilient. After the tortures of the British [during the EOKA years], we had a survival instinct. It makes you tough. You are not afraid of anything. For a couple of months, you sit down and cry. Then you get up, take the bull by the horns, and you just get on with it. You believe that nothing can stop you. In a strange way, a positive thing came out of this war.

Androula took her children, her mother-in-law, and her sick father and went to stay in the house of Father Marcos, the priest of Kalo Chorio. She told us,

> During the Turkish invasion in 1974, August 14 and 15, the Turks took Famagusta and the rest of the area. So, we came to Limassol, and we said, "Instead of staying here, let's go to the uncle's house in Kalo Chorio. We will be protected there, because it is mountainous. He said, "Normally, the Turks do not go into the mountain areas."

Figure 29. Papa Marcos by his home in Kalo Chorio.

When they reached the priest's house, they discovered 38 people had taken shelter there. My wife and I lived in that same house for a while in 2019, so we have a good idea of how crowded it would be for 38 people to occupy the space. Androula said,

> The old priest and his wife were so hospitable. I will never forget in my whole life. They didn't have running water, but he had a motorbike with a big container on the front, and he went into the village and filled it up and came

> back—over and over again—and they cooked for so many people. And they set up beds for everybody.... Petros was working with the electricity authority in Limassol. He was not in the mountains.

And there were other problems to solve.

"My son had a darkness phobia," Androula continued. "He could not sleep without a light." The priest's wife lit a candle inside a room, but out of fear of the invading Turks, they placed blankets over the windows to hide the candlelight so no one outside could see it. Androula shook her head and muttered, "Thirty-eight people in the house! I will never, never forget that." They bonded during their cramped time in the house, and their appreciation for the hospitality of Papa Marcos and his wife was great. On the other hand, their hatred for the Turks grew by the day. With time, some of the Greek Cypriot refugees relinquished their bitterness. Others did not.

Petros grew up in a neighborhood where Greek Cypriots and Turkish Cypriots lived in harmony, and he does not bear resentment toward them. Androula, on the other hand, grew up in a tense environment in Famagusta and often feared for her life when she was young. She said concerning the social gatherings that Petros had organized with Turkish Cypriots in recent years, "We argue about these meetings, because I don't want to live with Turks. I don't. God forgive me. I don't trust them." She added, "I didn't want to go with Petros to these meetings. All the time, my heart is racing. I didn't feel comfortable. So, I pretend like I enjoy the company, but I am pretending all the time. I honestly don't trust them."

Petros gazed lovingly at his sweet wife and said, "If we die, we die." "Yes," she replied, "but I don't want to die from a Turkish collar." Perhaps she meant a "Turkish yoke," a common expression for the condition of conquered peoples having to live under repressive and sometimes ruthless Ottoman rule. Turkish atrocities conducted prior to British occupation of Cyprus are deeply embedded in the collective memory of Greek Cypriots. In 1821, Küçük Mehmed executed Archbishop Kyprianos and brutally murdered other leading Greek Cypriots. Louis Lacroix, writing in the mid-nineteenth century, described the massacre as follows:

> The gates of the palace were then thrown open, and the bleeding corpses thrown into the square. This was the signal for a general massacre. The Convent of Phaneromene was at once occupied, and the priests strangled. I was told, says M. de Mas Latrie, that before killing them the Turks, with wild refinement of vengeance, saddled the priests as they would their horses, breaking their teeth to force the bits into their mouths, and making them caper under their spurs. The Greek houses were given over to pillage, massacres began again in all the districts of the island, and confiscation followed massacre. For six months universal terror reigned among the Greek population. (*Excerpta Cypria,* p. 464)

The 1974 conquest of northern Cyprus and the permanent expulsion of Greek Cypriots from their homes and farmland in the north did nothing to alter opinions of Turkish brutality.

Foolish decisions made by Greek Cypriot leaders, British diplomats, Greek military leaders, and Turkish leaders all combined to result in the disaster that is now permanent. But would knowing that fact change my opinion of those who drove me from my land, killed some of my relatives, and prevented my return to my property? I am often amazed at the attitude of Petros and others like him. Dafnis was from Limassol, so he did not lose his property; but he helped people during the humanitarian crisis. And until his dying day, he worked to reestablish good relationships between Greek and Turkish Cypriots.

Collapse of *Agria*

When Nicos managed *Agria*, the company prospered until the 1974 Turkish invasion. He had ordered 50 harvesting machines before July 1974, worth about £50,000. The *Agria* partners were not able to pay cash for the harvesters, so they got a bank loan. They were not worried. All 50 machines were pre-sold on credit, most to farmers in the north, especially in Kyrenia, Morphou, and Famagusta. The partners knew that 1974 was going to be a good year for the farmers, and after the harvest, all of them would be able to pay for the machines. Nicos said they anticipated getting £75,000, thus turning a £25,000 profit. But the Turkish invasion came, and all of their customers were wiped out. Nicos explained, "Some of them were killed. Others lost everything.... So what could we expect from those who had nothing? They were here [in the South] as refugees."

"What happened to the 50 harvesters?" I asked. "The Turks took them," he said. "We had a gap of one week from the first invasion to the second invasion, and I sent our people to collect as many as they could. We collected about 30 machines, and we put them in a garage north of Famagusta. But during the second invasion, the Turks took them all; and that was the financial destruction of our company." For a while, Greek Cypriots hoped that the crisis would end and they could return home and regain their possessions. But that hope slowly died.

As I interviewed Nicos, he was sitting beside Dafnis. Listening to these two old men describing each other was fascinating. Dafnis said that *Agria* benefitted financially from Nicos's management because he was a good businessman. Nicos said that Dafnis always had excellent ideas, but he was not able to put them into effect. Dafnis was an idea person, not a businessman, because he was a people-pleaser.

Conversations go different directions, and sometimes insights emerge unexpectedly. Dafnis suddenly decided to talk about his son, Thales, who sells Brazilian Bikinis. "He sells bikinis in more than 60 or 70 countries. Even in the Arab countries he sells these. But his worst customers are Greeks. They are in Greece. Utterly the worst! They do not pay him." One day Thales asked him for advice based on the mistakes Dafnis had made. So, Dafnis provided three bits of wisdom.

> *Number one:* concentrate. Don't spread yourself too thin. When I was in business, I did a lot of things, and I did not concentrate.
>
> *Number two:* do not sell on credit.

Nicos laughed and said, "That should have been number one."

> *And number three:* don't deal with relatives. And do you know what? He lost. Number one, he sold to Miss Israel $1,000 worth of bikinis on credit. She never paid him. And he went to Israel to collect. He came back without collecting. I asked him, "Did you at least get a kiss from Miss Israel?"

Some lessons are only learned the hard way.

Problems at Phassouri

What began as a positive experience at Phassouri Plantations for Dafnis did not end well, because his management philosophy differed from that of his boss. Dafnis said the chairman was born in Kyrenia, Cyprus, but he made his fortune in Africa paying his workers a pittance. He brought to Cyprus his philosophy regarding how to treat employees, but Cypriot workers belonged to unions and would not tolerate such abuse. Most of the plantation workers belonged to the Communist Party, and they insisted on eight-hour workdays and adequate wages. The chairman could not comprehend how to work with union members, and Dafnis was caught in the middle.

Dafnis's first two years managing Phassouri went fairly well in spite of labor problems between plantation workers and board members. The Rain Bird Company in California was a pioneer in irrigation technology, and Dafnis ordered a complete drip irrigation system from them and installed it at Phassouri Plantations. He also set up a computer system to control irrigation—the first such system in Cyprus. These innovations increased company profits. But the chairman chafed at the unions and their demands for fair pay and safe working conditions. He demanded that Dafnis break the unions, saying, "Dafni, before you do anything else, fire these 72 people." The 72 included the secretary, the treasurer, and all other key figures in the union.

Militant Communists controlled the trade union. Before Dafnis arrived at Phassouri, they had cut down 120 plantation trees to make a strong point against the management. So, Dafnis found himself in the middle of a major confrontation between workers and shareholders. He said to the top shareholder, "Mr. Chairman, two words are missing from your dictionary. Apparently, in Africa these two words do not exist, but here in Cyprus we must know them." The chairman asked, "What are the words that are not in my dictionary?" Dafnis said, "Trade unions and overtime. If they work overtime, you have to pay them!" The chairman retorted, "But we are losing money!" Dafnis replied, "You know that our accountant is a member of the trade union. He knows the accounts, and the trade unions have a copy of the profit and loss; and he knows that the year ended with nearly a million pounds profit." The chairman said, "Yes, you are right. But the profits *should* have been a million and a half. So we *lost* £600,000. Instead of making a profit of £1.5 million, we made only £0.9 million."

Andreas, general secretary of the trade union, wanted to come to Phassouri to discuss the labor stalemate, but the chairman told Dafnis, "If I see this man enter through the gates of Phassouri, you will go back to Ames, Iowa." "Okay, Mr. Chairman," Dafnis said. "What do you suggest that I do?" He said, "You tell him that he is not wanted on the Phassouri farm." After pondering the impasse, Dafnis called Andreas, whom he described as a reasonable person. Andreas had been a Member of Parliament, and he and Dafnis had worked together and become good friends. Dafnis called him and said, "Andrea, I have to deal with this lunatic who cannot communicate, and he ordered me not to allow you on the Phassouri Plantation. But I want to talk to you. Can I invite you to lunch at the nearby seaside restaurant to discuss these things." Andreas said, "Sure, Dafni." So they met at the restaurant and discussed everything.

Dafnis organized a party at Phassouri, where union workers were deferential toward the chairman, and the boss enjoyed himself. By working behind the scenes and choosing to promote peacemaking rather than confrontation, Dafnis avoided having to fire the 72 union members. He negotiated an amicable solution.

I told Dafnis that we had read a short article by Derek Sangster about this labor dispute ("Profit of Love," *Third Way: Towards a Biblical Worldview*, 1977, vol. 1, no. 25). Sangster reported that Dafnis was ordered to fire 82 workers (Dafnis told us 72) because the "unions and management were locked in intractable dispute," and the plantation was facing bankruptcy (p. 10). But under Dafnis's leadership, Sangster said, "This year the Phassouri Plantations has had its third successive record year for profits and productivity has risen 23 per cent over the past two years." According to the article, Dafnis explained that the order to fire the union members went against his principles. He had to figure out an alternative. Sangster quotes Dafnis saying,

> The firm was locked into a Marxian concept of the eternal battle between capital and labour, the war between "we" and "them". It was what sociologist Kenneth Boulding calls "the threat system". The union says, "Unless we get more, we will strike" and management says "unless you do this, you'll be fired". And every now and then each side has to carry out its threat so that it will not lose credibility.

The article went on to say that Dafnis asked the two sides to get together in the same room and pray. Both sides opposed his suggestion. Finally, however, he prevailed. The chairman sat by a mechanic, and after talking a while, "It broke the ice. We began to find the missing ingredient, which was love in the context of prayer." As a result, workers started to realize that the investors in the company deserved a return on their investments. And management began to have an authentic concern for the families of the workers. They also recognized that "a business has social responsibilities—concerning pollution and ecology." After a while, "the board of directors accepted the principle of returning part of the profits to the employees. The company had a new outlook which changed 'we' and 'they' into 'us.'" The article quotes Dafnis saying that peacemaking through love dissolves mistrust and selfishness. "We changed from conflict to collective effort—and it worked." Corporate profits and worker satisfaction both rose dramatically.

But as we listened to Dafnis describe his time at Phassouri Plantations, we wondered if Sangster's article painted an overly rosy picture of what happened. We asked where management and workers actually met for the prayer meeting and were surprised to hear Dafnis say it was in a small, old church on the Phassouri Plantations. He said that, after intense negotiations, he arranged for a voluntary liturgy for the management and the main staff of Phassouri. He made it sound like the event was no big deal.

I said, "According to the article, this meeting was difficult for you to arrange, and people resisted it; but once you finally made it happen, the chairman sat down next to a mechanic, and they started to get to know each other as people, and then one thing led to another. They started to cooperate and after three years the profit went up 23%." Dafnis replied, "This is true. It was very profitable." I asked for more details, so he said the following:

> Basically, my style of management was an open-door approach. We had a lot of newcomers, refugees from northern Cyprus, mostly women, who were in the packing house, packing grapes and oranges and so on, and they would come to see Mr. Dafnis or Maroula. As friends, we discussed personal problems and other matters, so there was a relationship established there. Not as the boss and the employee but as friends listening to each other. *All* of the employees came from nearby villages. They were farmers themselves, poor people—simple people. And the overwhelming majority of them were in AKEL, the Communist Party. Most of them were nice people who went to church. They did not understand what was going on, but they went to church, made the sign of the cross, and kissed the icons. These people did not know about biblical peacemaking or about the substance of Christianity.
>
> They grew up in a Greek Orthodox cultural environment where you go to church, you light candles, you kiss the icons.... But to *pray*—now that was something new for them. They did not *pray*. They went to

> church and made the sign of the cross, and it's finished. This is your duty. Most of the negotiation I conducted was done in small groups with only the managers—the plantation manager, the packinghouse manager, the export department manager—the managerial staff.

"So the prayer meeting itself was small," I said. "Yes," said Dafnis. "Small." He went on to explain that they only conducted liturgy in the church once a year on the anniversary of the agreement. Our impression was that Dafnis made definite progress, but problems persisted, including health hazards for workers.

At Phassouri he instituted a program introduced by the Israelis: biological pest control. In a lab they raised particular insects and released them to attack and eat the insects that destroyed citrus fruits. He was the only one in Cyprus employing this approach, and his chief plant manager wanted to use chemical pesticides. Dafnis said, "We were surrounded by farms where they used *a lot* of chemicals on grapes and citrus. So the atmosphere was polluted with chemicals and we had many cases of cancer. Staff died of cancer. And I had to go and deliver obituaries at their funerals." He and Maroula wondered what they should do. They liked the lovely setting at Phassouri, the greenery, the productive agricultural work, and all the activity and creativity. But the health hazards increasingly weighed on them.

Problems also continued because the chairman kept meddling in operational matters. Dafnis said the man's actions violated the principle that there cannot be two managers. "Here you have the chairman interfering in all details with his African style, and with me, who is supported by the trade unions and the staff." Dafnis's contract was for two years, and toward the end of that time, the chairman said, "We shall give you a good compensation and terminate the contract." The chairman offered to give Dafnis a car and a good severance package. Dafnis resigned as general manager of Phassouri Plantations in 1977 after only two and a half years.

Wheeling and Dealing

When Dafnis severed ties with the Phassouri Plantations, he started an agricultural consulting office in Limassol. His first order of business was to move back into their Limassol home. Two refugee sisters from northern Cyprus had been living in the house, so these women needed to find a new place to live. Once the sisters relocated, the Panagides family returned home.

Dafnis rented a nice office where, for two years, he shared the space with a friend from Colorado who worked as a contractor in Saudi Arabia. However, Dafnis said, "The Cypriots were not ready for professional consulting at that time. We were a little bit premature." He hesitatingly added,

> One of the things that we did—I don't know if we should talk [about this]—we were facilitating trade between Arabs and Jews. The Jews would come from Jerusalem, and the Arabs would come from Syria and Beirut to our office where they would make deals. To supply products, either export from Israel to Syria or from Syria to Israel, we would issue new invoices and new documents and place stamps on the items to verify that they were products of Cyprus exported to Israel or Syria.

Given the tensions between Jews and Arabs in the Middle East, such wheeling and dealing illustrates that, when money is to be made, people develop ways of circumventing national policies.

Final Political Campaign

Chaotic conditions in Cyprus finally caused Dafnis to run for office one last time. Greek Cypriots were passionately divided. Dafnis said,

> There was hatred; there was civil war. People were actually killed. Pro-Makarios forces assassinated the brother of Petros Avgustis, whom you interviewed.... Clerides, the president at that time,... said, "Dafnis, I have a request for you. I want you to play a role in bringing peace and reconciliation. It is hard to find somebody else to do it because everybody here was involved in some way or another. You were away, completely detached, and people trust you. You did not take sides on this conflict of the coup, so you can play a role in uniting the people." I asked, "How can I do this? I see we are deeply divided." He said, "You must agree to become a candidate for the Parliament again."

Clerides convinced Dafnis to run as a unifying candidate to bring together the pro-Grivas and pro-Makarios factions, but the strategy failed. Dafnis was soundly defeated. Voters rallied behind candidates who fought for the concerns of their own factions, who used fiery rhetoric to vilify their opponents. Voters rejected Dafnis, who sought a middle way to bring peace by listening to the concerns of both extremes. They refused to compromise and pursue what was best for their country. They saw those who disagreed with them not as people who hold different philosophies but as enemies. Such intense polarization nearly destroyed their democracy. And before long, Dafnis again moved out of the country.

CHAPTER 7
Allah, Sheep, and Surah

Quoting the Quran

Dafnis's consulting work in Cyprus flopped, and he made another disastrous investment, this time in real estate. In spite of all the money he had made at Phassouri Plantations, he was in serious financial trouble. His lifeline came from Saudi Arabia, where Arabs were making a fortune from vast oil reserves under the sand. An interesting sequence of events led him to the Kingdom of Saud from 1980 to 1996.

While Dafnis was an undergraduate at Iowa State University, he decided to take a class on the Middle East taught by a professor from Cairo. That class proved to be of profound importance for his career, for it caused him to ponder the beliefs of Muslims. What he learned about Islam at ISU later helped him gain the respect of important people in Saudi Arabia. Dafnis said his Egyptian professor gave a quiz in which students were to identify seven cities from the Middle East.

> The first day of class, the professor gave us six names of cities I could readily identify: Nicosia, Beirut, Cairo, Jerusalem, Amman, and Aden. But he also asked about one city that I could not identify. That was Sana'a, the capital of Yemen. I never heard of Sana'a. I said, "I live in the Middle East, and I don't know that the capital of Yemen is Sana'a." As a result of this quiz, I felt very ashamed of myself. I realized that I must understand the people who live there, so I decided to pursue a minor in Islamic Studies—to learn more about Arab history and Islamic history. I ended up reading a lot of books. I read the Quran cover to cover, and I studied about Mohammad. That was a good move because I ended up working in Saudi Arabia. Not only that, it also proved to be very helpful because the Arabs, the Bedouin, and the religious police accepted me because I knew their customs and their culture. I knew things that are very important for them.

His classes at Iowa State equipped him to conduct successful business with Arabs.

> Before I went to Saudi Arabia, I conducted a study for a member of the royal family regarding the establishment of a sheep farm in Medina. I quoted the Quran right after the title of my study: "A Feasibility Study of

> the Establishment of a Sheep Farm of 5,000 Sheep in Medina." I quoted a Surah about how nice it is to see the sheep coming from the meadow and something about Allah.

The British lady who edited these research studies insisted that he remove this quotation. But Dafnis argued with her and contended that it must remain. She finally gave in and let him keep the quotation.

Dafnis said, "When the king of Saudi Arabia was given this study, he looked at the first page and read this Surah, closed the book and said, 'Bring this man here.' That was all he read of my study." The king summoned Dafnis, a Greek Orthodox Cypriot who knew the Quran, and granted him access to an area where non-Muslims are forbidden entry. "Both Medina and Mecca are closed areas for non-Muslims," he said. "They have two kinds of work permits. One is brown for non-Muslims, and the white one is for Muslims. I had the brown one, so I could not go to Medina. But, by royal decree, I was allowed through, because the project was in Medina. And I spent a day there." Later he would become a trusted employee and friend of a Saudi prince. Sometimes scholars need to ignore the advice of editors who mean well but do not understand fully the implications of such things as quoting the Quran.

Working with Bedouin

Dafnis said three factors led him to Saudi Arabia: (1) financial woes—he was heavily in debt, and the only way he saw to get out of this financial hole was to accept a job in Saudi Arabia; (2) the adventure of going to desert lands in a Muslim country; and (3) the challenge of using his creativity in a culture with different social and economic norms.

Dafnis said that Saudi Arabia was "flooded with petrol and dollars."

> My boss was interviewed on a Texas television program. The interviewer asked him, "Doctor Abdul Assize, you are Minister of Finance. Here in the United States, we have a problem with inflation, with unemployment. What kind of problems do you have in Saudi Arabia?" And he said, "The only problem I can think about now is that every night when I go to bed, I am wondering how I am going to spend the money which comes to Saudi Arabia from oil." He had so much surplus money that he did not know what to do with it all.... They came up with a project called The Greening of the Desert as a way to distribute this wealth, which was, of course, in the hands of the royal family. Billions and billions.
>
> With American technical help, they set up an agricultural bank to make loans. "The widow of King Khalid once called me to her palace, and she explained that she wanted a loan! These people are millionaires, but they take out loans. One of them sent a Saudi 707 jet to Paris to buy flowers and bring her a bunch of flowers!" [He laughed and said,] "From Paris!"

My first trip there was to make a study with an Indian agronomist to develop wheat farms because they found aquifers of fresh water below the desert. Sometimes, when drilling for water, instead of finding water, oil came out. When that happened, we had to close the borehole and move to another place. But in many cases, we hit water at a depth of about 600 or 700 meters. We used big Caterpillar engines to pump fresh water.

The pipes and sprinklers operated in huge circles covering about 800 hectares—400 to 500 hectares in one round [one hectare = about 2.47 acres]. But problems arose when they tried to settle the Bedouins. The idea of settling the Bedouins had a political dimension also. The royal family thought, "How can you control Bedouins in the desert? You have to settle them in communities." So, they built houses, and they brought the Bedouins.... But in one or two months, they abandoned these. I saw many of these abandoned houses. And they went back into the desert with their camels.

During these first two months in Saudi Arabia, when I was working on this project, I met many important people—powerful people in the government, members of the royal family. And they invited me to return to Saudi Arabia, independently of my employer. So I ended up signing an employment contract with a powerful prince who was Minister of Defense in the army. He became a millionaire from selling armaments and buying weapons. And he decided to establish an agricultural company. When I met him, he had three employees in the office: an Egyptian agriculturalist, a Sudanese secretary, and a Yemeni coffee boy. He made me manager of this company, and over time we developed the enterprise into 15 different companies with over 7,000 employees. From agriculture we branched off into medical business and trading and manufacturing. It was very successful and remains so even today. Now the prince is retired, and his oldest son, Walid, heads up much of the enterprise.

In the culture of Saudi Arabia, priority goes to the first son. Walid complained to his father, Prince Nassir, "How come a *hawaja* could be the vice president for business development?" *Hawaja* in Arabic is an infidel, a non-Muslim, in my case, a Greek. He complained that his father, instead of making him the manager, hired a *hawaja*. And his father answered him, "Listen, Walid, when you go as many years to school as Mr. Dafnis went, and when you have the wisdom and the knowledge of his age, then you can take his place. Right now, you stay where you are."

Dafnis enjoyed working with Prince Nassir, but later he took a job with another prince.

Dafnis periodically traveled on behalf of his employers. Sometimes on these trips he encountered cultural differences that caused difficulties. He explained,

I was sent to the States on behalf of my group of companies as an official guest of the US Department of Commerce. I remember when I went to one of the hotels in Walla Walla, Washington, where there was a very big irrigation manufacturing company. I gave my name to the man at the hotel desk, and he said, "How are you going to pay?" I said, "By cash." He said, "We don't accept cash. Only credit card." I said, "But I have no credit card. What shall I do?" He said, "We don't accept cash."

The next day, we attended a meeting of the Chamber of Commerce, and I said, "I do not understand your system here. I have cash from your government, because we received a stipend to come here, but the hotel will not accept the cash." They explained that the credit card was a way to identify us. We had a lively discussion about this and other matters.

On this trip were representatives from various Saudi companies. One of them approached me, and he said, "Mr. Dafnis, would you be interested to join our company if we make an offer?" I said, "Who owns the company?" He said it was a very big agricultural company representing a major American irrigation equipment manufacturer—a leading company in the field called Arid. The man said, "I will make an appointment with my boss when I go back."

So, when we returned to Saudi Arabia, I arranged to see Prince Faisal Al Sudairi. He was from the royal family.... After we talked a while, he said, "I would like to hire you." The job sounded better and more challenging, so I joined Faisal Sudairi's company. Altogether, I stayed 16 years in Saudi Arabia working in the field of agriculture. We developed wheat farms and green houses, vegetables, and sheep and goat production. It was a healthy agricultural business, and I had direct contact with Bedouins.

I spent days and nights with Bedouins in the desert. And I learned some basic Arabic so that I could communicate with them. I met very nice people. That was, of course, before the rise of radical Islam, and we could comfortably sit and have tea together and eat together and make jokes and socialize.

When I was among the Bedouins, I always had an Arab assistant although I could say some things in basic Arabic. I could not tell jokes, of course, in Arabic; but they liked me, because I collected stories of Hodja. He lived in the Islamic Ottoman Empire. I collected these stories, and they loved them. For example, Hodja said, "You have to beat your wife every morning. You don't know why, but she knows why she is getting beaten."

Dafnis laughed when he quoted Hodja, and he said that the Bedouin found such sayings to be very funny. I wondered what was humorous about a husband beating his wife. Jokes are, of course, culturally imbedded. And hyperbole frequently plays a role in humor. But the sad fact is that Arab cultures have earned just criticism for their treatment of women.

Bedouin Generosity

Dafnis had positive experiences in other cultures, and because of his generosity and acceptance of others, he got along well with local people. He enjoyed the Bedouin, and some of them became his good friends. He benefitted from their hospitality, and he reciprocated and assisted some of them with business deals. Dafnis said, "During the very first few days I was there, I met a Bedouin father whose son went to a university to study Islamic theology. We became friends, and he asked me to help him get a loan from the Agricultural Bank—which I did." I wanted to know if it was unusual for a Bedouin to get a bank loan. "No," he said.

Dafnis was based in Riyadh, at the main office of the corporation, but he made frequent trips into the desert to farms where he provided technical services to farmers. Sometimes his visits were amusing.

> One day, I received a call that a pump we installed was catching fire, and we needed to go and see what was wrong. It was about 350 km away, but I love to drive through the desert. So, I went there and met this Bedouin. I said, "Start the engine." He started the engine, and then he told me that he tried to touch the exhaust pipe. And I said, "What?" He said, "Look, this exhaust pipe is too hot. It is getting fire." "No." I explained to him. "This is the exhaust pipe. The engine is perfect. You just keep away from this pipe, and don't touch it. The engine is okay." So, a big part of our job was to educate them.

He added that the Bedouin employed Filipinos to do both menial and skilled labor.

> The Filipinos would bring them tea. No Bedouin would work. All day they would sit in the tent drinking tea. Or they would be out with their camels. Filipinos did all the work on the farm, and they knew what they were doing. Or Egyptians, or Palestinians.... All expatriates. Expatriates did everything.

Dafnis said the generosity of some Bedouin amazed him. Once he told a man named Abdullah that he needed to buy a car, so he took Dafnis to a car lot.

> The very first day I met him he took me in his car to where they sold cars. We looked around, and I found one. I said, "This is a good one, but how much it is?" "Uh, 15,000 Riyals." Riyal was the currency. "But I don't have cash. Can we ask him to keep it, and I will come back tomorrow after I take money from the office?" He said, "No, Mr. Dafnis, I give you the money. You take the car now." And he paid 15,000 Riyals. I took the car right then. Abdullah did not even know me. He said, "Just take it and go."

Figure 30. *Dafnis and Maroula in Saudi Arabia.*

> Abdullah and I became very good friends and have remained so for 40 years. My wife became friends with his wife. And his wife told Maroula that Abdullah would get up in the middle of the night to pray and would say, "Allah, please Allah, make Dafnis convert to Islam, because I cannot be in Paradise without Dafnis." He took it for granted that he would go to Paradise, but I would go to hell.

Dafnis smiled and continued his story.

> One day, Abdullah came, and he was very distressed. He said, "Dafnis, Aziza left me." It was a catastrophe for a wife to leave. The other way around is fine, but for a wife to leave the husband, it is a catastrophe. I said, "What?" "Yes, she went to her mother." And he was very upset. They had five children already. He asked, "What shall I do?" I said, "Do you love Aziza?" "Yes, I love her." "Do you want her back?" "Yes, I want her back." "Did you ever tell her you love her? Did you ever tell her, 'Aziza, I love you'?" "Oh, no. She is my wife. I love her." "You should tell her. Call her now and tell her, 'I love you.'" He said, "I cannot. I cannot. What shall I do?" "Listen, Abdullah," I said, "you go now to the confectionary shop outside and buy a kilo of baklava and send it to the house of her mother and tell her, 'Aziza, this box of sweets is from me for you and the children.'"

> I convinced him, and he went out and he did it. Next day he came to tell me that they were together again. And perhaps I can be credited for the creation of two more children.

He chuckled and added, "By the time I left Saudi Arabia, they had seven children."

While he was in a nostalgic mood, I asked, "Do you think that, religiously speaking, you were ever influenced at all by Islam? Are you attracted to any part of it?" He responded with no hesitation, "On the contrary, actually."

> I have many books on Islam. I would say I am familiar with Islamic culture and history, but I found nothing attractive about the religion, because I experienced the segregation and the attitudes. My youngest daughter, Dora, came one summer, just to be with us. She was young, and she wanted ice cream. So we went to an ice cream place and of course, she saw a sign there: "No women allowed. Only men. Women on the other side." Having been educated in the United States, she said, "Dad, I am going to leave tomorrow, and I don't want to come back to this country again." She was very upset by this segregation of women.

Lynne asked, "How old was Dora?" Dafnis said, "She was 18 or 19."

Dafnis loved many Muslims, but he had little respect for Islam. He was far more tolerant of secular Muslims than he was of the fanatics. He appreciated his boss, whom he described as a true and faithful Muslim. But in general, when considering Islam as a philosophical, religious system, he could not endorse it. Dafnis said there are a "few good aspects of Islam, like paying five percent of your income for charity every year." But there is also "Jihad, which some Muslims interpret as war against any infidel, against any non-Muslim." He added that, in theory at least, because Christians and Jews are people of the book, they are respected.

His example was the protected status of the Monastery of St. Catherine near Mt. Sinai. In the monastery is a protection document that Mohammad had a follower write for him. "Because he was illiterate, he put his hand print on the paper. I saw it myself—on this document. And because of this document, none of the thousands of Muslims who have been around this monastery out in the middle of the desert has ever damaged it. Even now with this religious fanaticism of Islam, the monastery is there because of this document."

Fruit Fly Porn

Some of Dafnis's most humorous stories involved encounters with the *Mutawa*, the Islamic religious police in Saudi Arabia. The official title for this group of zealots is the Committee for the Promotion of Virtue and the Prevention of Vice. They rigorously enforced their version of Sharia Law, going around the marketplaces with their sticks and beating people for not dressing properly, for not closing their shops during prayer times, or for committing other supposed infractions. The most bizarre story Dafnis told about them had to do with fruit flies:

> While employed in Saudi Arabia, I was on vacation in Cyprus when I received an urgent telephone call from my boss, Prince Faisal. He said, "Dafnis, you are wanted by the religious police, so delay your return to the Kingdom because you are accused of importing pornographic material into the Kingdom." I said, "Prince, I was never interested in pornographic material, but I suspect that probably one of our American farm managers thought that if he ordered some material in my name, it would not be opened by the customs. I shall check with him."

Prince Faisal agreed with the plan, but he insisted that Dafnis not return to Saudi Arabia until the matter was cleared.

At this point, Dafnis was really enjoying telling his story. He leaned forward and continued, "I checked with a farm manager and said, 'Tell me the truth. Did you order any pornography?' He said, 'No! I never did!'" So, Dafnis asked the man to investigate the accusation. The manager finally gave his solemn report. Dafnis said the man

> found that I had ordered some books, and among them there was a book on entomology. This book contained a chapter called "The Sex Cycle of the Mediterranean Fruit Fly." Now, in order to be able to control any insect, any pest, you need to know the insect's reproductive cycle. You know, what is the correct time to spray, when is it correct to put out the traps, and so on. And we were very concerned about the Mediterranean Fruit Fly. These little flies are so very small you can barely see them. But they do a lot of damage to fruits. They lay eggs that turn into worms, and these go inside the fruit, and they ruin the fruit. So this book had a complete article about their whole reproductive cycle. But it used the word sex in the report. So the religious police put a black mark and they underlined these words, and they said, "Sexual reproduction"—of the fruit fly, of course.

At this point, we were laughing hysterically. "This was a serious accusation," Dafnis said. "And after the prince made certain contacts, the *Mutawa* destroyed the book."

Dafnis flashed his contagious smile and concluded his story, "I went back to the Kingdom—and I had a good laugh, of course. I told Prince Faisal all the book was about, and I said, 'Don't worry. I'm going to re-order the book and have it delivered in Cyprus.'" Dafnis paused and looked at the bookshelves lining his office. "It must be here somewhere," he said. "I shall photocopy the chapter, and the next time I come I shall bring it just for you to have a laugh." Then he added in a more somber tone: "I barely escaped being put in prison and accused of promoting pornographic material."

Dafnis loved telling such stories. On another occasion, he told us,

> In Saudi Arabia I received a call from [a man in] Jeddah. He said, "Mr. Dafnis, our shipment of paint *pig*ments was rejected at the customs. The Customs will not allow the container because it contains pigments." I said, "Are you sure about this?" He said, "Yes. Talk to the Customs officer." I said, "Pass him on to me." The Customs officer said, "It says *pig*ments." I said, "What do you understand this is?" He said, "Small pigs." I said, "Why don't you open it, and if you find small pigs, throw them into the Red Sea. But if you find something else, please send the container here to us in Riyadh." We got it finally, but this was the situation. Pigments.

Sometimes, we had difficulty knowing when Dafnis was being serious and when he was joking. He could tell the most outrageous stories with a completely solemn expression on his face.

Woes, Women, and Mutawa

Dafnis also said he got caught violating the rules of the Islamic religious police pertaining to being with a woman in public. His offense? He took a woman to a market to shop. Dafnis explained,

> One time, I went shopping at the Panda Supermarket, accompanying a British nurse. The religious police approached me and asked, "Who is this woman?" I told them her name and explained that we came to shop. "She is my friend. I am helping her because she had nobody here, and who is going drive her for the groceries?" The *Mutawa* said, "Yes, but you are here in the Kingdom, and you know the laws. You are not supposed to accompany this woman because she is not your wife; she is not your mother; she is not your daughter; she is not your grandmother; she is not your aunt; she's not six degrees of relationship. You must know the rules." I said, "Okay, sorry. She wanted to go shopping, and I was just trying to help her." They sternly replied, "Okay, we will issue you a warning." So they issued me a warning, which I still have in my files somewhere. It states something like, "This man was seen accompanying a woman who was indecently dressed [Dafnis gestured with his hands that the nurse was not wearing a black robe from shoulder to feet—and maybe did not have her hair covered properly], and she was not related to him; and this paper is given to him as a warning. Signed, the Committee for the Preservation of Religious Ethics and Morals."

I assume that Dafnis meant the Committee for the Promotion of Virtue and the Prevention of Vice that he mentioned earlier, but I am not positive.

The abuses of the *Mutawa* could be the focus of an entire book, so egregious and numerous were their mean-spirited actions. In an email that Dafnis sent to a woman in the United States in 1996, he mentioned a friend from Texas who, while working in Saudi Arabia, got into trouble with the religious police: "She was falsely accused of 'practicing prostitution' simply because she went shopping in a supermarket with a female friend of hers without being accompanied by their father. They were sentenced to 90 lashes each. How cruel!" On a brighter note, in 2016, the Saudi government sharply curtailed the activities of the *Mutawa* following decades of their abusive behavior. They no longer have the authority to arrest and detain people suspected of not adhering to their grotesquely harsh interpretation of Islam. Crown Prince Mohammed bin Salman led the way in bringing Saudi society back to a moderate Islam following years of fundamentalist terror. But Dafnis lived in Saudi Arabia during the darker days of oppression.

Lies in the Name of Allah

Another encounter with the *Mutawa* also involved a woman, and Dafnis *really* enjoyed describing this one—partly because it illustrates his rhetorical skills in tense situations.

> A few years later, there was an American nurse from New York: Doris. I remember her name: Doris. [In another telling of this story, he remembered her name as being *Jenny*.] Her mother was dying, and she urgently wanted to go see her mother. We had a travel office. One of the companies we had was NABA Travel and Tourism. So, I said, "Okay, Doris, I will arrange for you to get your ticket, and I will take you to the airport, and you will leave tonight for New York." So, I went outside the hospital, and there was Doris, who got into my car, and immediately after—the Religious Police were watching around the corner—and they *BOP* [he made a gesture of being nabbed by the police]. And they said, "Who is this woman?" I said, "This woman is my daughter." He looked suspicious and said, "Your daughter?"
>
> Saudi Arabia has different work permits. The brown one is for non-Muslims, and the white one was for Muslims. We both had, of course, the brown. He checked the permits and said, "But this woman does not seem to be your daughter." I said, "Listen, I am 92 years old." [In another telling of the same story, he said that he told them he was 75 years old, and Jenny was only 22] "Oh, are you," he said. "You look younger." I said, "I am, *Hamdullah*." Always, you must throw this word in: *Hamdullah*. [In Arabic the word means "praise be to Allah." The longer version is Al-hamdu lil-lāh.] This is a hot button word. *Hamdullah*.

Dafnis digressed to interject further humor, lampooning Arabs.

> In fact, I established a college in Saudi called the IBM: The IBM College. The "I" stands for *Inshallah*: "God willing." Always you must throw in this

word. Always. "*Inshallah, Inshallah, Inshallah, Inshallah*." Usually, they ask no further questions. "Are you Muslim?" "*Inshallah*." Finished. No argument. "If Allah wants, Yes, I shall become a Muslim." So, "I" stands for "*Inshallah*." "B" stands for *Bukera*. *Bukera* means "tomorrow." And the rule of this school of management is "Never do today whatever you can postpone until tomorrow." *Bukera*. And "M" stands for *Malish*—"Never mind." "Never mind. It doesn't matter." IBM School of Management I called it. It was a smashing success. It took off right away. Everybody was talking about this school of management.

Dafnis then returned to describing the serious encounter with the *Mutawa*—but he did so with his customary humor. We heard several versions of the story with differing details. Here is the more developed version.

They took us, but they made a very big mistake. They left us together in the car. They said, "Come, follow us." And I told Doris, "Listen, we need to keep the same report, both of us. Whenever they ask us, we must answer the same thing." [In other words, they must have their stories consistent so they did not contradict each other when being interrogated. So they rehearsed what they would say.] Okay, we went there, and they put us into two separate rooms to write down the facts.

After hours of waiting, the interrogation commenced. I started my comments by saying, "In the name of Allah, the merciful, the most merciful, the benevolent"—these are the starting verses of the Quran—always, always you have to recite these verses—But I confess this to you, I never told so many lies in my life as I did in the name of Allah, the merciful, the most benevolent. So, Doris in the other room wrote the same—exactly the same. So, the man said, "Congratulations. I never saw a non-Muslim telling the truth as you did. Why don't you become a Muslim? I said, "*Inshallah*." He asked, "Can we meet again?" I said, "*Inshallah*."

So, the *Mutawa* were sitting there with their beards, like this. [Dafnis acted out the men's posture.] They use this incense, which is objectionable to me. Anyway, they put their beard over the incense smoke to change the color a little bit. And it smells something like bullshit, actually, when you burn it for two or three days that way. But they like it. And one guard accused me, "You violated the rule." I said, "I violated the rule? But I did not violate the Holy Quran." He said, "What are you talking about?" "I did not violate the Holy Quran," I repeated.

He had three copies of the Quran on his desk. So, I tapped one Quran with my finger and said to him, "Open this book and show me where the Prophet, blessed be his name"—you must always say these words—"where he says 'When a woman has a mother who is dying in the hospital and has *no* husband and *no* brother and *no* other relative, and she needs *desperately* to go to the airport, that you should let her mother die without seeing her daughter?' *Show* me this page." He said, "Okay, I will let you go, but please I want you to return here tomorrow to convert to Islam." I said, "*Inshallah*."

The guard asked me if I knew the Quran, and I answered, "Yes, I know it very well. I have read it three times." He gave to me a copy of the Quran in Arabic with annotations, and then he insisted, "You *must* convert to Islam." I replied, "*Inshallah*." In other words, "If it is the will of Allah, it will happen." That stopped the discussion, and the guard let us go.

Dafnis pointed to an ornate copy of the Quran on his bookshelf and said, "That is the Quran that the guard gave to me." It was definitely a handsome volume. But the ugly and oppressive way the *Mutawa* used the Quran to abuse people in the name of Allah fundamentally opposed Dafnis's philosophy of life: that love is the highest expression of godliness. In his mind, we please God when we accept people regardless of whether or not they agree with our beliefs.

Dafnis did engage in animated debates over beliefs and policies that he rejected. But his close friends included those whose political and religious philosophies differed from his own. We participated in social gatherings with his friends where, in the same room, were committed, left-wing-atheist Communists and fervent, right-wing-Orthodox Christians. Somehow, with the mediating presence of Dafnis, these philosophically diverse individuals enjoyed each other's company and engaged not just in civil conversation but also in friendly banter. They did not check their beliefs at the door, but they did check their animosities toward others at the door and congenially embraced their common humanity. It was a great model of how people can be friends and love each other, even though they do not agree on central beliefs.

Dafnis's brand of politics and religious principles focused not on exclusion but on acceptance. He focused on what we have in common, not on what makes us different. Instead of limiting his circle of colleagues and friends to those who shared his viewpoints, he widened that circle to include a diverse set of people. Did he get frustrated with others and criticize their actions? Absolutely. We have seen him express anger loudly and in no uncertain terms. But people understood that he loved them, and that awareness allowed them to see past his outbursts.

Christians in Saudi Arabia

The *Mutawa* do not share Dafnis's acceptance of people with other belief systems. Being a Christian in Saudi Arabia can be very bad for your health. I said to Dafnis, "From what I have heard, you took some dangerous chances meeting with

Christians while you were in Saudi Arabia." "I did," he replied, and continued,

> I could be deported. I could be put into prison. I could be lashed 39 times because I organized and participated in religious activities. Every Friday we had an underground religious service. The people who started these Christian services were American army personnel who came for the Iraq war—to liberate Kuwait [1991]. They had military Bibles with military colors for the Army. In the American camps, it was safe to meet together for fellowship. The religious police could not touch you. However, I did not live on an army base. On Fridays we had our meetings in the nice villa where I lived. The villa belonged to the prince, and he let me live there. It was very spacious with a swimming pool....
>
> Another thing that I was involved in could have landed me in prison: I was involved in what is called a prison ministry. We had a charity for taking care of people who were in prison and had families. Most of them were Filipinos, but other nationalities were also in prison. On one occasion, we received news of the arrest of a Filipino who was a pastor of the Filipinos in what they called the CLIM fellowship. CLIM means "Christ Lives In Me." Hundreds and hundreds of Filipinos belonged to CLIM. Every Friday they would go to a secluded area in the desert. Most were born-again Christians, and their celebrations were noisy with music and guitars and dancing. Finally, somebody noticed they were there, and they were arrested and put into prison. This happened when George Bush the senior was president. Not the stupid one; the other one, his father. And they told me that the Filipino pastor would be beheaded on Christmas day. Beheadings are on Friday.
>
> I was really alarmed, and I went to the American embassy, and there I talked to a Mrs. Kennedy. I told her, "Listen, this is very serious if it happens, and you need to intervene—right now." So, she called George Bush Sr., told him what was happening, and insisted that he needed to stop the execution. Bush picked up the phone and called the king and convinced him to intervene. Then Mrs. Kennedy called me, and she said, "Dafnis, go early in the morning to the prison. They will release him. And take him straight to the airport to leave the kingdom." A few days later, the Filipino ambassador called and invited me to his office. He knew what had happened, and he said, "I want to thank you on behalf of the embassy."

I asked Dafnis what happened to the other Filipinos who were thrown in prison. He said, "They were just deported."

We were interested to know more about the meetings that Christians held out in the desert. So, Dafnis provided additional details—perhaps with a bit of his normal hyperbole.

> And every year at Christmas time, we had the Christmas concert. Hundreds and thousands [??] attended in *wadis*, which are valleys in the desert. They used secluded areas. Germans who worked in the various ministries organized these events. One of the key organizers was an employee of ours, Manfred Kerner, who provided the transport vehicles. He represented a German military truck manufacturer, and these people were agents of our company in Saudi Arabia. Another German, who will hopefully come to Cyprus before you leave, was the key person who set up the music. We had a concert with Christmas music in the desert, and it was really a big celebration that was crowded and well attended.
>
> Later on, the governor of Riyadh at that time—who is now the king of Saudi Arabia—Salmon—he called my boss and he told him the *Mutawa*, the religious police, were going to raid the Christmas concert. "Please tell your people not to do it." Of course, we did not organize the concert that year. We cancelled it. And the Mutawas took bulldozers, and they put huge rocks at the mouth of the *wadi* to make it inaccessible so we could not drive our cars into the canyon.

"How often did you meet with these Pentecostal Filipinos?" I asked. "Every Friday," he said. In a letter dated 6 June 1984 to Roy Calvocoressi, Dafnis sounds like a Pentecostal.

> Roy, thanks and praises to Jesus who made it possible for us here in this desert land to worship him despite the high risk of being imprisoned or deported. Any worship other than Islam is strictly forbidden. But in "Christ Lives in Me" Fellowship we praise him and worship him every Friday. The CLIM Fellowship is more than 600 strong. I was touched by the Holy Spirit the other day and together with Maroula we fell down and the elders put their hands on us and prayed. Prayer healing is a matter of routine. It is done every Friday at the end of the church service. Praise the Lord. In Him we find new power every day.

By the time we interviewed Dafnis in 2017, however, he seemed far removed from such activities. Indeed, he seemed hesitant to talk much about people being slain in the spirit, speaking in tongues, and getting healed. But in Saudi Arabia in the 1980s, Filipino Pentecostals evidently had a significant impact on Dafnis.

"Which Christians participated in the Friday group meetings in your villa?" I wanted to know. "In my villa," he said, "we would have between 30 to 50 people. Most of them were nurses from the hospitals. Our meetings did not involve loud music. Mostly we were pretty quiet." I asked, "How did you make sure that nobody came in and spied on you?" Dafnis shrugged his shoulders and said,

> Because we knew they were all expatriates. But one day one of our employees, Sayid Mossary, a fanatic Muslim, came to me, and he said, "Dafni,

we notice that on Fridays there is a lot of movement in your office [villa?]. And I think you are doing something that you should not." I feared that he might report us, but he never did, probably because I had the support of my boss, who was a Prince. This fanatic man was a manager in the company, and now he might be a Jihadist. I don't know. He left the company to start his own business.

Figure 31. *Dafnis and Maroula.*

One day I heard that Sayid was in prison. He entered into an agreement with a bus company to take pilgrims to the Hadj. Two or three million pilgrims go every year to perform Hadj, so there is money to be made from busses and so on. Something went wrong with his agreement, and they put him in prison. One day, I told Maroula, "We should go to visit him in prison." So, Maroula and I went to the prison. And when he saw us, he started crying. He said, "You are the only ones who came to visit me. And you are not Muslims." Sayid was very touched by this.

So much for Muslims showing compassion and taking care of their own! To be fair, it reminds me of a popular Christian preacher who was caught in an infidelity and disgraced years ago. He said that the only one who called to check on him was an atheist friend. Bitterly, he said, "What I learned from this whole affair is that Christians shoot their wounded."

I was curious to know how often Maroula visited Dafnis in Saudi Arabia. He said,

She would come two or three times a year and stay two months. Our children were here in Cyprus, and Saudi Arabia is not a friendly country for foreign women. However, Maroula told me that some of her happiest days were in Saudi Arabia because we were able to create our own little microcosm. And we were happy because we could ignore what was out there. Maroula got along well with Saudi women.

Business in Saudi Arabia

"You lived in a big villa, and you worked for the prince," I said. "You must have been making a ton of money. I don't understand why you are not rich." Dafnis smiled and said, "What kind of question is this? How do you know I am not rich?" I replied, "Well, you don't act like it." He laughed and continued.

I borrowed a lot of money to pay my expenses. You see—before I went to Saudi Arabia—my brother and sister, and my brother-in-law, and a distant relative in America, we decided to set up a company. We planned to develop some of our land here in Limassol by building a multi-story building and then sell it. But we started at the wrong time. It was in the early 1980s, during the time of Ronald Reagan, and the interest rates shot up to 18%. Our American relative dropped out, saying, "Sorry, I cannot go through with this deal."

We decided to call the building Happy Life, and we set up a company. But after our American partner dropped out, we were left with a heavy loan that we could not pay. We failed, and we had to abandon the project. When the project failed, we had a large loan that had to be repaid; and that is the main reason I went to Saudi Arabia. I had to absorb the loan myself. Without repaying the loan, the bank would auction all our property, and we would have nothing left. I had signed an agreement with the bank that decided to foreclose the mortgage.

But just as they were ready to foreclose, another bank bought the bank. And Evagoras, the chairman of this other bank, was a close friend of my father, and a personal friend of mine also. So, I went to him, and I told him, "This is the situation," and I signed an agreement that I would repay the loan. I told him that I could pay £500 per month. He told me, "My dear Dafnis, don't tell the bank this. Tell the bank £300, because if you tell them £500, and you only send £400, the bank will be very upset. But if you tell them £300 and you send £400, the bank will like you. I followed his advice, and most of my money went to repay the loan. And so I saved the property here. Later we built the shops on Georgiou Griva Digeni [the main street just north of his house], and now my children have some income from these shops. But somebody else completed the building we were going to name Happy Life.

Figure 32. Dafnis at his desk in Saudi Arabia.

A friend of mine named Brian asked me, "How come we handle so many millions

> of dollars, and we are penniless—unlike the Lebanese and the Iraqi accountant who embezzled $3 million?" About that accountant, I asked the prince, my boss, "What shall we do? He took $3 million." He said, "Dafnis, what shall we do? Allah wanted it this way. We shall let him go."
> The man took the $3 million and he disappeared.

I shook my head and said, "So, it is okay to behead a Filipino pastor for leading a Christian worship service, but they let the guy who embezzled $3 million go free without penalty?!"

Greed and scandalous behavior were rampant in Saudi Arabia. Dafnis gave another example.

> We had an American employee in charge of maintenance of agricultural equipment: combines, harvesters, and so on. One day he said to me, "Dafni, come with me. I will take you to the site of the biggest robbery of the century." And he took me to a farm belonging to one of the royal crown princes. He said, "This is the site of one of the biggest robberies. This prince bought 150 combine harvesters from John Deere. He bought 50 tractors, and other equipment costing millions and millions of dollars. Yet he paid not a single penny.
>
> A few months later, two Lawyers from an office in New York City came to see me. They said, "We came to talk to you, because John Deere hired us to take action against this prince. What do you advise?" I said, "I advise you to go back to John Deere and to write off these tractors as 'Charity for American aid to the Kingdom of Saudi Arabia.'" They were shocked. I said, "You will achieve nothing." They said, "But there is a contract."
>
> They went to the crown prince, Abdulla. And I waited for them in a lounge. After about two or three hours, they came back; and their faces showed that they had been unsuccessful. "Mr. Dafnis, exactly what you told us is true." "What happened?" They said, "We told the prince that he bought these things, and he must pay. We said, 'You have a contract.' And the prince said, 'Show me the contract.'" And they gave him the contract. He tore it up and threw it into the wastebasket. Then he said, "This is your contract." And he threw them out. And not only that, he also confiscated their passports. He said, "I have your passports here." Consequently, they had a problem getting out of Saudi Arabia.

"Sounds like a great place to do business!" I said. Dafnis smiled.

Desalinization Scam

Dishonest people from various countries sought to cash in on the vast quantities of money flooding Saudi Arabia. One of the more creative attempts was by a French engineer working with a Lebanese facilitator. Dafnis said,

> When I was in Saudi Arabia, Prince Faisal Abdul Rahman al Sudairi was my boss.... Prince Faisal called me to his office to show me a letter from a Lebanese guy living in Paris claiming that he had a connection with a French nuclear engineer who found a way to convert seawater into fresh water for agriculture and for domestic uses. I said, "This cannot be true because such an invention would bring him the Nobel Prize at least. Not to mention making headline news."
>
> He said, "No, it is! It is!" This Lebanese man wanted $20 million to sell the rights to our company, and he called his device Blue Water. So, I got on a plane and I flew to France to investigate this matter and decide whether we should pay $20 million to buy the invention.... The French engineer and his wife came to meet me. I was representing the prince, bringing $20 million, so of course I received a royal welcome.

At this point, Dafnis laughed loudly. Then he continued his tale.

> They put me in a nice hotel there, and the nuclear engineer, who worked for the French atomic energy committee, did not speak English, but his wife did. She said, "Okay, we will pick you up tomorrow morning and take you to see the equipment. It is top secret. We have it in a farm some kilometers away from here. And nobody knows about it."
>
> I was laughing to myself, because I did not believe his invention was legitimate for the simple reason that up until now there is no such device. Desalinization plants use membranes, most of them made by DuPont in America, to filter out the salt. It's a very expensive process, and you cannot use it for agriculture; you can only use it for domestic uses for drinking. But this invention was supposed to bring tons of seawater through the machine and produce fresh water to irrigate fields. Fantastic! So we reached this farm and there was this shed and a little machine, which was a prototype. They brought it out, and we were about to start testing the machine.

They tested salt water with the standard salinity for the Mediterranean Sea, and the engineer claimed that he could convert this saltwater to fresh water. Now Dafnis got really animated.

> All of a sudden, a heated quarrel started between the husband and wife with shouting and fighting in French. I wondered what was happening. It went on and on, and then she told me, "You know, we need a catalyst, and he forgot to bring it." He forgot the chemical catalyst. And she was blaming him that my report would be negative, and the $20 million deal would be thrown out the window. I said, "No, calm down. We will stay here. Let him go to town to bring the chemical." She calmed down and we stayed there alone, and he went to get his catalyst.

Dafnis decided to tell the wife about Maroula spilling soup on him at their engagement meal. Indeed, he told us that entire account yet again. Then he got back to his main story.

> About that time the engineer arrived with his little bottle of chemicals, and he was surprised to find his wife in a pleasant, laughing, smiling mood. She walked up to him and gave him a kiss. We went ahead and tested the machine, and the results, of course, were a complete failure. It did not work. He must have been daydreaming. And I saved the prince \$20 million. The Lebanese man who approached the prince regarding the desalinization device had told me privately, "You'll get a good share of the \$20 million. It will go to your bank account in Switzerland. But, of course, I never had a bank account in Switzerland.

Dafnis's honesty in this matter contrasted with the ways other people sought through fraud to get rich. In other areas of life, however, he was not transparent.

Clandestine Activities

Sometimes when we were interviewing Dafnis's good friends, they volunteered information that shocked us. Our first window into his clandestine activities came early in our 2017 trip to Cyprus, when we participated in a cordial luncheon with ten friends at a seaside restaurant in Zygi. An accomplished, professional woman from Nicosia called Dafnis a womanizer. Others nearby laughed. She said it as if she thought his behavior were cute. Dafnis smiled and seemed to take the comment as a compliment. At the time, we wondered what exactly she meant.

My wondering ceased when I interviewed a businessman who met Dafnis in Saudi Arabia around 1989. Dafnis invited him to join a group of internationals who went on hikes in the desert. Sometimes they stayed overnight or late into the night to observe the moon and stars in the clear desert sky. He said, "We even had ambassadors and diplomats in these groups. But the most important part of these gatherings was *girls*. It was for dating—for men and women to meet out away from the religious police." Then he dropped the bombshell: "Dafnis was always the playboy. He was the one who chatted all the girls. And all the girls liked him, because he is a good entertainer."

I was curious about these desert hikes, and I pointed out that Dafnis was a married man. He shrugged and said,

> Dafnis loves women…. Even though his wife may be in the house, in front of his wife he tries to impress women…. I think that Maroula knew but didn't care. She was not stupid. I think that she became more like a sister to him than a wife. To my knowledge, even here in his own house women were sleeping in his bed. I don't know how he does it, but women love Dafnis.

"What was the attraction?" I asked. "He was a lot older than these women." The friend said, "He is a smooth talker, and he listens intently to women when they talk to him. He flatters them and makes them feel so nice."

We also heard comments about Dafnis and women from some of his close relatives. A cousin of Dafnis was working in Saudi Arabia before Dafnis went there. The cousin told Dafnis about some of the possibilities for employment. But he cautioned Dafnis, "As long as you are strict with the laws, and you don't go out with the nurses, it's okay." The cousin looked at me and added, "But that is exactly what happened." When I asked for clarification, there was an awkward pause in the conversation, followed by nervous laughter. So, I said, "Why did you hesitate so much when I mentioned something about Saudi Arabia and nurses?" He said, "Dafnis prefers the company of ladies rather than men."

A more revealing conversation happened when a sister of Maroula came to Dafnis's house, accompanied by her husband. We asked questions about her memories of Maroula and had a pleasant time talking about how sweet Maroula was. Dafnis was in the room, translating for us, and he commented about how frequently he brought people home for a meal without telling Maroula that they were coming. He merely expected her to fix meals for them. "How did you manage to live to be this old?" I asked him. And everyone laughed. But then things got awkward. Maroula's sister's husband said, "I remember a friend of Dafnis named Gretchen. She was coming here EVERY summer. One month. One and a half month." Dafnis interrupted to explain.

> She was Dutch. I met Gretchen at the Agape Camp—the ecumenical camp in Italy. And we became friends at that time. And she used to come to see me. She worked with the European Parliament in Strasbourg, and she spoke seven languages, including Greek. Her job was with the Dutch delegation. And the thing is that, at one time, she wanted to marry me. But Maroula won, and Maroula felt sympathetic for Gretchen. And they were excellent friends. We have many, many experiences together. She was part of our family. When I was in the detention camp, she sent me a box of vitamins, because she thought that I was not fed properly. She was a very good friend. She would send me information on what was happening in the European parliament regarding Cyprus.
>
> Anyway, I am often accused of not delivering on time things that I promised to do. It takes me time, okay, because I do too many things. And on one occasion, I promised to send [to Gretchen] some special pencils. She was painting things. And I sent her a package. And she wrote me back and said, "I am glad that you delivered what you promised to me six years ago."
>
> She took her driving test 16 times and kept failing it. On the 17th time, she finally got her driving license. And every time I went to visit her

> in Luxembourg, I was very afraid to ride with her in the car because she would go through red lights. She said she could not concentrate because I was sitting in the car next to her.

He laughed. I turned to the sister's husband and asked, "Did you finish saying what you wanted to say about Gretchen, or do you have more to say?" "No," he said. "I did not finish." Then he added, "She was a good person—very artistic. I don't know if she had a secret with Dafnis. But Maroula was very fair with that girl."

After an awkward pause, Dafnis repeated the story of how he met Gretchen at the Christian work camp in Italy and how she took up for him when two British students slighted him. Then Dafnis attempted to change the direction of the conversation. He described an occasion when he told Maroula that they were invited for a luncheon at a fancy hotel in Limassol, so she should dress up and be ready to go. She spent the entire morning getting ready for the luncheon, but when they got into the car to go, Dafnis looked at the invitation and realized that the event was scheduled for the following week.

Lynne said to Maroula's sister, "I have one more question. Why do you think that Maroula was so patient with Dafnis and with other people?" Dafnis ignored her and kept on talking. Only this time his story pushed into the forbidden zone.

> Maroula prayed, "Lord, give me patience to cope with my husband." But the worst case happened in Saudi Arabia. In Saudi Arabia, we lived in various places, but on one occasion we lived in villa with an upstairs and a downstairs. We had a woman doctor who visited us, and I asked Maroula, "Did you water the plants downstairs?" She said, "I am not sure, so I better go to check." When she came back, she saw me holding the hand of this woman doctor.

I said, "So, you were holding hands with a female doctor in Saudi Arabia, and your wife came into the room." He averted his eyes. Nervous laughter followed. Finally, Dafnis continued.

> And then Maroula came back and she said nothing. But afterwards we drove this doctor to the airport to say goodbye because she was leaving for the UK. When we came back, Maroula told me, "Listen, I want you to know that what you did was wrong. And you should think, not about me, I don't care. But you should think that eventually you will have to explain what you are doing to the Lord at the last judgment."

Lynne said, "So, you knew what she was talking about?" "Of course I knew," he said. "And I knew what I was doing, as well. Holding the hand of this doctor. Well, okay, we are made of flesh. I am not an angel." He explained to his sister-in-law in Greek what he told us—and she laughed. And Dafnis laughed. Lynne and I locked eyes for a moment. Then Dafnis continued in a joking way, "I told Bishop Athanasios, 'Did you ever hear me claiming that I am an angel?' He said, 'You and I are both too fat to be angels.'"

Dafnis continued to make light of his actions and reminded us of a story he told us on more than one occasion.

> When Maroula appeared at the Golden Gates, she was asked to produce her I.D. So, she produced her I.D. The angel said, "Okay, I have to give this to my master." He went in to St. Peter's office and showed this I.D. St. Peter looked at his super computer briefly until he located Maroula, wife of Dafnis Panagides. St. Peter asked for clarification about her identity. She said, "Dafnis was my husband for 48 years." "Ayee. For 48 years?" St. Peter told the angel, "Take this woman and put her next to Jesus himself."

Dafnis laughed loudly. Lynne and I exchanged another glance.

We noticed a cultural acceptance by both men and women that married men may have extracurricular activities with other women. That outlook emerged again when I spoke with an elderly couple who had been close friends of Dafnis for decades. The wife said, "You see, he is so secretive." Her husband added, "Even though he is very open, there are some secret things that he keeps for himself. For instance, when Maroula was still living, Dafnis would bring girls from Sweden or other countries, and sometimes he would bring them to Pachna. Pachna is my village, and they would sleep up there because Dafnis did not want to put them in his house." The man's wife said, "Yes, but Maroula knew about the girls." The husband said, "She knew, but she pretended she did not know." The wife looked at me and asked, "Did you ever hear this before? Noooo?" Then she laughed.

Her husband continued,

> I have a house in Pachna... and they used to go up there many times on the weekends to the house where I was born. So, one day, I see one girl coming down the ramp from my house, and I said, "What do you want?" She told me, "Dafnis sent me." So, I kept her there for a couple of hours, and then Dafnis came. And they spent the weekend there. *They* spent. I was not there.

The wife chuckled and shook her head as her husband told the story. Then she spoke about Dafnis living in Saudi Arabia.

> Lots of women who were mostly nurses were there—from many different countries. And they would come to Dafnis's place to visit on their way back to Saudi Arabia or on their way back to their home countries. They would make a stop in Cyprus, and they stayed with Dafnis. Maroula knew a lot of them because of meeting them in Saudi Arabia. When they came to Cyprus, they used to stay with Maroula and Dafnis in their house—maybe even months. There was one woman from Sweden, and the way the beds were arranged in the room—anyway, one time she jumped out the window to run away so that Maroula wouldn't see that she was there. Things like that, you know—extracurricular activities.

> Maroula was there. Since she knew most of these women from Saudi Arabia, she sort of trusted them.

She paused, took a deep breath, and added, "as much as she could." Then she laughed a knowing kind of laugh, which caused me to say, "Ohhhh." At this point, she caught herself and said,

> But I am sure that Dafnis was a good boy. He was just, uh, full of life, as always, and enjoyed the company of women around him all the time—any kind of women—okay, from the most religious to the worst kind.... And if they needed help in any way, he was always willing to be there for them, whether economically or—*whatever*. Any kind of help. He was always [pause] *willing*. He did help many of them. They are still friends. He gets calls from all over the world.

The husband grunted, and the wife laughed nervously.

I said, "When we were having lunch by the sea at Zygi, one of the women told Dafnis that he is a womanizer. I thought, 'Well, that's odd,' but it sounds like..." I did not finish the sentence, so she finished for me: "*This* kind of stuff." "That's correct," I said. But then she qualified her comments, "Womanizer has a negative meaning." I did not understand the distinction, so I said, "But if he was sleeping with women who were not his wife in his own home...." I left the implication unstated. So she responded, "It looks bad. So, you can use it or not use it. It is up to you. But we want to see Dafnis not as a saint, but you know what I mean."

Grateful Friend from India

Sami, who owed his life to Dafnis, was extremely grateful and looked upon him as a father figure. His actual name, *Swaminauton*, is common in the southern part of India where he was born. His first daughter had died, and he had no money, so he went to work in Saudi Arabia out of desperation. He was hired as a foreman, but two months later, his boss demoted him, and he had to work as a laborer in extreme heat (52 degrees Celsius = 125.6 degrees Fahrenheit). He almost died.

Sami's boss would not pay him for months at a time, and he paid only half of what he promised. Sami was starving, but his employer threatened to send him back to India if he complained to anyone. We frequently heard such stories about Arabs abusing their workers. Unfortunately, we also learned that some Greek Cypriots mistreat their foreign workers. However, it is illegal in Cyprus—and people can get prosecuted for it. When Sami was in Saudi Arabia, employers could abuse their workers with impunity. Sami noticed people coming on Fridays to Dafnis's villa, and he concluded that they were Christians. He went to Dafnis at night and asked if he could join the group. Dafnis let him meet with other Christians for prayer meetings.

Sami's employer relocated him farther away from Dafnis, but on weekends he walked eight kilometers to see his benefactor. Sami said Dafnis helped him a lot—paying him to do odd jobs on weekends. Maroula got clothes for him and checked on him every week when she was in Saudi Arabia. When he later came to work in Cyprus, he would take a taxi from Nicosia to see them once a week. Maroula arranged for him to do various jobs around Limassol to increase his income. Sami said that Maroula always did what she promised, but he added that Dafnis sometimes says he will do something that he is not able to do. "He promises," said Sami, "but he does not follow through." He added, "But when Mama Maroula said she was going to do something, she always did it."

Sami told us, "I was in a very bad condition 20 years ago after I came to Cyprus." Dafnis would give him money, and when Sami tried to pay him back, Dafnis would not take it. Dafnis got a job for Sami with his psychiatrist friend in Nicosia, who appreciated the man's reliability. Sami told us he taught his sons in India *never* to promise anything to anyone unless they were going to keep their promise. Regarding his own parenting, he said he gives his sons more freedom than his parents gave to him. He told them if they want to marry a girl, they should come to him and ask. He will check out the girl and her family, and if she is a good prospect, then he will give his permission. "Young men are not wise enough to do this," he said. He loves his sons, but he does not believe they have much common sense.

When we asked what lessons he had learned from Dafnis, he said that the big thing is that Dafnis treats everyone the same. "He does not treat poor people differently than important people. He helps lots of people." He added, however, "But he makes lots of promises that he does not keep." Sami reflected a minute and said, "My wife is very generous to poor people in India. Every day women come to her and she helps them."

His beloved wife, Lilly, is 12 years younger than Sami. He said that he went 25 km to a village to meet her, and he thought, "She was too skinny and too dark. But I had prayed to God (Hindu god) to show me the girl I should marry. I could not know the heart of the lady, so I trusted the god to direct me. I was not impressed with Lilly at first, but I agreed to marry her." They had never spoken to each other before they got married.

Sami and Lilly went through extremely difficult times, and Lilly's wealthy father never helped them. Interestingly, to marry Lilly, Sami became a Christian. He believes that a Hindu god directed him to Lilly, but he believes that God has no problem with people praying to different gods because they are really all praying to the same God. He believes that God helped him to buy land at the right time—land that several years later became worth much more. After all the trials he endured earlier in life, he is optimistic about his future and was looking forward to returning home to India. His gratitude toward Dafnis and Maroula is profound.

In the Shadow of Dafnis

Dafnis's only son, Thales, was born in Ames, Iowa, and considered himself to be an American. When Dafnis returned to Cyprus in 1974, Thales was hesitant to move to the island. He said, "I was not a happy camper, and it took me about a year to adjust to Cyprus. I came when I was ten years old, and I remember writing on a piece of paper, 'America, I love you and miss you.' It was a poster, and I pinned it on the wall in my bedroom." He felt self-conscious about not being able to speak Greek. To help Thales adjust to the new environment, Dafnis and Maroula sent him to an English school. Over time he came to love Cyprus.

In 2017, I asked Thales if he ever felt intimidated being the son of Dafnis. "No," he said,

> I don't operate the way he does.... I like to live my life more the way my mom did: calmer, quieter, peaceful, and serene. Whereas my dad is the opposite: the chaos, the thriving in the noise and the action. So, "No." He is popular. Always in the streets, everybody is [saying], "Mr. Dafnis, blah, blah, blah." Even to this day, wherever I am, if I see an older man, if I ask, "Do you know my dad?" he will say, "Of course I know your dad. You are the son of Mr. Dafnis." It does not surprise me any more. Dad liked presenting—he was an amazing storyteller. And I often wondered how much of the story was true. And then I think of what your son said, which is so fitting, "Why let truth get in the way of a good story?" He does it because it is fun. And it is all in good nature—nothing to hurt anybody. He is not a gainful opportunist. He does everything innocently, playfully.

At this point I observed, "It is amazing to me that he has no more money than he does. He talks about going to Saudi Arabia to work for a prince. I would think he should be wealthy, but he is not... People tell us that he is a great guy who is always thinking big picture, but he is a lousy businessman." Thales smiled, paused, and then said,

> True. You are spot on. He admits it. He is an ideas man—incredible ideas. He just does not execute or implement them. He is very bad with money. He will admit it. We have concluded that he would have made an outstanding academic. He should have pursued the academic life: a professor somewhere; publishing; writing books; researching; teaching. But he ended up having to go to Saudi Arabia because of a bad deal that left him in debt. And he had to pay this debt.

He told about the failure of the Happy Life Building and added something I had not yet heard.

> Another thing that forced my dad to go to Saudi—because he went on two occasions; it wasn't just one long stint—he owed back taxes on his salary from Phassouri. An accountant ill advised him. It was like £15,000,

> which at the time was about $30,000 that he had to pay to the government. He was lousy with money. He is still lousy with money. He is a free spender also. He pays for everybody. He won't let anybody else pay. That is another thing I remember. When we were in restaurants, when we had guests—20 or 30 people—Dad would pay the bill. Over and over and over again, he did this.

That tendency was so pronounced with Dafnis that I had to develop clandestine ways of paying for things—sometimes to the extent of humorously covert maneuvers. Once, when I paid for his hotel room, Dafnis got agitated and insisted that I had done a bad thing and embarrassed him. I smiled and said, "You win some; you lose some." Lynne and Maria laughed. He was probably about out of money anyway.

I asked Thales if he learned more about parenting from Maroula, because she was home much more than Dafnis. He said that Dafnis "did play a role—as much as he could—but from a distance." While Dafnis was still in Saudi Arabia, Thales returned to the United States for four years to earn his undergraduate degree, then two years for his MA, and then he spent ten years in Brazil. He seldom saw Dafnis, but he indicated that he was never bothered by his father's absence. "It was a nice feeling to know that a loving and giving father was there with advice. And if I did need money, he helped. Even though he was absent, I felt his love."

Thales added, "Mom played a huge role in Dad being able to operate at the level he did. She made it possible for him to do what he did. She did the cooking, the cleaning, the logistics—she did all of it." "How about the money managing?" I wanted to know. He said,

> She had a notebook, and she would record all of her expenses. I got that habit from Mom, not Dad. My dad admits that he is a lousy money manager. Even today we joke about this matter in emails. He gets a small stipend from his retirement and a small stipend from the shops. And I say, "Dad, here is your month's income. Please spend it wisely." And he says, "Son, I am more careful this year. I am more diligent. I will try to make it to the end of the month." But the joke now is, "Dad, at your age, you can do whatever you want. Spend it wherever you like. Eat whatever you want." But he takes advantage of this age thing. Yesterday, we heard that little heated talk with my sister. He said, "Excuse your dad. I am getting older." When I talk with her, she says, "No! Just because he is old does not mean he can get away with it. Eating whatever he wants, saying whatever he wants, doing whatever he wants."

He smiled and said regarding his sister's frustration, "Dad has to be accountable, right? That's the American way. She has a Midwestern Protestant mindset."

Two More Years for Tuition?

Dafnis said he wanted to retire and return to Cyprus at age 65, but he stayed two extra years to pay tuition costs for graduate studies for his youngest daughter, Dora. He added that he went to Saudi Arabia in 1980 because he needed the money: "I had my four children in college." Such memory lapses were common. He was, after all, 88 years old. When Dafnis left for Saudi Arabia in 1980, Lydia and Louisa had already finished their college education, Dora was 17, and Thales was only 13 years old.

With chagrin, Dafnis said Dora had a full scholarship, but she called [in 1986] to say she was quitting college. He was not happy. Dafnis asked what she was going to do. She said she wanted to go to Brazil to learn Portuguese and recuperate. "Portuguese?" he said. "Who cares about Portuguese?" Dora explained that Portugal is part of the European Union and "millions of people in the world speak Portuguese." She convinced him, and she dropped out of her graduate program at the University of Iowa, went to Brazil, and lived with a Brazilian family.

Dafnis said that six months later, Dora called him to say she wanted to go to Johns Hopkins because they had an excellent program in public health. When he asked, "What does this mean?" she replied, "This means that I need \$26,000 for tuition fees." Dafnis groaned, rolled his eyes, and said, "Oooo! \$26,000!" He said that he and Maroula decided that he should renew his contract in Saudi Arabia for two more years to get their daughter through college. However, the dates are problematic. Dafnis returned to Limassol from Saudi Arabia in 1996. Dora started a Ph.D. program on full scholarship at the University of Iowa in 1986 and dropped out in 1987 after she realized that the program was just not for her. She did a M.H.S. at Johns Hopkins from 1988 to 1990, finishing her graduate work six years before Dafnis returned to Cyprus. She was well into her career by 1994—two years before Dafnis returned to Cyprus. Dora is amused by Dafnis's claim that he spent two extra years in Saudi Arabia to pay for her tuition, but she said he had told her the same story.

Remembering things accurately can pose problems, and written documents can correct our memory defects. I have a scan of a letter from Dafnis to Roy Calvocoressi dated 11 November 1990 in which he says his employment had just been terminated. The Gulf War (2 August 1990 to 28 February 1991), interrupted a lot of business in Saudi Arabia, and Dafnis became unemployed as a result. Deeply disturbed by his financial insecurity, he wrote to Roy,

> It came as a surprise to me because it came earlier than what I planned or expected or even what I can afford. Maybe it is the will of God but I am not quite sure if he wants to put me again in new financial stresses and tribulations. The truth of the matter is that if I retire right now I have no income at all, other than a small pension of about £180/month to support

> my son's studies, the family, and also to meet the monthly payments on the balance of the loans. I discussed the matter with Maroula and the children and of course I am telling you everything for your advice and counseling....
>
> If my employer honors his legal commitments, I am entitled to a termination payment of about £12,000. This will mean a lot. I asked him to settle it, but I do not know how soon he will be able to do it or whether in fact he will do it. Another option available to me is to sign a contract for one more year in Saudi Arabia with another company. There are possibilities but everything now is very uncertain. For my son's schooling I can cash my insurance policy in the USA. It should give me enough to cover him for at least the two years he needs to graduate. My youngest daughter found a job in Kapoeta Southern Sudan.

Thus, in November 1990, part of Dafnis's financial commitments involved helping Thales with college expenses, but Dora had already finished her degree at Johns Hopkins and was working in South Sudan at the time.

In a December 1992 Christmas letter Dafnis wrote from Riyadh, Saudi Arabia, he gives a short description of what each of his children is doing. Regarding Dora, he wrote,

> The American and US troops who reached Baidoa [Somalia] on the 14th of December were surprised to find a small team of aid workers already there caring for people dying of hunger or wounds. My youngest daughter, Dora, was one of them. She is with the International Medical Corps, and during the last two years, she has been evacuated from "hot" spots such as South Sudan and more recently Angola.... She is happy to be right in the center of this massive international and humanitarian effort and her parents share her happiness.

In 1992, brave Dora was on a medical team assisting people in horrible circumstances, and she had previously been working in other dangerous environments. Apparently, the reason Dafnis remained in Saudi Arabia until 1996 was to pay off his bank loans, but somehow over the years he got firmly planted in his mind the belief that he stayed two extra years to pay for Dora's tuition.

However, when he returned to Limassol at age 67, he was in good health, and he set about hiking trails in Cyprus and enjoying the beauty of his homeland. He also made spiritual journeys to places like Mt. Athos and Mt. Sinai. And most important of all, he became increasingly involved in raising the consciousness of Cypriots to care for the natural environment of their lovely Mediterranean island. When he retired, he did not just sit in an easy chair. He remained very active and became increasingly influential in his homeland.

CHAPTER 8
Father of Environmentalism in Cyprus

"A writer has got to have a pretty good—a reasonably attuned—memory of his past. And the stuff that I can't remember, I just make up."
—Bruce Springsteen[1]

Leadership in Retirement

In many ways, Dafnis's education and work experiences prepared him to do his most significant work after he retired. He maintained a hectic lifestyle, but he directed his efforts toward improving the environment of his beloved Cyprus and enhancing the lives of all the diverse populations who live on the island—with the possible exception of wealthy Russians who have flocked to Cyprus to take advantage of the shortsighted immigration laws passed by the Cypriot Parliament.[2]

When Dafnis returned to Cyprus from Saudi Arabia, he reconnected with his Eastern Orthodox traditions, made trips to Mt. Athos to explore matters of spirituality, began to push for stronger environmental laws to protect animal species, pushed for better farming techniques to produce higher yields but also protect the land, pioneered sustainable tourism to protect Cyprus's natural resources while maintaining the revenue stream from the millions of tourists who visit the island,

---

[1] "The Boss: A Homecoming," in *AARP: The Magazine* (October–November 2020), p. 39.

[2] Russians have cleverly used the system to gain access to the European Union markets that would otherwise be closed to them. They enjoy the moderate climate and are buying up the waterfront in Limassol and building large complexes along the beach. They now have sufficient numbers to form a voting block. In 2020, *Al Jazeera* conducted an undercover sting operation that exposed criminal behavior at the highest levels of Cyprus government and society, videoing individuals explaining how they sell citizenship and passports to criminals who want to take advantage of a Cyprus program to lure foreign investment. https://www.aljazeera.com/news/2020/10/12/cypriot-politicians-implicated-in-plan-to-sell-criminals-passport. The news reporters posed as representatives of a Chinese man who barely escaped from China after he got caught money laundering. He supposedly had a lot of money that he would invest in Cyprus if he could gain a Cypriot passport. The exposé caused such outrage in Cyprus that politicians abolished the Citizenship Investment Program (CIP) effective 1 November 2020: https://www.aljazeera.com/news/2020/10/13/cyprus-abolishes-citizenship-through-investment-programme.

advocated better protection of nature preserves, and fought against the human trafficking scourge on the island. The relationships he built with Cypriot leaders over the years, in addition to the friendships he cultivated with people from countries around the world, provided a valuable network for accessing intellectual and material resources to work for good. He became an advocate for land reform, for environmental awareness, for cleaning up the mess left behind by careless use of plastics, for planting trees, for protecting endangered species, for seeking economic growth in the small villages in the mountains where aging populations and economic stagnation are problems, and for illuminating abuse of foreign workers.

Unknown Places

Dafnis knew virtually every inch of Cyprus, but he had no interest in becoming a licensed tour guide. He said, “I'm interested in off-the-beaten-track places where there are not these huge tourist buses.” He smiled and added, “Father Gennadios wanted to see some of the unknown places in Akamas. At one time, Akamas was considered the small Mt. Athos because there were so many monasteries and churches and caves where hermits lived.”

Dafnis took Gennadios to see the ancient church of Agia Paraskevi, which is visited by few people. As he and Fr. Gennadios were preparing to enter a gorge to walk to the church, two men arrived in a rental car and asked if Dafnis knew the way to Agia Paraskevi. He said,

> “We are going there ourselves; you may follow us. But who are you?” And this guy said, “I am the manager of the Cyprus Tourism Organization. This gentleman is an Italian journalist who came to Cyprus as our guest to write about religious tourism. He wanted me to bring him to Agia Paraskevi, but I had no idea where is Agia Paraskevi.”

Traveling with Dafnis was like touring with a living encyclopedia, and he loved to tell us about the history and ecology of wherever we went on the island.

Embracing his Orthodox Faith

Dafnis's sister, Chloe, was attracted to the Baha'i religion for a while, but she returned to her Orthodox roots. In the late 1980s, when Dafnis was home from Saudi Arabia on a brief vacation, she pressured him to speak with Fr. Athanasios. He responded, “Look, I grew up around priests. I'm tired of being around priests. I have had enough of all that!”

I asked Dafnis about his spiritual journey. Did he set his Orthodox beliefs aside for a while and then return to them after he retired? His answer was nuanced.

> I grew up in a Christian Orthodox environment, but my father was a very open-minded man with an ecumenical spirit. So, I have always been in

the liberal, ecumenical tradition. In other words, when you ask if I am Orthodox, my answer is "Yes, I am." I am baptized Orthodox, and I follow the Orthodox Church rituals and so on. But I'm not so much a person of ritual and formalities and NO-NOs and all these things. The outlook, which I inherited from my father, is open-minded.

We had the first ecumenical camp at Kakomallis in 1954, sponsored by the World Council of Churches, years before the Ecumenical Movement started. And now the question of dialog with other churches has actually *split* the Orthodox Church. Last year there was a synod in Crete, and five or six Orthodox churches *refused* to attend because they did not want to participate in a meeting officiated by the Ecumenical Patriarch of the Orthodox Church, a man who communicates with the Pope and participates in services with the Pope. And recently, just two weeks ago, the Archbishop of Athens refused to go to the island of Corfu because the Ecumenical Patriarch was there. He said, "No, I don't want to go and meet this heretical archbishop."

The Ecumenical Patriarch of Constantinople (Istanbul) plays a significant leadership role in the Orthodox Church, although each region has its own archbishop. As with any denomination, infighting can be intense among Orthodox Christians. Dafnis was much more tolerant than some. He said, "I try to keep out of these narrow things."

Because he did not answer my question, I rephrased it: "I asked you about your spiritual journey. Were you ever, like some of your friends, into a movement that involved Buddhism?" "No. Never," he said.

Kissing Icons

"You kiss icons," I said, "yet you say you are unconcerned about rituals." He shrugged his shoulders, and said, "Yes, I kiss icons. It's part of the Orthodox ritual." He explained. The controversy over icons lasted a hundred and fifty years in the ninth century (sic.). Many people were killed and many icons were destroyed. Cyprus stayed out of this conflict [called the Iconoclasm]. And many icon painters came to Cyprus to avoid persecution. This is why we have so many frescos and icons in our churches, because they came here where it was safe. We Cypriots never took part in this controversy. The issue was finally resolved with the affirmation that the respect given to the icon passes through the icon to the person depicted in the painting.

He felt some ambivalence toward kissing icons: "If I go to church I rarely kiss the icons unless there's a special occasion because I want to say a little prayer."

His graduate work at Ames dramatically influenced his beliefs, but one would be naïve to say that his academic studies completely altered his mindset. At heart, he was an open-minded Orthodox Cypriot.

> I was always in the Orthodox Church tradition. I grew up with it, and I stayed in it, and I continue to follow the sacraments of the Orthodox Church and the basic beliefs of the Orthodox Church. But I would say I am very moderate in my practices when it comes to rituals and formalities, which, I would say, have no spiritual context. For example, I am not supposed to eat certain things during fast days. But I am flexible when it comes to fasting. I don't follow the strict fasting rules that on certain days you must not eat olive oil or you must do this or that. I think the spiritual aspect is a personal experience, which Fr. Athanasios preaches. It is a matter between you and your Lord.

Dafnis said he "participated in very fundamentalist Protestant prayer meetings" in Saudi Arabia. More serious from an Orthodox perspective were his Catholic connections. And most serious were his prayers with Muslims. He spent much time with Bedouin in the desert. While with them, he participated creatively in their calls to prayer. He explained a Muslim legend about Allah and the calls to prayer.

> Muslims pray five times a day, and they have to mention the name of Allah 56 times every day. Originally Allah wanted the prophet Muhammad to mention his name 5,000 times. But the prophet found it impossible. "How could I mention your name 5,000 times?" And he negotiated with Allah, and slowly, slowly, slowly, he bargained with him and Allah brought the number down to 56. Of course, bargaining with Arabs is part of their culture. You have to bargain. You never take the price as an answer. If they say, "Five," you say, "No, I give you one." And you bargain.
>
> Their first prayer is early in the morning, but the time changes three minutes every day. It moves according to the moon, or the sun. And in the desert, in the tents, there is always an elderly person whose job is to go around and to knock to wake people

Tricky Diagnosis

A neighbor in her early 80s came to visit Dafnis, and he asked about her health: "Did you ever have yourself checked?" She said, "No, never." Slyly, he said, "Show me your hand." He carefully examined it and said, "You have high blood pressure; you have high blood sugar; and you have high cholesterol." She listened intensely, so he added, "And maybe you have some arthritis in your joints. Madame Maria, why don't you go to the hospital–just to get tested?"

After three days, she returned and said, "I am very upset with you. You are a doctor and for so many years I did not know it. When I got the results from my tests, everything you told me showed up in the analysis." He laughed about his prank and said, "Now, there is no way that I can convince her that I have no knowledge of medical matters."

> up to attend the morning prayers. When I was with the Bedouins, I had to adapt and to pray.

He added, "I also participated in Catholic services. I spent a few days in a Trappist monastery."

Such openness got him in trouble when he first journeyed to Mt. Athos, the very heart of archaic, Orthodox spirituality. Several times he recounted to us his unusual encounter with an old monk who demanded that Dafnis be re-baptized.

> When I first went to Mt. Athos, the monks did not like this idea of me praying with Muslims. I had decided to see a spiritual leader at a monastery, Fr. Pavlos [Paul], and it turned out that he was the strictest confessor in the Orthodox world. We spent a couple of hours together, and I told him that in Saudi Arabia, I prayed with Protestants and with Catholics—secretly of course, because we could be in serious trouble if we met in the open. I also told him that, on many occasions in the desert, I joined Muslims—Bedouins in their tents—during the five times prescribed by the Koran that you have to pray. And I was in line with them, but while they were reciting verses from the Koran, I would recite the Lord's Prayer or the Apostle's Creed or some prayer of my own.
>
> Fr. Pavlos was unhappy with what I told him, and he said I could not receive communion until I was re-baptized. He said, "I am sorry, Mr. Dafnis, but when you prayed with Muslims you denounced the Orthodox faith, and you must be re-baptized." I said, "I never denounced it. They were praying in Arabic, '*Allahu Akbar,*' but I was saying, 'I believe in God the Almighty, the one God,' and so on. You know, the creed." But he said, "No!" So I said, "Okay, father. I came by my own will to Mt. Athos. So, I will do what you want me to do."
>
> Then he said to me, "I will make a special baptismal service, and after that you may be readmitted to the Orthodox faith." I remember it was Palm Sunday Eve. At midnight in Mt. Athos, where there is no electricity, it was absolutely dark. I could see nothing. I could not even see who was next to me. And Fr. Pavlos was officiating the liturgy, and it was about one o'clock in the morning when I saw him carrying a candle. He came out of the altar place, and then he started going from stand to stand [seats where people either sit or stand in Orthodox churches]. And I was wondering what he was doing.
>
> He was looking intently at the people in the room, and when he came to me, he said, "Oh, you are here." I said, "Yes." He said, "How are you doing?" I said, "I am doing fine." "Are you not tired?" I said, "I took a short sleep." He said, "Better to sleep in the church than on your comfortable bed." But then he told me the following. He said, "Dafnis, forget what I said this afternoon, because just now I received a message from

> the Holy Spirit telling me 'Dafnis should receive communion today.' So, you can receive communion. I received inspiration while praying." He believed the message came from the Holy Spirit or from some angel who told him, "Dafnis should receive communion today." So he said, "Come to receive communion." I prayed, and I received communion. It was a very significant experience in my spiritual life.

Some of Dafnis's friends considered Fr. Pavlos's reversal of opinion to be a miracle.

Revisiting the Shepherd Story

The matter of divine revelations at Mt. Athos also emerged in a message he sent to Roy Calvocoressi, the peace activist with whom he dialogued extensively about Christian peacemaking through non-violence. In an email that Dafnis sent to Roy on 18 April 2000, he mentions his encounter with the literate shepherd at Avgorou who asked whether or not Jesus would use bombs and guns against the British. The email reveals that Dafnis had been discussing this event with Orthodox monks.

> I came back from a most wonderful time on Mt. Athos. I was able to go into deeper investigations of the spiritual life there, and it had a significant impact on my life. In fact, Chloe detected a general change in my attitude, which I believe will stay. One of the strongest experiences was the revelation by a hermit that the shepherd who asked me the question, which turned me from a terrorist into a Christian Pacifist, was in fact an angel disguised in the form of a shepherd.

Dafnis had obviously told the story of the shepherd to Roy. But now he indicated that he knew via a divine revelation that the shepherd was an angel in disguise.

The fact that Dafnis did not drive to Avgorou in 1959 to deliver Andreas's list of debts to his widow did not prevent him from telling his fabricated story frequently to different audiences. I do not know when he began to insert the story of an encounter with a literate shepherd into his imaginary trip to Avgorou, nor can I explain why he attached so much significance to something that never happened—or why he persisted in telling the story so often. Perhaps he viewed his elaborate tale as useful for validating his pacifist position. I will never know.

In his 18 April 2000 email to Roy, Dafnis transitions to the central issue of his friend's life: peacemaking—telling him what a monk had to say about this topic.

> Another elder made clear to me that there will be no peace [in Cyprus] unless and until the Greek Cypriots, starting with the Orthodox hierarchy, publicly apologize for all the crimes committed over those years. This of course has to be done irrespective of whether the other sides—Turks and British—apologize and repent or not. Bishop Athanasios of Limassol suggested it to the synod, but he was voted down and actually called

> names by the Bishop of Paphos. We are not ready yet, but we shall keep trying.

The mere suggestion that the Orthodox Church needed to repent of its actions during the EOKA rebellion and afterward brought angry responses from some Cypriot clergy. But Dafnis trudged forward on the path toward peace. He was still making progress that direction right up to the day he died. Establishing harmonious relations between Greek Cypriots and Turkish Cypriots continued to occupy his thoughts, and he facilitated people learning to love each other as friends. We personally attended a few of these events and witnessed genuine affection between the Greeks and Turks. They represented a small fraction of the total populations, to be sure, but their actions demonstrated on a micro level how peace is possible. As Dafnis would say, "from the ground up."

Dafnis had times in his life when he inclined more toward a spiritual mindset. When he retired and returned to Cyprus, he began to spend more time dialoging with Orthodox monks. This environment pushed him toward increased reflection on spiritual dimensions of life. Our environment certainly shapes our thinking and behavior. We also tend to adapt our speech patterns and topics of conversation to the people with whom we communicate. Roy was a spiritually minded British evangelical whose language reflected his biblical worldview. Dafnis concludes his email to Roy with a benediction that imitates words Roy would use—the likes of which we *never* heard from Dafnis: "Let the passion of our Lord and Savior touch our hearts and renew our commitment to Him and to His commandment of love."

Pilgrimages to Mt. Athos

Being retired allowed more time for Dafnis to travel to places that enhanced reflection. I asked him to tell us more about his trips to Mt. Athos. He replied,

> I've never gone alone—always with two or three friends. One time I went with Kyriacos Markides, because Athanasios asked me to accompany Kyriacos. He told me, "Dafnis, you know your way on Mt. Athos, and Markides wants to go there. I want you to be with him because Markides *may* have a problem, knowing his background with the oriental religions and spiritualism." Kyriacos describes this trip in one of his books. I think I told you how it was the beginning of Lent, and Kyriacos did not realize the demand to abstain from eating food and drinking water. The monks pray continuously for three days.

True to form, Dafnis did not arrive when he said he would, so Kyriacos stayed in Thessaloniki for days waiting and repeatedly going to the airport to meet him.

Dafnis admitted that Kyriacos's description of the situation in his book was very polite, saying something like, "I was disappointed. I went back to my hotel, and then two days later, Lavros [his name for Dafnis in his books] called me and said, 'I am here in Thessaloniki and let us go.'" Dafnis said, "I explained to him there was no point going to Mt. Athos; we would not be allowed in; everything would be closed. And that was my excuse." He did not bother to explain to us why he had been late arriving in Thessaloniki. Those who knew Dafnis would not be surprised. People had a tendency to get angry with him for subjecting them to such inconvenience, but once he finally arrived, they would have lovely adventures with him. I could tell such stories about my own experiences with Dafnis.

Mysteries of Mt. Athos

Dafnis was intrigued by what he experienced at Mt. Athos, but he remained skeptical on some matters. He clearly believed that supernatural things happen in this center of conservative Eastern Orthodox spirituality. Some of his best friends among the Cypriot Orthodox clergy were monks from Mt. Athos. He had great respect for them, but he was able to critique their actions and attitudes. The abilities of some of the holy men fascinated him. He described a Romanian monk who went to Mt. Athos when he was 21 years old, and when Dafnis met him he was 92 years old and completely blind. Yet Dafnis said the monk could see through his blind eyes. "He could describe everything—in a mysterious way he could describe you and he could see like this." He mimicked the blind man. Dafnis said that he asked the monk, "Okay, you are already in Paradise yourself because you live here in the forest and have the blue sea of the Aegean; but tomorrow we go back to the city. We are surrounded by temptations, by tribulations, and we have to work hard. What is your advice?" The blind monk said, "My advice is one word only, but strangely enough people find it extremely difficult to follow this one word. They try to follow advice which is in books that involves so many words, but they don't realize that the advice is only *agape*." That one word of advice had a profound effect on Dafnis. *Love* became central to his belief system. "If there is something spiritual," he told us, "it is a dimension of *agape*."

Dafnis held two worlds in tension. His time at ISU in Ames, Iowa, instilled an empirical, Western mindset. Prof. Timmons and others taught him to be analytical when considering evidence. We noticed, for example, that he was capable of evaluating the beliefs and practices of his good friends Bishop Athanasios and Fr. Gennadios in light of the cultural influences that Mt. Athos had on them. Yet he was also open to believing that monks teleported from one place to another and dead monks sometimes appeared to people to provide insight or direction.

Sometimes I pushed him regarding his beliefs. Once I asked, "Do you believe in hell?" From what I knew of his core beliefs, I was not surprised when he said,

> Do I believe in Hell? In fact, I think it does not make sense. Why? Suppose I live 20, 30, 50, 100 years, and every day I sin. Would you believe in a loving God who will punish me for eternity when I only sinned for 60

> or 70 years? Is this God a loving God? I believe Origen is right, because Origen believed that, in the long run, God will forgive even Lucifer.

He grew reflective, looked at me and asked, "What do you think?"

Figure 33. *Two of the depictions of judgment and hell in Panagia Asinou.*

I said, "It makes no sense to me that God would impose everlasting punishment for finite sin. But I was curious what you think." Dafnis replied, "So, we agree on this." I said, "Oh, yes. The idea that God would take delight in burning people for all eternity makes no sense to me." Dafnis said softly, "I don't think that either." But how did he fit his viewpoint into Eastern Orthodoxy? I added, "At Panagia Asinou near Nikitari, we saw scenes of the great judgment in some of the frescos. They reminded me of Dante's *Inferno*. People were hanging over flames on big hooks. In my opinion, those frescos are morbid." Dafnis skirted the issue by saying, "Okay, the fresco of the great judgment is a way to send a message. The problem with that is people take these metaphorical, symbolical images as real. The message is that there will be punishment for certain violations, a certain way of life. That's it." I was not convinced that the artist who painted the frescos would agree that the scenes he depicted were merely metaphorical, but Dafnis, at least, rejected the belief that God vindictively and brutally punishes human beings for all eternity.

Maroula and St. Catherine

Maroula was a more faithful Orthodox Christian than Dafnis, but after his return to Cyprus from Saudi Arabia, Dafnis took a greater interest in Orthodoxy and went on pilgrimages. Twice, Dafnis took Maroula to St. Catherine's Monastery at the base of Mt. Sinai because her connection with St. Catherine was deep and mysterious. He said,

> Maroula had strange visions of St. Catherine, which I was not aware of myself. In the middle of the night, she would disappear. I would wake up and think, "Where is Maroula?" I would find her outside, praying, and as I listened, I realized that she was praying to St. Catherine. Her connection was so strong that she died on St. Catherine's Name Day. Her health became fragile, but she wanted to go to St. Catherine's Monastery for some reason. So, I asked her doctor, "Can she go to St. Catherine's?" The doctor said, "I don't see why not." Maroula was so happy. So, we went, and she enjoyed it. She did not go up Sinai Mount where supposedly Moses got the 10 Commandments, but I did. At that time, I was still strong enough to walk to the top, although it was very tiring. Others would ride camels or donkeys up the mountain. But Maroula waited for us down at the bottom.

Actually, Maroula had a stroke on 25 November—Saint Catherine's name day—and she died on 5 December 2002. Her passing put Dafnis into a time of deep reflection and despair. His response to her death reveals a dark state of mind. He told us he had visions of Maroula, but he did not know if he actually had contact with her or whether these were simply dreams.

On 9 January 2003 Dafnis wrote to Roy Calvocoressi. In typical Dafnis fashion, he opened with a humorous comment about why he had not responded to messages. Then he said seriously,

> I can come up with scores of excuses, and of course I can fabricate many more. The one valid explanation, the one which I confidentially shared with Stahis and Joy, is that since last December I have not been able to come to terms with myself. Takis Evdokas the psychiatrist who knows me very well believes that it usually takes between 3 or 4 years to come to terms with their new life style. Some never can make it. Very few, including myself, he believes, can recover within a year or so. I know I am not the same person, and despite my strong faith I go into periods of depression and at times I retreat into myself, not caring about the hundreds of emails, telephone calls, letters, and personal visits which come my way. Recently, I see some improvement, thus this message.

On 23 February 2003, Dafnis again emailed Roy, and again he began humorously by complimenting Roy for being so adaptable that he can dress up to meet with the Queen of England one day and a few days later meet with an African chief the bush. He good-naturedly jests with Roy about Orthodox Christians like himself being pagans, because they kiss pieces of wood. Then, on a somber note, he adds:

> As for myself, Roy, I cannot say that I have adjusted to my new situation without Maroula. As I told Athanasios who stood by my side and gave me

> a lot of spiritual power and counseling, it is one thing to read or lecture about death, and another thing to face death in the eyes. I am carrying my cross with the help and prayers of friends and spiritual brothers and mentors like yourselves and others.
>
> We shall have Maroula's 3-month memorial next Sunday and then I shall take off to Saint Katherine's on Mt. Sinai for a period of contemplation and ascetic practice. I found that Maroula had a mystical connection with St. Katherine and I expect that I may be able to communicate with Maroula if I stay at the monastery for some time.

In 2017, he was quite reticent to admit that he wanted to go to the monastery to try to communicate with Maroula. By that time he would only confess to having dreams about her.

Dafnis told us he returned to St. Catherine's Monastery with a small group of friends a year after Maroula died. And something unusual happened. He said his friends did not know about Maroula's special relationship with St. Catherine. Yet three people from his group talked with him privately and said, "You know, the relic of St. Catherine is kept in this monastery—and I felt the presence of Maroula when I was by the relic." He grew pensive and said, "These are mysterious things. I don't research them. I am just telling how they felt. Three different people told me the same thing: when they thought of Maroula, they smelled a strong aroma and felt her presence." He added, "In the Orthodox tradition, if there is a good spirit in the room, there is a sweet smell. So, this is how you experience the presence of a good and benevolent spirit. Some people have this experience, and this is what happened at St. Catherine's Monastery."

In 2017, his assessment was more detached when he described his grieving process. He repeated Dr. Evdokis's prediction that Dafnis would recover sooner than others, but in this telling the predicted time was only one year. "My psychiatrist friend told me, 'I know you. Normally, it takes between three and four years for a person to overcome the loss of a spouse. But in your case, I think in a year's time, you will come back to normal.' But it was not a year. It was only three months."

I have heard stories about dead saints appearing to people, and I asked Dafnis if Orthodox Christians believe non-saints like Maroula also appear to the living. Dafnis said, "Yes. They believe the spirits of people can appear." He added that most Orthodox believe that one should be cautious about going to a spiritualist because even the devil can transform himself as an angel of light. So we can be deceived. He told a story to illustrate his ambiguous feelings about this matter.

> There are many stories—okay, you can go back to experiential psychology. We have this story of Nikos Kazantzakis, a famous Greek author. When he was 12 years old, his father took him to the cemetery to put

> some flowers on the grave of his great grandfather, Captain Michalis, a famous man in Greek literature. And Grandmother Kazantzakis says his father went into a trance and said, "Listen. Do you hear the voice of your grandfather? He is talking to us." Kazantzakis heard nothing. But his father heard his grandfather talking to him. Who was right and who was wrong? According to experiential psychology, you cannot tell me "You are wrong," because I am experiencing something that is my own experience. If I believe so, it is so. Who cares if I am right or wrong? I feel this way.

He laughed nervously and added, "I am curious sometimes. Dale Carnegie said, 'Life is to live it, not to understand it.'" And with that comment, he was done.

Dafnis and the Mukhtar

Panicos, the Mukhtar (Mayor) of Louvaras, engenders affection from others. People in his village have so much respect for this soft-spoken, organized man that they unanimously elected him to be their mayor for a second term. He is wise and innovative and provides excellent leadership. Dafnis arranged for us to interview him at the Kakomallis Campground, located up the hill from Louvaras, and he served as our interpreter. Panicos said, "I met Mr. Dafnis at the vespers when Bishop Athanasios came for the first time [to Kakomallis]... Dafnis is active, interesting,

Figure 34. *Lynne and Dafnis at Kakomallis Campground. The right section is an expansion on the original building.*

devoted to social activism—a significant person who reminds me of my father, and I love him like my father."

Panicos explained that Solomon Panagides started Kakomallis as a site for summer youth camps, and for years Dafnis and others used the grounds effectively. But the EOKA struggle, the political turmoil following independence, the fact that Dafnis spent eight years in the United States and sixteen years in Saudi Arabia —all these factors degraded the health of Kakomallis. The facility was neglected until Panicos reinvigorated its use. He organized an outdoor vespers service at Kakomallis and invited Bishop Athanasios of Limassol to join them. The bishop was so enthusiastic about what he saw that he provided €10,000 from church funds for maintenance work and repairs. Then he set up an association called Friends of Kakomallis Forest and entrusted the campground keys to the Louvaras council.

On 23 August 2017, the day after we arrived in Cyprus, we went with Dafnis and Maria to Kakomallis to attend the concluding ceremony of a weeklong camp for volunteer firefighters from six different nations: Cyprus, Russia, Germany, Sweden, Switzerland, and Greece. These men and women belong to an international NGO called Firemen of the World, and their morale that night was high. A series of speeches occurred during the banquet, and Panicos spoke on the seminal role that Dafnis played in the construction of the camp and in its ongoing operation. After the speeches concluded, the drinking and dancing began. We were amused by the dancing competition between Russian and Greek firefighters. Flamboyantly, they exhibited their finest moves.

According to Panicos, Kakomallis is a blessing for Louvaras and the entire surrounding area, and he plans to upgrade the facilities so the camp can accommodate 70 people. The maximum now is about 30. They want to make Kakomallis available for conferences and meetings as well as youth group gatherings. He admitted that bureaucratic obstacles block their way, but he asks Dafnis to intervene for them, and he always helps. Panicos smiled and added, "The Mukhtar of Kalo Chorio complains that Mr. Dafnis takes better care of Louvaras than he does of Kalo Chorio, his own village."

Panagides Foundation

Solomon Panagides exerted a profound influence over many Cypriot youth. Some of his former students started the Panagides Foundation in 1967 to carry on the spiritual work of Solomon and to address major social problems in Cyprus–including drug addiction among youth. To fund their efforts, they started the first recycling program in Cyprus.

An island-wide economic crisis in 2012 wiped out their investments, and an earthquake damaged the building where they held their meetings. The leaders of the Panagides Foundation have hope for the future, but only time will tell if the work continues. The founding members are old and dying. Will new, vigorous leadership emerge?

Yet Panicos complained: "Sometimes, Dafnis upsets me because I try to reach him on the phone, and he never answers." Dafnis replied, "The first one to complain today was my daughter Louisa. She said, 'What happened to you? Since yesterday, I have been trying to reach you; and it is urgent!'" Dafnis added, "Sometimes when I do not respond, he [Panicos] has to take into consideration that I am carrying on my shoulders almost 90 years of weight. The best communication is person-to-person. The worst communication is electronic communication." With that comment, they both laughed and hugged each other.

Dafnis said he went to the Kalamaras Restaurant in Arakapas to say "Hello" to the owner, and he saw the Minister of the Interior sitting at a table with Panicos and chairmen from 17 surrounding villages. So he walked over and greeted the minister, whom he knew, and he said good things about the group members. Later, Panicos told Dafnis that, because he intervened on behalf of the local chairmen, immediately after the meeting, the Minister of the Interior granted the necessary permits. "Unfortunately," Dafnis said, "in Cyprus you need to have connections."

Panicos also expressed appreciation for the way Dafnis had helped Louvaras to receive an award for sustainability practices during an annual meeting of the Sustainable Tourism Initiative (STI). A few weeks after we interviewed Panicos, we attended an STI meeting in Paphos with Dafnis and Maria that included a slate of speakers from other countries. During that conference, Louvaras again received the top prize for sustainability practices in Cyprus.

On another occasion, Panicos told us more about his efforts to preserve and improve not only the Kakomallis campground but also the surrounding Forrest. His efforts were not without difficulties. He said,

> We see a lack of interest from the appropriate authorities in government, so we are trying to initiate action to get more government involvement. Last year we gathered together about 200 people, and we walked seven kilometers around the forest, and then we returned here to the campground for a picnic—a big celebration. We will have another such celebration on the 29th of October. Will you be in Cyprus? Will you join us?

"Yes," I told him. "We would love to come." He was aware of my Nikon D750 camera, so he added, "Do you promise to walk with us and take pictures?" We assured him that we would.

On 29 October, we had a pleasant time with other participants hiking from the Kakomallis campground to the top of a nearby mountain and back again. Clouds filled the sky that morning. When we were about a mile from Kakomallis on the return walk, rain began to fall. On the arid island of Cyprus, complaining about precipitation is ill advised, so we marched through the mud in good humor. Dafnis could not participate in the hike, so he stayed at the campground.

Once we reached the campground, Lynne and I filled plastic plates with food and sat alone at a dilapidated picnic table because all of the other seats were taken.

But then Maria found us and said we were expected at the VIP table on the other side of the bunkhouse. We followed her and discovered a much more elaborate table setting. Dafnis introduced us to several members of the Cyprus government who came to the event as guests—they did not go on the hike! I was seated next to the Director of the Interior. He was pleasant, but mostly I had a revealing conversation with an engineer who worked with the Director of the Interior. He confided in me that he could accomplish a lot more if he did not have to go through so many other people. Government bureaucracy slows down everything he does. Some frustrations are universal!

Troubles with Truffles

Although Dafnis was an agriculture expert, he fell for a scam involving truffles—a failed venture with a Turkish professor who specialized in fungus. Reluctantly, Dafnis explained how he was duped.

> The man was working as a professor at the University of Bonn, in Germany. He told me that he had succeeded in inoculating truffles, which are very expensive—maybe €2,000 per kilo. He said, "I succeeded in the lab at inoculating this fungus onto the roots of an early fig tree." The professor said he had tried it in Saudi Arabia, and he showed me pictures of the results. I said, "This is a fantastic idea." It was when Tassos was the president of Cyprus [Tassos Papadopoulos was president from 2003 to 2008], and he went to France on a state visit, and they went out to a restaurant. Tassos ordered spaghetti. When the bill came, he asked the French president, "Can anybody tell me another place where spaghetti costs €45?" He called the waiter and said, "There was a mistake." The waiter said, "Mr. President, it is not the spaghetti that you are paying for, it is the truffle sauce."
>
> On the plane back to Cyprus, Tassos said, "We must do something about these truffles." My Lebanese friend, whom you know, was part of the delegation, and he told Tassos that Dafnis would know about such things: "We have to get in touch with Dafnis about these truffles." So he called Dimis, who called me the next day and said, "Come to Nicosia. We are going to negotiate how to push truffles. We have to do it because the president wants truffles."

Dafnis and the others fell prey to an elaborate con job. I got further details from the Lebanese friend who recommended that Tassos contact Dafnis. Same story—different details.

He told us that a Kurdish professor [Kurdish Turk?], who conducted research at Hanover University in Germany [instead of the University of Bonn, as Dafnis said], claimed that he could inoculate trees, especially olive trees [instead of fig trees, as Dafnis said], with fungus, and when the tree was planted in a field, it would produce truffles. The idea sounded great to Dafnis.

The Lebanese friend funded the project, and he and Dafnis hired workers to "inoculate about 15,000 olive trees." Dafnis coordinated the effort, which received much attention. "Everybody was talking about it. Even the president said, 'You are a genius. This idea will make Cyprus very rich.'" They should have researched the matter more. As it turned out, the Kurdish/Turkish professor was working for a Saudi prince, and this "professor" inoculated some 150,000 trees in Saudi Arabia with the fungus. Foolishly, Dafnis and his friend entered into a partnership with the man and started paying fees for his supervision of the project.

Because of the media hype, they sold inoculated trees to the Orthodox Church, to the government, and to entrepreneurs. The Lebanese friend continued,

> But we didn't sell 15,000. We sold a maximum of 2,000. It was a big issue for two years, and we were spending money but getting no income from truffles. We sold enough plants to make a little bit of profit. But the professor was taking most of the money. And I was naïve. I was not very clever. Dafnis was also not a good businessman to advise me on the business side—to be more careful. He is older and should be wiser, but he is not. Without him, I would not have financed the project. But he studied the matter, and he believed the man's claims. Later, we found out from people in Saudi Arabia that they kicked the professor out of their country. They said he was going to the market and buying truffles and going to the fields at night and burying them in the sand by his trees. And in the morning he called the prince and said, "Let's go search for truffles." He would say, "Dig here." And, of course, they found truffles. The man was an international crook.

Ironically, the fungus caused the olive trees to grow quickly and produce abundant numbers of olives. The farmers were not allowed to use chemical fertilizers that would have killed the fungus. As long as the fungus was on these trees, they grew fast and produced more olives. Because of increased yields of olives, those who purchased the inoculated trees were not upset about getting no truffles. Olive trees typically produce numerous olives one year and less the next year. But the fungus olive trees consistently produced great olive harvests, and farmers sold their olives at a higher price, because they were organic.

He concluded by saying that Dafnis had no wisdom when it came to money. Maroula was a much better money manager. "She would take his salary, put it in her pocket, and give him one pound at a time. Otherwise, Dafnis spent it…. He is nice and intelligent. You cannot deny that a discussion with him is very interesting. He is wise. He is educated."

What if a lion eats me?

Dafnis's youngest daughter, Dora, and her husband, Michael, lived and worked in Zimbabwe for seven years; and in 2006 Dafnis traveled alone to see them. The three of them rode the Blue Train on a side trip to South Africa—an overnight excursion from Pretoria to Cape Town. Among other adventures, they stayed in the Makalolo Lodge in the immense Hwange National Park in Zimbabwe. Three years later, in 2009, Dora and Michael invited Dafnis and Maria to come and celebrate his 80th birthday in Africa. They lodged at Stretch Ferreira Safaris in Mana Pools National Park, Zimbabwe. By the time Dafnis told us about this trip in 2017, however, he had conflated the two trips. In his memory, he and Maria stayed at Makalolo National Park and together they rode the Blue Train from Pretoria on a three-day trip to Cape Town. Dafnis said, "It is the most luxurious and most expensive train in the world, and I was very embarrassed." He said he complained to Dora and Michael about spending too much money, but they told him he spent two additional years in Saudi Arabia to pay tuition for Johns Hopkins, so "What we are doing now for you is nothing." Thus, by 2017, Dafnis had incorrectly but firmly fixed that tuition connection in his own mind and merged it with his birthday trip.

Dafnis's journal entries for his 2006 Africa trip indicate that, at age 77, he loved hiking on a wildlife tour. His reflections also reveal his philosophy of the environment. He wrote,

> Our "civilized" way of life separated us from our environment and alienated us not only from our natural world but also from our fellow human beings, from ourselves, and from our Creator. Instead of taking up our role as custodians of our environment, we quickly became profit-maximizing exploiters. The realization and confirmation by scientific research that we are headed towards a global catastrophe in not too many years came, perhaps, too late.

The Makalolo Plains awed Dafnis: "One must let oneself feel the freedom of the vast openness.... One must come face to face with the vast biodiversity in order to realize that one is part of this wonderful creation." Their guide led them across the savannah where they saw an amazing number of animals on their walking safari.

> We would go in a jeep and then we would step out and walk in a row, one behind the other—no more than seven people in a group so we would not make noise and disturb the wildlife. The safari leader was an expert. He had been doing this work for 25 or 30 years, and he carried his gun—just in case. But the strange thing was that, out of the seven people in the group, all the wild animals singled out *me*. The guide told me, "I don't know why. I never experienced this before." I said, "Probably it's my size; I have more to eat."

Dafnis shrugged and added, "But I survived."

Then he waxed comically philosophical and again conflated the 2006 and the 2009 trips. "Before I left to go to Zimbabwe, I went to Fr. Athanasios and I said, 'I have decided to accept the invitation to celebrate my 80th birthday in the jungle, among the wild animals. So I want to know, if a lion eats me for lunch, do you promise to declare me a saint of the Orthodox Church?'" He said as an aside, "Many saints were eaten by lions in Rome, in the Coliseum." Then he continued.

Figure 35. *Dafnis in 2009 on a Safari in Mana Pools National Park, Zimbabwe.*

Athanasios thought about it a little bit and he said, "Okay, Dafnis. *IF* while you are in the jungle a lion approaches you and asks you, 'Mr. Dafnis, do you denounce Jesus Christ?' and you say 'No, I don't denounce Him,' and the lion eats you up, then I promise your icon will be in the St. Trinity Church next to St. John the Baptist and the others." He continued, "But you know what? I doubt that such a lion exists in South Africa, and what I suspect will happen is that the lion will eat you up and then will say, 'Thank you, God. This was a very tasty meal for me today.'"

Dafnis could bring out humor from most people, including Orthodox bishops.

Dafnis and Maria loved their trip. In 2009, he was mobile enough to participate in all the activities. But by 2017, his knees bothered him and he walked painfully with a cane. Nevertheless, in 2018 he and Maria flew to Rome to visit Dora and Michael; and he walked around the city much more than I thought he was capable of doing. From the photos we saw, he greatly enjoyed the trip. He remained an adventurous spirit, filled with curiosity.

Figure 36. *Maria and Dafnis in Africa in 2009.*

Involvement in NGOs

In his retirement years, Dafnis became involved in volunteer organizations and served as a board member for some of these. I asked him to list the organizations to which he belonged. He said,

> Currently, I am a member of the board of trustees of CHIPS (Christian International Peace Service), a Christian peace-making organization based in England, with projects in Africa and elsewhere. I am also a member of the board and one of the founding fathers of the Cyprus Sustainable Tourism Initiative (CSTI), which focuses on bringing the benefits of tourism to small Cypriot communities in a sustainable way with respect to the environment and the culture—not through moving large numbers of tourists on buses. I am a member of the board of ASPIS, which is a youth against drugs organization that for years was directed by Kleitos, but now we have a new chairman. I am a member of Bird Life, an environmental organization that focuses on birds. We participate in activities like bird watching, bird reporting, and lobbying against hunting and illegal trapping of birds. Also, I am one of the oldest members of Friends of the Earth—an international environmental organization. I am also a member of the Cyprus Herpetological Society. This is why you see posters of snakes everywhere around the island. I am a friend of the snakes. I hope they realize it, and they are my friends also…

Lynne interjected, "And stop eating your birds." Dafnis smiled and said, "I killed that one. I followed the Jewish rule: a tooth for a tooth. It was a *just war*." He laughed and continued.

> I am a member of another environmental organization called The Environmental Committee of Limassol—a federation of environmental organizations to which various environmental organizations belong. I was one of the founders of this committee. At one time, we had 67 organizations in Limassol interested in the environment. Now the number has declined because some of the organizations were politically motivated, and we decided to keep politics out. Some parties were only interested in the environment for political reasons.

Dafnis added that he is a member of the Cyprus Green Party, which represents the Federation of Environmental and Ecological Organizations, with 16 NGO members who are active in the fields of ecology, environment, culture, and human rights issues.

The last volunteer agency he mentioned was the one that occupied the majority of his time. He said,

> Finally, I am a member of the Shelter for Victims of Violence, which is under the auspices of the Orthodox Church. The Vietnamese women you

> see at my house are overflow from the shelter. Because it is full, we put the women with families until their cases are processed. They are victims of violence. And, irrespective of religion or nationality, we help them. I serve as about 70% director of this shelter.

Lynne said, "You explained recently your definition of violence, which, as I recall, contained five different points. What were they?" Dafnis responded,

> First of all, physical violence. We have cases of physical abuse, such as the one involving Luon, a Vietnamese woman. When she came to the shelter, she had bruises on her body from her boss, who was a Turkish Cypriot teacher. Second, we have economic exploitation when they are supposed to work for eight hours and then after six days to take one day off. But they were forced to work for 12, 14, 16 hours per day, cleaning the house of the mother and of the sister and of the other children—yet not paid accordingly. Third, we have sexual exploitation, which, unfortunately, is very common. Fourth, we have psychological blackmailing. "If you don't do this, tomorrow I will send you back to your own country." And, of course, the women are horrified because they don't know their rights. They are scared. They think their boss can take them to the airport. And fifth is the way they are exploited in their own countries by employment agents who charge exorbitant fees. To pay the fees to come here, the women end up mortgaging their homes to get money.
>
> These abused women are lucky when they are connected to a committee called *Charity (Philoptochos*, friend of the poor). We have women who look for such abuse cases, and they help financially and in other ways. When they hear of a case of abuse through a neighbor or somebody else, they refer them to us. Yesterday, I handed some serious cases to one of the ministers of the interior. And I have their papers here, and I am waiting for him to return my call. If he never calls, he will regret it.

I said, "When we were here in 2011, you were working with a lawyer; and you were involved in liberating women who were victims of human trafficking over in the eastern part of the island. Was that part of this group?" Dafnis nodded and said,

> Yes. And we succeeded in liberating two of them. They were in Sotira village near Ayia Napa. We took the case to the court in Larnaca. The poor girls were trembling because the woman employer was very belligerent and shouting and saying, "I will send you back to your country tomorrow!" When she said something in the court, I said, "Madam, you are not the one to decide. It is the honorable judge." And the judge immediately said, "You have to pay €1,820 immediately." And she said, "We don't have the money now, but we shall pay it." So, I took these girls to Sotira, and they collected the money. We placed them with two other employers for a while. Both of them are back now in Viet Nam.

"When we think of human trafficking," I said, "we usually associate it with sexual trafficking or telling a person, 'We are going to employ you,' but then making a slave out of the person when he or she gets there." This comment elicited another story.

Deception and Bluffing

Under the tutelage of Colonel Grivas, Dafnis grew talented at bluffing, and he was a fine practitioner of the art of deception. After he retired, he sometimes used these skills to benefit others. He explained that a young woman from Moldova came to Cyprus to work as a waitress in order to support her sister who was a university student in Italy. When she arrived, however, she learned that her job, her employer, and the restaurant were not what she was promised. Dafnis explained,

> She was put in a night club, a gentleman's club, and she was given instructions on how to put drugs into drinks and how to solicit clients and how to sort the money—€30 for her and €70 for the club. She was a student of civil engineering in her country, but she ended up being forced to become a prostitute. [In another telling of the story, Dafnis said she had graduated with a degree in civil engineering.]

"Who owns this club?" I asked. "Was he a Russian?" "No," Dafnis replied. "He was a Greek Cypriot." He continued,

> Rose was her name—a beautiful girl. And after three or four days, when she went to serve somebody, she started crying in the nightclub. She was crying, crying, crying, and one of the clients of the nightclub asked, "Why you crying? Why do you look so unhappy?" This guy was a carpenter I knew very well. And she told him her story: "I am a civil engineer. I work as a waitress. I came here to work in a restaurant, and this is what happened to me." And he felt sorry for her, and he said, "You are lucky to come to my table. I shall send you to somebody who will help you."

The man instructed her to walk out of the nightclub through a certain door at a precise time and immediately get into a cab parked at the curb. She followed his directions, jumped into the cab, and the driver sped away.

Dafnis was very animated and dramatic as he continued his story.

> So, in the middle of the night, someone knocked at my door, and I opened it, and I saw this angelic creature. She was tall and really beautiful with blonde hair. And the taxi driver said, "So and so asked me to bring this woman to you." I don't know what the taxi driver thought. And then he told me the name of the man, and of course I knew him. I said, "Okay." He went away. She told me her story. I said to her, "You can stay here tonight, and tomorrow morning I shall accommodate you until you have your papers." And she said, "But all my belongings are with this man." I said, "I shall take care of these things."

> So next morning I went to a public [phone]booth, and I telephoned so that he could not trace the call. When he answered, I said, "Are you the employer of Rose?" He said, "*Who are you! Are you the one who took the most beautiful and the most accomplished [girl] from my business? And you are ruining my business.*" I said, "Watch out, because if you know who you are talking to, by tonight your head will be on one side of the road and your body on the other." The man calmed down, and I added, "Then I'm going to blow up your Cabaret, and I'm going to blow up yourself!"

Here Dafnis laughed loudly and said,

> Of course, I could not do any of these things. But I told the man, "At four o'clock you are to have her luggage ready outside the apartment, and the luggage will be picked up by someone I am going to send—*AND* don't dare ask who he is or where he is taking it if you want to be alive tomorrow."

I asked, "Did you learn all these things from Grivas?" He smiled and said, "I did." Then he added, "You see, I knew the owner [of the club], and I knew that he was a dangerous man in the night life here. He could pay somebody to exterminate you." The driver Dafnis hired went to the apartment as directed and found the luggage outside as Dafnis specified. He took the luggage back to Dafnis's house, and they never heard from the criminal employer.

Rose was severely traumatized, so Dafnis arranged for Dr. Evdokas to meet with her and provide psychiatric therapy. He helped her to recover, and she was finally able to return to Moldova. Dafnis concluded the story on a happy note.

> She called me a few days before Christmas two or three years ago. And she said, "Mr. Dafnis, I want to tell you I am happily married and live in the Peloponnese.... We have a restaurant, and we have olive trees and we produce olives. AND I AM PREGNANT! And I invite you and Dr. Evdokas to come for the baptism." [In another telling of the story, Dafnis said, "And two years later, Rose called me from the Peloponnese in Greece. She said, '...I am married, and I live in *Kalamata*, Greece, where they make the *pizzolis*. We have an olive grove, and we have a baby. We want you and Dr. Evdokas to come to the baptism of our daughter at Christmas time.' We never went, but still it was very nice of her to invite us."]

Dafnis was pleased that Rose was happily married. His effective bluff secured her deliverance and safe return home. Dafnis smiled and said, "I can threaten to do *dangerous* things."

I wanted to know if Dafnis got the police involved and if they shut the place down. "Well, it was a licensed business," he said. "As far as the police [were concerned], there was no case. Now, of course, because of the European Union, there can be much more effective work against exploitation." Cyprus became part of the EU in 2004, so I am not sure when Rose was in Cyprus.

Exploitation of Foreign Workers

Most domestic workers in Cyprus come to the island because of economic stress, and Cyprus has regulations regarding the rights of these workers. Dafnis said,

> Take Vicki, my housekeeper—I have legal and financial responsibilities for her. She is assured medical insurance, accident, and all these things. And there are agencies here—one that we work with closely—that have a list of prospective employers, mostly old people and people with terminal diseases or handicaps. Every employer has to post a guarantee of €850 to the Immigration Authorities, and they issue a temporary visa. On the basis of this visa, the foreign workers come to Cyprus.
>
> Agencies in the other countries recruit the women to come to Cyprus. Unfortunately, the agencies in Viet Nam exploit these women and make them pay €5,000 for their services. The agencies in Viet Nam lie to these poor women and tell them, "You will get €1,000 or €2,000 per month." So of course, these women think, "Okay, I will borrow €5,000 against my mortgage." But the women have to pay the fee before they leave Viet Nam, and when they get to Cyprus, they discover that they only make €330 per month. In Viet Nam, there is no control over such unscrupulous activities. Here in Cyprus, there is some control. With some countries, like the Philippines, there is a lateral agreement between government agencies. This is why the Philippine women get a higher salary: €400 per month. With Viet Nam, there is no government agreement, so when Vietnamese women come here, they get stuck with only €330 per month.

Figure 37. *Foreign workers celebrating Dafnis's 80th birthday.*

> These women must pay the agency, and they must pay their families to support them—their husband, their children's schooling, and so on. If they have a good boss who allows them to do extra work—to iron or to clean around the neighborhood—then they can get additional income, about €800 or €900 per month. But this is not always the case.... Some women are so stressed financially that they sell their body. It is very sad.
>
> The ones who suffer the most are the Vietnamese because there is no government agreement, and they are being exploited. But if we have an employer, we bypass the agency in Viet Nam and save the women the money. I have two cases now, if we get approval, the workers will go directly through an employer in Cyprus and save the €5,000 fee.

During his retirement years, Dafnis expended considerable time and money helping abused women. Sometimes, he won. In one case, he and the consul of Cyprus in Brazil exposed a Russian company that was chartering planes and trafficking Brazilian women to Cyprus. This company was banned from ever doing business in Cyprus again.

Justice for Foreign Workers

Dafnis had a German friend named Franz, who moved to Cyprus in 2010. He lived with a Vietnamese woman for five years in Limassol and grew very troubled by the abuse of foreign women. He and his girlfriend had an apartment with three rooms, and they began to keep one bedroom for abused women. Word spread that women could go to them and be protected. In 2017, Franz happened to be in Cyprus, and he came to Dafnis's home so we could interview him. A tall and muscular fellow, his size probably worked to his advantage when arguing on behalf of diminutive Vietnamese women.

Franz told us that when he went to the Labor Office with some of these women, he observed how poorly the legal system treated them. He heard about the work Dafnis was doing to provide shelter for abused women, so he went to see Dafnis, who was more experienced with the legal system in Cyprus. Franz was impressed that Dafnis, who was in his early 80s, was such an energetic and fearless advocate for abused women. The two men began to work together. Sometimes Dafnis would call and say, "We need to go to such and such village to deal with a problem." So, Franz would arrange to go with Dafnis after work.

Franz became increasingly aware that some Cypriots do not think Vietnamese women have the same rights as Cypriot women. Some employers believed they could do whatever they wanted with these workers. Franz developed a tactic to shame these Cypriot employers. He asked them, "What would you do if someone treated your daughter like that?" or "Would you like it if someone treated you like that?"

Franz also said the police in Cyprus could be abusive and calloused toward the plight of these women. He gave an example of a Vietnamese woman who was forced to work very hard and was not getting paid. Franz said, "She was very skinny—a bag of bones." Yet the police officer was completely unsympathetic. He said, "She has run away. I will deport her and send her back to Vietnam." Franz chided the policeman for his attitude.

He explained: "Cypriot employers use the threat of deportation as a means of having power over the women. But if Dafnis gets involved in handling these cases, the women are not treated in the same way. They are shown more respect." He added that Dafnis had helped hundreds of women in Cyprus to find new employers who are not abusive. Franz sadly had to explain to the Vietnamese women not to run away because then the police might treat them like criminals if they do not have sponsors in Cyprus. Because he speaks Vietnamese, the foreign workers would come to him for help, and he would accompany them to the Labor Office to present their cases.

While Franz lived in Cyprus from 2010 to 2015, he gained great respect for Dafnis. He told us that Dafnis genuinely cared for those who are disadvantaged; and because of his numerous connections in Cyprus, he was often able to solve problems without going through government procedures. The crafty old student of Grivas knew how to use his covert skills for good.

Sustainable Tourism

Dafnis helped create the Cyprus Sustainable Tourism Initiative (CSTI), and he saw in Philippos Drousiotis a man with the skills needed to develop this organization. Philippos earned degrees at a university in Iowa, and when he returned to Cyprus, he decided to help his uncle run the Droushia Heights Hotel near the towns of Polis and Latchi in northwest Cyprus. The hotel is located off the main roads, and the view of the Mediterranean Sea from its outdoor pool is stunning.

Philippos met Dafnis when a group of professionals helping children with special needs started coming to Droushia Heights for their meetings. The scholars in this group fascinated him, and he enjoyed listening to their lectures and conversations. "Dr. Evdokas," he said, "was probably one of the most educated people in Cyprus at that time." Philippos continued,

> Running the hotel was easy for me, and I needed something else to keep me busy. So I created a lecture series. Every last Friday of the month, we had a lecture at the Droushia Heights Hotel.... I was really impressed by a lecture that Dafnis delivered.... He forgot to bring his notes, but he spoke for an hour without repeating himself. And it was much applauded by everybody. I organized more than 300 lectures at Droushia, and Dafnis's presentation was one of the best. One time we had him do a workshop

about archaeology in the Akamas area. He lectured in the evening, and the next morning, we did an excursion. We went with Dafnis to find out what happened in the Akamas. He was always full of energy and full of enthusiasm.

The Sustainability Initiative Foundation began in England in 2003 as a non-profit organization promoting sustainable tourism in destinations where British people vacationed. Because many vacation in Cyprus, the members of the Sustainability Initiative chose to work there. They created a steering committee and chose Dafnis to lead because he emphasized sustainability and environmental concern going hand in hand. The goal was to extend the benefits of tourism from resorts in cities to villages. Dafnis worked with village leaders to get tourists into the villages. When Philippos moved to Limassol in 2004 to manage another hotel, Dafnis involved him in CSTI. Through his influence, Philippos became chairman of CSTI.

Dafnis persuaded Philippos of the need to educate tourists about their obligation to enhance the welfare of Cyprus. He believed that tourists would not mind paying a little extra if they thought they were doing something good for the island. He also believed they would become "repeaters," people who return to Cyprus instead of going to Egypt or Turkey the following year.

At first CSTI was small, and most of the work fell on Philippos, but over time it grew enough to have a board. According to Philippos, Dafnis consistently came up with excellent ideas. He suggested placing a statue made of cans and bottles in the airport as a means of conveying the message to travelers that they should recycle while on vacation. It was somewhat successful.

Philippos calls Dafnis the father of CSTI, adding that without Dafnis the Initiative would never have happened. "Dafnis is always giving without wanting anything back—unlike some of the people who join the board." Philippos explained that Cyprus did not have adequate drinking water, so they imported water on ships from Greece. But after the CSTI members tackled the problem, within six months, the island saved more than half a million Euros through water savings. The project was so successful that other arid countries began to take notice. Because Dafnis personally knew the environmental commissioners and the president of Cyprus, new opportunities arose for CSTI.

Philippos leads seminars for hotel management teams to teach them how to lower their impact on the environment. He explains, for example, that tourists waste much more food with buffets than they do if they pay for each item. Hotels that have a fixed rate for the room, food, and drinks encourage waste. Tourists tend to get a beer, drink half of it, and leave it when it gets warm and get another beer. The same principle is true with water use.

In 2017, three million tourists visited Cyprus. But the island has limited water, and tourists use *far* more water than do the locals. The amount of water waste is staggering. Philippos teaches hotel managers how to diminish water consumption by tourists. The Mediterranean Sea is becoming a pile of plastic trash, so he teaches how to reduce plastic waste by using filtered water instead of bottled water. Businesspeople oppose anything that cuts their profits, so Philippos has to convince them that conservation increases their revenue. He pressures politicians to pass environmentally friendly legislation. For example, as of January 2018, grocery stores must charge five cents for every plastic bag used for patrons' groceries. This law encourages people to bring re-usable bags for their purchases, thus reducing the immense environmental problem caused by plastic bags. Because of CSTI's efforts, sustainability became fashionable in Cyprus.

Philippos appreciated the fact that Dafnis was interested in doing what was good for his country—not just enriching himself. With disdain, he told us about government ministers who came to his hotel in Droushia and expected to be given free room and board. Dafnis was different. He paid his bills. He did not expect a free ride. He did not do things to enrich himself. He did what he thought was right.

Philippos also respected Dafnis for opening his home to foreign women trying to escape abuse by unscrupulous Cypriot employers. "We respect him," said Philippos. "His little house is so full of history, so full of knowledge. He shares what he has, and he is by far more active and energetic than most people his age.... He is intelligent.... He is amazing. I have seen people his age who do nothing. He keeps his mind strong and his health strong, and he is giving all the time."

The Wine Festival

In 2017, Dafnis insisted that we attend the Wine Festival at Limassol. When we reached the entrance at the appointed time of 8:00 p.m., we found that Dafnis had already purchased tickets for us. We knew better than to argue with him. Once inside the gate, we walked past a statue of a Greek man holding a wine goblet. Underneath the statue was written, "Established 56 years ago." Dafnis said casually, "I was on the committee that organized the first wine festival."

People were obviously enjoying themselves: talking with friends, buying food from vendors, sampling different wines, and watching demonstrations of how Cypriots used to stomp on grapes with their bare feet to produce grape juice for wine making. Various groups of musicians entertained people. At the end of the main concert, performers formed a line and began dancing around the audience, inviting members of the audience to join them. Lynne jumped up and quickly learned the dance steps as the participants moved in a circle around those of us who were less adventurous and remained seated. She rejoined me when it was over, flushed with the exertion and smiling with pleasure at being able to participate.

Figure 38. *Friendly gathering of Greek and Turkish Cypriots (and a few foreigners) at the Kakomallis Campground. Dafnis and Maria are in the middle of the second row.*

In the early days, Turkish Cypriots attended the wine festival—and some still do. Two buses from the North had transported Turkish Cypriots to Limassol to participate in the festivities. We saw Turks enjoying the food and wine and entertainment. Dafnis commented that the politics of wine differ from geopolitics. Normal citizens navigate inter-communal relations better when government officials stay out of the way. Dafnis located the woman who led the Turkish contingent to the Wine Festival and said, "Let's get together again and show that we can live in peace." He invited her to attend an inter-communal event at Kakomallis on 24 September. We joined this event, and a nice contingent of Turkish Cypriots drove down from the North. Dafnis, the senior spokesman of this group, created their motto: "Building peace from the ground up." In a short speech, he said, "Establishing peace from the top down, letting our elected leaders take the initiative, has failed miserably. It is up to us, the common people, to show the way forward."

We witnessed good will between those of Greek and Turkish descent as they ate together, sang together, and hiked together up to the fire lookout tower. I spoke with a Turkish Cypriot civil engineer who is restoring 20 Orthodox churches and monasteries in the North—buildings that were severely defaced. He gets money from the United Nations to do the work. To my delight, I learned that his crew had restored the St. Andreas Monastery at the tip of the Karpas Peninsula. When Lynne and I visited this once thriving monastery in 2011, it was literally crumbling from neglect.

Father Gennadios

Father Gennadios, Abbot of the Monastery of Archangel Michael, was Dafnis's spiritual father/confessor. The two men met in 1996 at one of the monasteries on Mt. Athos and discovered they shared common interests. Gennadios supervised the garden at a monastery, so he gladly benefitted from Dafnis's expertise in horticulture. He described Dafnis as a happy and witty person who was a fascinating conversation partner. When Gennadios's spiritual father sent him to Cyprus to restore the Monastery of Archangel Michael, he and Dafnis resumed their friendship.

Fr. Gennadios said Dafnis enjoyed life and had a special desire to help others. When they discussed Dafnis's difficulties in trying to help certain people, Gennadios told him that he needed to be more direct and tell them what they needed to do in order to improve. But Dafnis admitted, "I cannot do that." Gennadios told him if he could not say "No" he must say, "I cannot help you." Dafnis replied, "But I cannot keep from trying to help."

During our interview, we talked about the book Dafnis was supposedly writing. Gennadios smiled and said, "He has been going to write that book for the past 15 years. I have encouraged him to go ahead and write the book, but he just does not get around to it."

Figure 39. *Dafnis at work in his home office in 2017.*

> He has a good heart and loves to help others. Financially, he is poor, because he spends his monthly allotment within 15 days. One time when we were driving down a road, Dafnis asked me, "Do you have €20?" I said, "Yes." Dafnis said, "Okay, give it to me, and later I will repay you." So, I gave it to him, and in a few minutes, he stopped his car close to somebody; and he gave to him the €20.

Gennadios described Dafnis as a good person who enjoyed tricking people. He also mentioned Dafnis's tendency to be late. He said once they were going to the Nissi Beach Hotel near Ayia Napa, so he asked, "What time shall we start?" Dafnis answered, "We shall leave from here at 3:00 p.m." Later, he called from a village near Larnaca and said he was delayed. Finally, he came three hours late to the monastery to pick up Fr. Gennadios. The monk laughed when he recounted the story. He paused and added, "He does not do it intentionally. He just gets involved doing other things and loses track of time."

Fr. Gennadios said he asked God to allow Dafnis to live a few more years, because, "We still need him. He is very useful. He is old, but he still has a lot to give to the world. The way he behaves is like a saint. He is not afraid of death. He is ready to die any time. He doesn't have bad thoughts.... Such a person is a very huge gift." Toward the end of our pleasant conversation in the quiet, rural setting of Archangel Michael Monastery, Fr. Gennadios added that when Dafnis expressed hesitation concerning my writing a book about his life, he told Dafnis, "By the time Cosby finishes his book, you will be dead. What are you worried about? The book is for others, not for you to read." He was right.

CHAPTER 9
Legacy of a Legend

"For everything, there is a season" (Ecclesiastes 3:1)

On 12 February 2019, we began another journey to Cyprus. Months earlier, we had concocted covert plans with Dafnis's children to surprise him by joining the celebration of his ninetieth birthday on 17 February. But our dear friend died unexpectedly in his sleep on 5 February, and the entire purpose of our trip changed. A deep sense of grief replaced our anticipation of merriment. We flew across the Atlantic Ocean with heavy hearts to mourn his death with his family and friends. When we arrived at our destination, we noticed both the dreary grey of the overcast sky and the vivid green of lush vegetation, which we had not seen before on this arid island.

We had never experienced Cyprus in the rainy season—only the parched dryness of late summer, fall, and early winter. Maria had told us that we really must come again in the spring to witness the beauty of blooming flowers that produced an explosion of colors across the island's landscape. Dark clouds are a prelude to new life. The winter of 2018–2019 brought almost record rainfall to Cyprus. After decades of drought, relentless downpours refilled depleted reservoirs, inflicted erosion on the rural landscape, and signaled the rebirth of the island's vegetation. Death and rebirth. The cycles of nature. Sadness and joy. "For everything there is a season… a time to weep, and a time to laugh" (Ecclesiastes 3:1–2, 4, NRSV).

Dafnis's son, Thales, met us at the airport in Larnaca and drove us to Kalo Chorio, the village of Dafnis's birth. We stayed in the house of Stahis and Joy Panagides, located just across a narrow walkway from the house where Dafnis was born in 1929. His cycle of life was complete. His children and grandchildren continue his line. "A generation goes, and a generation comes, but the earth endures forever" (Ecclesiastes 1:4).

We spent much time bundled up in the chilly house in February and March. Old Cypriot homes are not insulated, and cold air pours through gaps around doors and windows. Bake in the summer. Shiver in the winter. Cycles of the seasons. Dark, dripping clouds. Bright flowers. "The sun rises, and the sun goes

Figure 40. Almond blossoms at Kalo Chorio.

down.... The wind blows to the south, and goes around to the north.... All streams run to the sea, but the sea is not full" (Ecclesiastes 1:5–7).

In between rainstorms, we hiked the hills around Kalo Chorio, photographing the beautiful almond blossoms, smelling the sweet fields of flowers, and watching the bees feeding on nectar to produce honey. We experienced moments of sadness and joy as we pondered the life of our friend and revisited some of our favorite places in the countryside. "A time to mourn, and a time to dance" (Ecclesiastes 3:4).

A few days after Stahis and Joy arrived from Bethesda, the four of us went to the cemetery in Limassol to pay our respects at the family grave. In accordance with Cypriot custom, family members share the same tomb. Dafnis's body was added to the remains of those who died before him. In the same grave were already buried his father, mother, wife, brother-in-law, and sister. The following information was carved on the communal tombstone. In English translation it reads.

> "My children for whom I am again in childbirth-labor
> until Christ be formed in you." (Gal. 4:19)
> Father Solomon Panagides 1892–1964
> Maria Solomontos Panagidou 1906–1969
> Maroula Dafni Panagidou 1931–2002
> Antonis Christodoulou Ioannou 1934–2008
> Chloe Solomontos Ioannou 1931–2012

At the bottom of the gravestone would be added "Dafnis Solomon Panagides 1929–2019." This Cypriot tradition of family burial sites resembles the custom of family graves mentioned in biblical passages. For example, Genesis 25:8–9 says, "Abraham breathed his last and died in a good old age, an old man and full of years, and was *gathered to his people*. His sons Isaac and Ishmael buried him in the cave of Machpelah." To be *gathered to one's ancestors* meant to have your bones placed in the same burial cave as theirs. In the United States, the custom has been

Figure 41. Stahis, Lynne, and Joy at the Panagides family tomb with a huge number of commemorative wreaths placed on top.

more to bury family members in separate graves beside each other instead of in the same grave. But the symbolism is similar.

Another custom in Cyprus is to show respect for the deceased by bringing to the burial site a wreath of flowers with your name printed on a ribbon surrounding the wreath. Heaped on the Panagides family tomb were dozens of wreaths. We recognized numerous names of friends and extended family members written in Greek on these wreaths. We also read the names of dignitaries, including the president of the Republic of Cyprus. Dafnis lived a long and productive life, and his contacts were extensive. His death represented the end of an era: "A time to be born, and a time to die" (Ecclesiastes 3:2).

"Of making many books there is no end" (Ecclesiastes 12:12)

To capture Dafnis's life, I drew from the complex collection of voices we had recorded in 2017. Different perceptions pepper the pages of our transcribed interviews. Many of the interviews presented Dafnis's own distinct voice, describing events from all phases of his lengthy life. He loved to tell stories, and he was so fond of some that he told them multiple times, often with minor variations. Sometimes he disagreed with himself. Sometimes his memory was foggy and the details he declared were confused. These problems existed both in his oral versions and in his written accounts of the same events in his book, *Bitter Leaves of Laurel.* His written versions recounted stories in the same manner as his oral deliveries—except without the benefit of his voice inflections and facial and hand gestures. Believing his written version to be more accurate than his oral accounts would be naïve. Both comprise an oral history complete with differing details. Dafnis was not a stickler for taking the time to make sure what he said or wrote was accurate. He was a storyteller, not a historian. In addition, I always had to be alert to his tendency to embellish and invent elements in his accounts—as well as his fondness for fooling me.

Seeking to separate truth from fiction was a necessary component of my writing. I fact-checked historical details where his story intersected with published accounts by others. And I was able to interview historians such as Andreas Karyos, who pointed out that some of Dafnis's stories were completely fabricated. A sobering realization emerging from the oral history of Dafnis is how far from precise history books are generally, for so much is based on the less-than-precise memories of people who tell their stories. I have long been aware of the tendency of ancient authors to embellish their accounts and to totally create some of the stories they report as history. While conducting interviews with or about Dafnis, I became increasingly aware of the same tendency in modern storytelling. I was simply unable to corroborate some claims in the stories we recorded, so I quote what people said and occasionally comment on the probability of accuracy. Stories grow over time; and people tend to exaggerate details that make themselves look better and to downplay details that make them look bad.

One learns to look at the larger narrative and expect conflicting viewpoints on details. Although I could not verify all claims made by participants in the oral history of Dafnis, I became progressively acquainted with the primary properties of his person. Certain characteristics emerged consistently, and I am confident these attributes were authentic. I could ignore comments that seemed to be outliers, but when I heard the same comments independently from a number of people, I concluded that they revealed the truth. Dafnis was a loveable collection of inconsistencies, many endearing, some not.

Be kind to the poor (Proverbs 19:17)

According to Dafnis's friends and family, he was lovable, generous, interesting, and caring. They also indicated that he was irresponsible, cavalier with respect to time commitments, unconcerned with keeping promises, insensitive to the expectations of others if he found them uninteresting, and inept in his business dealings.

In his own words, Dafnis said he was "unpredictable, spontaneous, and incorrigible." And Maria added, "Unreliable."

Over and over, we heard how wonderful he was—how he loved people regardless of their ethnic backgrounds or their places in society. His love for others and desire to help them revealed much about the man. He enjoyed being the center of attention, and he attracted people with his charismatic personality. But he was also adept at doing menial tasks for others in a selfless manner. His tireless advocacy for foreign workers endeared him to those he saved from abuse by unscrupulous employers. He truly cared for the welfare of others, and he expended considerable time, energy, and money seeking to help them have a better life.

Dafnis was an unabashed tree hugger and lover of all things natural. His idealism and innovative ideas provided major motivation for environmental movements in Cyprus. At a meeting of the Cyprus Sustainable Tourism Initiative in Paphos in 2017, we witnessed grateful leaders of the group present Dafnis with an award designating him the Father of Environmentalism in Cyprus. His tireless efforts resulted in an enlightened environmental movement on the island. He sought to provide a better life for island residents—both human and otherwise. All life was sacred for Dafnis. He seemed to do his best work when he developed innovative ideas that others put into practice. He often got distracted with something else and followed his whim of the day, forgetting or ignoring other tasks.

Figure 42. *Dafnis (right) accepting the "Father of Environmentalism" award from Philippos Drusiotis, Head of the Cyprus Sustainable Tourism Initiative (left), and Panicos, Mayor of Louvaras (middle).*

Lynne and I learned to be flexible with scheduling as we passed time with Dafnis, and we found ourselves influenced by his generosity. Culturally speaking, Cypriots practice more hospitality than is common in the USA—where people might talk about generosity on a philosophical level more than they implement generosity on a practical level. Sending a check to a benevolence society is more comfortable than inviting needy people into your home. Cypriots tend to be generous with each other but don't talk a lot about generosity. Of course, we noticed examples of hypocrisy and greed in Cyprus, as we would find anywhere. Overall, however, as I witnessed generosity, I found myself wanting to follow their example.

Generosity flows more naturally when it is a cultural expectation, and social interactions involving generosity provide increased cultural cohesion due to such give and take. One nice aspect of a more homogeneous cultural context as opposed to the ethnic and cultural diversity of the USA is greater consistency of expectations. One day I may give; the next day I may receive. The resulting social contract binds people together. Cypriots are much less fragmented than Americans when it comes to social norms, but they are every bit as fragmented when it comes to political matters.

Cypriot attitudes toward non-Greek Orthodox people vary considerably. They might or might not show hospitality to those who are outside their own group. Some Cypriots like Dafnis treated Filipino and Vietnamese kindly and with dignity, but others view these foreigner workers as an underclass and exploit them. Increased tourism and immigration have brought cognitive dissonance. Wealthy Russians have earned disdain from island residents by their arrogant conduct and dismissive attitudes toward Greek Cypriots. However, some Greek Cypriots are happy to make a lot of money from the Russians because of lucrative real estate transactions. Greed is a consistent problem in most human societies.

Although many Cypriots are as addicted to their mobile phones as people are in the USA, their emphasis on social gatherings brings greater cohesion to society and more of a sense of belonging. Due to the small size of the island, Cypriots often live closer to their extended family members and experience less social isolation than Americans do. Those of us in Western societies would do well to ponder how to foster a greater sense of belonging by spending more time interacting with our neighbors and less time in front of TV or computer screens. Often we do not live close to our extended families, so Dafnis and his friends provide a helpful model for increased social interactions in order to experience a greater sense of belonging.

"A time for peace" (Ecclesiastes 3:8)

Dafnis always had pacifist tendencies, but after his involvement in the bloody EOKA rebellion in the 1950s, his commitment to nonviolence escalated into a lifelong passion. He concluded that Jesus's command to "Love your enemy" precluded killing your enemy. He insisted that we conquer animosity through love. Violence is counterproductive—*always.*

From his perspective, the only remedy to the long-standing enmity between Greek Cypriots and Turkish Cypriots was for members of both groups to meet together and get to know each other as fellow human beings—not as adversaries. They must become friends on the basis of their common humanity—to seek what is best for *both* groups instead of trying to extract concessions from each in an effort to promote only the self-interest of one's own group. And he led by doing.

He warmly invited Turkish Cypriots to join with Greek Cypriots in friendship meetings at the Kakomallis Campground and elsewhere. We witnessed delightful examples of common humanity at these meetings where Greeks and Turks ate together and sang together and hiked together and generally enjoyed getting to know each other. For over 40 years, political leaders have failed to find common grounds for peace in Cyprus, but Dafnis led in developing a grass roots movement. All who attended those Kakomallis gatherings recognized him as the Patriarch of Peace.

Societal fragmentation in the USA continues to increase—to the point that violence is an ever-present danger. Many people feel alienated in society. There is a strong sense of not only rejecting the ideas of those who disagree politically and religiously but also of viewing them as enemies. We would be wise to ponder the fact that disintegration of Cypriot society resulted from ethnic differences where Greek and Turkish people mistrusted each other, then hated each other, and then killed each other. And much violence had no basis in ethnicity but focused on differing political beliefs. Among Greek Orthodox Cypriots, those who held right wing, nationalist philosophies hated those with socialist views; and over time they began killing them. Of course, those with socialist beliefs reciprocated, and murders became common. Political differences almost destroyed their democracy.

As extreme political affiliations escalate in the USA and people increasingly find themselves not just disagreeing but also hating those who hold different views, a nation-wide commitment to peace has become more urgent. If we do not find a way to see our common humanity with those who hold different religious and political views, we will move toward mutual destruction. Instead of arming ourselves and preparing to fight each other, we need to adopt Dafnis's approach of befriending people representing a wide array of beliefs. Sharing meals and engaging in congenial conversation will help us to appreciate our common humanity and stop viewing others as enemies to be subdued. For years, feelings of animosity ran so high in Cyprus that coffee shops catered to specific groups. Communists went to their own coffee shops to visit with other Communists. Right wing nationalists sat in their own coffee shops talking only with those who were like-minded. Sometimes these coffee shops were directly across a street from each other. The philosophical divide between the hostile groups was far greater than the distance between their respective coffee shops. Only a conscious effort by both sides to bridge such divides can lower tensions and lead to greater cooperation—or any cooperation at all.

"Forgive your neighbor" (Sirach 28:2)

Dafnis's friends did not ignore his faults; they put up with them. His tendency to be late for appointments, or to fail to show up entirely, was legendary. He was such a free spirit that he simply got lost in whatever he was doing, considering it to be more important than his other obligations. Friends wasted time waiting for him to arrive, but he was so fun that they forgave him and enjoyed his presence. Sometimes he promised things that he had no intention of doing. He enjoyed pleasant conversations, and he often avoided confrontations, sometimes to the point that he might leave Cyprus rather than face a conflict situation.

As one of his friends said, "We are not changing Dafnis." With age, I have reached that conclusion with my friends. I am not changing them. They are not changing me. We need to focus on pleasant activities that we can share, rather than wasting time dwelling on what annoys us about each other. If we dwell on what separates us, we become more separated. If we focus on life experiences that we share, we learn to support each other in spite of our differences. And it must be on a local level. Focusing on peace efforts as a philosophical exercise for people in society as a whole is not going to change the way we interact with our neighbors. We need to do more listening and less preaching. If I try to understand others instead of figuring out ways to make them agree with me, there will be progress. If my focus is on winning arguments, greater distance develops.

Dafnis had close friends who disagreed with his religious and political beliefs. Sometimes he had feisty debates with them about why he did not agree with their views. But they knew he loved them when he expressed his differences. They could disagree as friends as they sat around a table sipping coffee with each other. They were not shouting and waving placards in each other's faces. Peace comes from the ground up—or from the grounds up, if we are drinking coffee.

I am not saying that we must befriend everyone; but most people, even grouchy ones, respond positively to friendly gestures. Admittedly, some folks simply have a terminal case of being obnoxious, and befriending them might not be possible. To be truthful, I would not invite into my home some of the men I meet while kayaking. They are so crude that I do not want them around my wife. Yet some of these crusty fellows are more likely to watch out for my safety when going through challenging whitewater than some religious zealots I meet—people who talk a lot about God but are simply not there if someone needs them. Life is filled with ironies and insincere people. That is a given. But we can all help to dial back the corrosive rhetoric.

"Those who are generous are blessed" (Proverbs 22:9)

Dafnis was generous to a fault. He typically insisted on paying for everything—whether he could afford it or not. He enjoyed the attention and acclaim he received from paying the bill at restaurants. Something in his personality drove him to spend lavishly even when he had insufficient funds, and his compulsive generosity sometimes created hardships for his family. Although innovative and forward thinking, on a practical level he was not good at business. He was well aware of this problem, yet he could not change. He did not care about acquiring money, and he often found himself in debt. When working in Saudi Arabia to pay off the debts he amassed in Cyprus due to failed business ventures, he enjoyed himself and spent his money freely. He loved living in the large villa provided by the prince, and he relished entertaining other foreign workers.

Some people took advantage of his generosity, yet his kindness endeared him to people. To be fair, he was also adept at manipulating others. He had lots of friends, and he loved interacting with them. He felt good about himself when talking with others, and he loved fostering a sense of community. He groused about his TWs (time wasters), but he relished the way people wanted to be with him. Our time with Dafnis taught us the difference between *spending* time and *passing* time. The ability to relax and be in the moment and not fret about what we were not accomplishing was a valuable lesson. Dafnis's Mediterranean mindset would not earn him a Nobel Prize, but in his disorganized life, he accomplished a great deal because of his personal relationships. He was a riot of contradictions. And he was a riot to be around.

I am more task-oriented and focused on what I set out to accomplish. Consequently, I am much more likely than Dafnis to finish a large project. For years, he talked about writing his memoirs of the EOKA years and the early Republic of Cyprus. For years he procrastinated. For years he said he was almost finished, even though he had not yet started. Finally, he focused enough on the task to almost complete it. I could not live like that. I do not want to live that. My personality differs from that of Dafnis. But he rubbed off on me and helped me to relax and pass time. For example, I am not so concerned any more with what I am not getting accomplished as I pass time with my grandchildren or neighbors who stop by to chat. People take precedence over projects.

People should eat, drink, and enjoy themselves (Ecclesiastes 8:15)

In 2011, at the conclusion of our time in Cyprus, Lynne and I agreed that Dafnis was the most intriguing person we met on the island. We found his stories to be captivating, and we were amazed at the volume of projects he spearheaded. In 2017, we set about to write the story of his life because we wanted to show how one person can make a difference in the world. When we spent time with Dafnis day after day, what we discovered removed naïve assumptions we had at the beginning of our project. Yet we remain convinced that his life story provides significant value for contemplating how individuals can make a difference in the world.

Trying to fit into a mold is counterproductive. Each individual is unique. We all have strengths and weaknesses. For me to imitate Dafnis would be complete folly. I need to make a difference in the world with my own skill set. Dafnis's life shows that imperfect people can accomplish great good. We all have quirks and inconsistencies, but we can adopt his enthusiasm for life and expand our horizons to meet new challenges. We need to stop wishing we had the abilities of someone else and set about appreciating who we are and developing our unique capacities to compliment each other in community—to benefit from each other's strengths without being envious of each other.

Few of us will ever be as much of a free spirit as Dafnis was. Indeed, life would be chaos if we all exhibited his tendencies. But if we all shared his love for nature, our planet would be much healthier. And if we all shared his central goal of loving other people, our contribution to society would be immense. As his friend in Kalo Chorio told Dafnis's son, when all is said and done, "Only love remains, nothing else."

The End

Select Bibliography

Arbel, Benjamin. "Cyprus on the Eve of the Ottoman Conquest." Pages 37–48 in *Ottoman Cyprus: A Collection of Studies on History and Culture*. Edited by Michalis Michael, M. Kappler and E. Gavriel. Near and Middle East Monographs, vol. 4. Wiesbaden: Harrassowitz Verlag, 2009.

Asmussen, Jan. *Cyprus at War: Diplomacy and Conflict during the 1974 Crisis*. London: I. B. Tauris, 2008.

Barker, Dudley. *Grivas, Portrait of a Terrorist: The Fascinating Story of the Greek Leader of the Cyprus Revolt, General George Grivas*. London: Cresset Press, 1959.

Botswain, Tim. *A Traveler's History of Cyprus*. New York: Interlink Books, 2005.

Borowiec, Andrew. *Cyprus: A Troubled Island*. Westport, CT: Greenwood Publishing Group, 2000.

Bowersock, G. W. "The International Role of Late Antique Cyprus." 14th Annual Lecture on the History and Archaeology of Cyprus. Nicosia, Cyprus: The Bank of Cyprus Cultural Foundation, 2000.

Bryant, Rebecca. *Imaging the Modern: The Cultures of Nationalism in Cyprus*. New York: I. B. Taurus, 2004.

Cassia, Paul Sant. *Bodies of Evidence: Burial, Memory, and the Recovery of Missing Persons in Cyprus*. New York: Berghahn Books, 2005.

Crawshaw, Nancy. *The Cyprus Revolt: An Account of the Struggle for Union with Greece*. London: George Allen and Unwin, 1978.

Cobain, Ian. *Cruel Britannia: A Secret History of Torture*. London: Portobello Books, 2012.

Dionysiou, George. "Some Privileges of the Church of Cyprus under Ottoman Rule." In *Επετηρίδα Κέντρου Επιστημονικών Ερευών* 19 (1992) 327–334.

Divided Cyprus: *Modernity, History, and an Island in Conflict*. Edited by Yiannis Papadakis, Nicos Peristianis, and Gisela Welz. Bloomington: Indiana University Press, 2006.

Duckworth, Henry Thomas Forbes. *The Church of Cyprus*. London: Society for Promoting Christian Knowledge, 1900. Reprint, Boston: Adamant Media Corporation, 2003.

Dodd, Clement. *The History and Politics of the Cyprus Conflict*. New York: Palgrave Macmillan, 2010.

Durrell, Lawrence. *Bitter Lemons of Cyprus: Life on a Mediterranean Island*. London: Faber and Faber, 1957.

Ebied, Rifaat, and David Thomas. *Muslim-Christian Polemic During the Crusades: The Letter From the People of Cyprus and Ibn Abi Talib Al-Dimashqi's Response (The History of Christian-Muslim Relations)*. Leiden: Brill Academic Publications, 2005.

Εγγλεζάκης, Παῦλος, Ἀρχιμανδρίτης. *ΕΙΚΟΣΙ ΜΕΛΕΤΑΙ ΔΙΑ ΤΗΝ ΕΚΚΛΗΣΙΑΝ ΚΥΠΡΟΥ (4ος ἕως 20᾿ ος αἰὼν). ΑΘΗΝΑΙ: ΜΟΡΦΩΤΙΚΟΝ ΙΔΡΥΜΑ ΕΘΝΙΚΗΣ ΤΡΑΠΕΖΗΣ*, 1996. [20 Studies by the Church of Cyprus (4th through 20th Centuries). Athens: Educational Foundation National Bank, 1996]

Excerpta Cypria: Materials for a History of Cyprus. Translated and edited by Claude Delaval Cobham. Cambridge: Cambridge University Press, 1908; reprinted, British Library Historical Print Editions, 2011. Available on-Line via OpenLibrary.org.

French, David. *Fighting EOKA: The British Counter-Insurgency Campaign on Cyprus, 1955–1959*. Oxford: Oxford University Press, 2015.

Friedman, Herbert A. and Ioannis Paschalidis. "Psychological Warfare: Cyprus 1954–1959." http://www.psywarrior.com/cyprus.html

Grivas, Georgios. *Guerrilla Warfare and EOKA's Struggle: A Politico-Military Study*. London, 1964.

_____. *The Memoirs of General Grivas*. Edited by Charles Foly. New York: Praeger, 1965.

Hackett, J. *A History of the Orthodox Church of Cyprus*. London: Methuen, 1901.

Hadjianastasis, Marios. "Cyprus in the Ottoman Period: Consolidation of the Cypro-Ottoman Elite, 1650–1750." Pages 63–88 in *Ottoman Cyprus: A Collection of Studies on History and Culture*. Edited by Michalis Michael, M. Kappler and E. Gavriel. Near and Middle East Monographs, vol. 4. Wiesbaden: Harrassowitz Verlag, 2009.

Hill, George. *A History of Cyprus*, 4 vols. Cambridge: Cambridge University Press, 1940–1952 (reprinted 2010).

Holland, Robert F. *Britain and the Revolt in Cyprus, 1954–1959*. Oxford: Oxford University Press, 1998.

Ιστορία της Κύπρου, εκδιδομένη υπό την διεύθυνσιν Θεοδώρου Παπαδοπούλου, Λευκωσία: Ίδρυμα Αρχιεπισκόπου Μακαρίου Γ΄, Γραφείον Κυπριακής Ιστορίας. [*History of Cyprus*. Issued under the direction of Theodoros Papadopoulos. Nicosia: Foundation of Archbishop Makarios III, Office of Cypriot History, 1977–]

vol. Α΄: Αρχαία Κύπρος. Μέρος Α΄: Φυσιογεωγραφική εισαγωγή. Προϊστορικοί χρόνοι. Σχέσεις προς ομόρους χώρους, 1977 [*Vol. 1: Ancient Cyprus Part I: Historical Introduction*. Prehistoric Times. Contacts with Neighboring Areas, 1977].

vol. Β΄: Αρχαία Κύπρος. Μέρος Β΄: Αρχαία Βασίλεια – Ελληνιστική Κύπρος, Επαρχία της Ρωμαϊκής Αυτοκρατορίας, Αρχαία Θρησκεία, Αρχαία γραφή, Γραμματεία και Φιλοσοφία, Αρχαία τοπωνύμια, Βιβλιογραφία, Χρονολογικοί πίνακες, 2000. Επιλογή και επιμέλεια Ανδρέας Δημητρίου, 2000 [*Vol. 2: Ancient Cyprus Part II: Archaic Kingdom Hellenistic Cyprus, Province of the Roman Empire, Ancient Religion, Ancient Writing, Scribal Office and Philosophy, Ancient Toponyms, Bibliography, Chronological Tables*, 2000].

vol. Γ΄: Βυζαντινή Κύπρος. Ιστορικογεωγραφική εισαγωγή, Θεμελίωσις της Κυπριακής Εκκλησίας, Πολιτικός θεσμός, Το Θέμα Κύπρου, Αραβικαί επιδρομαί, Η Κύπρος υπό τους Κομνηνούς, Βυζαντινή Αρχιτεκτονική και Τέχνη, 2005, Πίνακες. Επιλογή: Χαράλαμπος Γ. Χοτζάκογλου, 2005 [*Vol. 3: Byzantine Cyprus: Historical Introduction, Foundation of the Cypriot Church, Political Institution, The Topic of Cyprus, Arab Raids, Cyprus under Komnenoi, Byzantine Architecture and Art, 2005*].

vol. Δ΄: Μεσαιωνικόν Βασίλειον – Ενετοκρατία. Μέρος Α΄: Εξωτερική Ιστορία – Πολιτικοί και Κοινωνικοί θεσμοί – Δίκαιον – Οικονομία – Εκκλησία, 1995, Γενεαλογικο Πίνακες [*Vol. 4: Medieval Kingdom – Venetian Rule. Part I: Foreign History – Political and Social Institutions – Justice – Economy – Church*, 1995. Genealogical tables].

vol Ε΄: Μεσαιωνικόν Βασίλειον – Ενετοκρατία. Μέρος Β΄: Πνευματικός βίος – Παιδεία – Γραμματολογία – Βυζαντινή Τέχνη – Γοτθική Τέχνη – Νομισματοκοπία – Βιβλιογραφία, 1996 [*Vol. 5: Medieval Kingdom – Venetian Rule. Part II: Spiritual life – Education – Literature – Byzantine Art – Gothic Art – Coins – Bibliography*, 1996].

Hitchens, Christopher. *Hostage to History: Cyprus from the Ottomans to Kissinger*, 3rd edition. London: Verso, 1997.

Karageorghis, Vassos. *Cyprus: From the Stone Age to the Romans (Ancient Peoples and Places)*. New York: Thames & Hudson, 1982.

Karpat, Kemal. *Turkey's Foreign Policy in Transition: 1950–1974*. Leiden: E. J. Brill, 1975.

Karyos, Andreas. "EOKA, 1955–1959: A Study of the Military Aspects of the Cyprus Revolt." Unpublished Ph.D. Dissertation. University of London, 2011.

Ker-Lindsay, James. *The Cyprus Problem: What Everyone Needs to Know.* Oxford: Oxford University Press, 2011.

Koumarianou, Catherine. *Avvisi (1570–1572): The War of Cyprus*. Nicosia: Bank of Cyprus Cultural Foundation, 2004.

Κυπριανος, Ἀρχιμανδρίτος. *ΙΣΤΟΡΙΑ ΧΡΟΝΟΛΟΓΙΚΗ ΤΗΣ ΝΗΣΟΥ ΚΥΠΡΟΥ.* ΕΚΔΟΣΕΙΣ Κ. Venice, 1778 (3η ἔκδοση, ΛΕΥΚΩΣΙΑ: ΕΚΔΟΣΕΙΣ Κ. ΕΠΙΦΑΝΙΟΥ, 2001).

Λεύκωμα κρατητηρίων και πολιτικών κρατουμένων, Ε.Ο.Κ.Α. 1955–1959. Λευκωσία: Εκδοση Συνδέσμου Πολιτικών Κρατουμένων Ε.Ο.Κ.Α., 1989. [*Album of Holdings and Political Prisoners: EOKA 1955–1959.* Nicosia: The EOKA Association of Political Prisoners, 1989]

Luke, Sir Harry. *Cyprus Under the Turks, 1571–1878: Record based on the Archives of the English Consulate in Cyprus under the Levant Company and After.* London: C. Hurst, 1921 (reprint 1969).

Λυσιώτης, Ρένος [Lyssiotis, Renos]. *Αγαπητέ μου Ρένο [My Dear Reno].* Nicosia: MAM, 2019.

_____. *Γιγάντιες Ψυχές [Giant Souls].* Nicosia: MAM, 2011.

_____. *Το ημερολογια του D.P.743: 1956–1959 [The Memoirs of D.P. 743: 1956–1959].* Nicosia: MAM, 2012.

_____. Προσωπική μαρτυρία: Ο D.P. 743 στα Κρατητήρια Πύλας [*Personal Testimonies: D.P. 743 at the Detention Center Gate*]. Nicosia: MAM, 2018.

_____. Στρατάρχα μου, παραδίδομαι... και 19 άλλες ιστορίες. Nicosia: MAM, 2016. English translation: *My Marshall, I surrender ... and 19 other stories.* Nicosia: MAM, 2016.

Μακαριωτάτου Ἀρχιεπισκόπου Κύπρου. ἡ ἁγία νῆσος, ἔκδ. Β΄. Λευκωσία, 1997.

Mallinson, William. *Cyprus: A Modern History*. London: I. B. Tauris, 2005.

Markides, Kyriacos C. *Mountain of Silence: A Search for Orthodox Spirituality*. New York: Doubleday, 2003.

_____. *The Rise and Fall of the Cyprus Republic.* New Haven, CT: Yale University Press, 1977.

Michael, Michalis N. "An Orthodox Institution of Ottoman Political Authority: The Church of Cyprus." Pages 209–230 in *Ottoman Cyprus: A Collection of Studies on History and Culture.* Edited by Michalis Michael, M. Kappler and E. Gavriel. Near and Middle East Monographs, vol. 4. Wiesbaden: Harrassowitz Verlag, 2009.

Michael, Michális Stavrou. *Resolving the Cyprus Conflict: Negotiating History.* London: Palgrave Macmillan, 2011.

Mitford, Terence Bruce. "Roman Cyprus." Pages 1285–1384 in *Aufstieg und Niedergang der romischen Welt: Geschichte und Kultur Roms im Spiegel der Neueren Forschung* II. 7.2. Edited by Hildegard Temporini and Wolfgang Hasse. Berlin: Walter de Gruyter, 1980.

Muller, Gerhard P. and Klaus Liebe. *Cyprus.* Munich: Verlag C. J. Bucher, 1986.

Neophytos, Metropolitan of Morphou, editor. *Holy Bishopric of Morphou: 2000 Years of Art and Holiness.* Nicosia, Cyprus: Bank of Cyprus Cultural Foundation and the Holy Bishopric of Morphou, 2002.

Oberling, Pierre. *The Road to Bellapais: The Turkish Cypriot Exodus to Northern Cyprus.* East European Monographs, No. 125. New York: Columbia University Press. 1982.

Παναγίδης, Δάφνης Σ. (Panagides, Dafnis S.). ΠΙΚΡΟΔΑΦΝΕΣ: ΚΥΠΡΟΣ 1954–1974 (*Bitter Leaves of Laurel: Cyprus 1954–1974*). Dafnis's family published his memoir posthumously in 2019. His brother, Stahis S. Panagides, translated the book into

English: *Cyprus: Island in the Storm: An Individual Encircled by Violence becomes a voice for Reconciliation and Peace*. Pittsburg: Dorrance Publishing Co., 2021.

Panteli, Stavros. *A History of Cyprus: From Foreign Domination to Troubled Independence*, 2nd edition. London: East-West Publications Ltd., 2000.

_____. *Place of Refuge: A History of the Jews in Cyprus*. London: Elliott & Thompson, 2004.

Papadakis, Yiannis. *Echoes from the Dead Zone: Across the Cyprus Divide*. London: I. B. Tauris, 2005.

Papageorghiou, A. *Christian Art in the Turkish-Occupied part of Cyprus*. Nicosia, Cyprus: The Holy Archbishopric of Cyprus, 2010.

Pericleous, Chrysostomos. *The Cyprus Referendum: A Divided Island and the Challenge of the Annan Plan*. London: I. B. Tauris, 2009.

Portelli, Alessandro. *The Death of Luigi Trastulli and other stories: Form and Meaning in Oral History.* Albany, NY: State University of New York Press, 1991.

Rapp, Claudia. *Holy Bishops in Late Antiquity: The Nature of Christian Leadership in an Age of Transition*. Berkeley: University of California Press, 2005.

Salem, Norma, ed. *Cyprus: A Regional Conflict and its Resolution*. London: Macmillan, 1992.

Salin, Ibrahm. Cyprus: *Ethnic Political Components*. Oxford: University Press of America, 2004.

Smit, Anneke. *The Property Rights of Refugees and Internally Displaced Persons: Beyond Restitution*. New York: Routledge, 2012 (pp. 51–54 on Cyprus).

Smith, M. "Explaining Partition: Reconsidering the Role of the Security Dilemma in the Cyprus Crisis of 1974." Unpublished Ph.D. Dissertation, University of New Hampshire, 2009.

Solsten Eric, ed. *Cyprus: A Country Study.* Washington, D.C.: Library of Congress, 1991.

Stavrides, Theoharis. "Cyprus 1750–1830." Pages 89–106 in *Ottoman Cyprus: A Collection of Studies on History and Culture*. Edited by Michalis Michael, M. Kappler and E. Gavriel. Near and Middle East Monographs, vol. 4. Wiesbaden: Harrassowitz Verlag, 2009.

Studies on the History of the Church of Cyprus: 4th–20th Centuries. Edited by Silouan Ioannou and Misael Ioannou. Brookfield, VT: Ashgate Publishing, 1995.

Σωτηρίου, Γεώργιος Α., editor. *Τα βυζαντινά μνημεία της Κύπρου*. Αθηναις: Γραφειον Δημοσιευματον Ακαδημιας Αθηνημων, 1935. [Sotiriou, George A., editor. *The Byzantine Monuments of Cyprus*. Athens: Publishing Office of the Academy of Athens, 1935].

Thomson, John. *Through Cyprus with the Camera in the Autumn of 1878:* Vols 1 and 2. New edition, London: Trigraph Ltd., 1985.

Tofallis, Kypros. *A History of Cyprus: From the Ancient Times to the Present*. London: The Greek Institute, 2002.

Τρίτος, Τόμος. *Μεγάλη Κυπριακή Εγκυκλοπαίδεια*, #3. Λευκωσία, Κύπρος: Φιλόκυπρος, 1985. [Tritos, Thomas. *Great Cypriot Encyclopedia*, #3. Nicosia, Cyprus: Philokypros, 1985].

Van Deun, Peter, editor. *Hagiographica Cypria: Sancti Barnabae Laudatio Auctore Alexandro Monocho*. Corpus Christianorum, Series Graeca, 26. Brepols: Leuven University Press, 1993.

Varnavas, Andreas. *A History of the Liberation Struggle of EOKA (1955–1959)*. Translated into English by Philippos Stylianou. Nicosia: The Foundation of the EOKA Liberation Struggle 1955–1959, 2004.

Von Falkenhausen, Vera. "Bishops and Monks in the Hagiography of Byzantine Cyprus." Pages 21–33 in *Medieval Cyprus: Studies in Art, Architecture, and History in Memory of*

Doula Mouriki. Edited by N. Patterson Ševčenko and C. Moss. Princeton, NJ: Princeton University Press, 1999.

Walter, Christopher. *The Warrior Saints in Byzantine Art and Tradition.* Burlington, VT: Ashgate Publishing, 2003.

Wideson, Reno. *Portrait of Cyprus.* The Hague: Deppo Holland, nd.

Zartarian, Giragos. *Photographs: 1935–1950.* Edited by Stavros G. Lazarides. Nicosia, Cyprus: Cultural Centre Marfin Laiki Bank, 2007.

Made in United States
North Haven, CT
28 June 2022

20709208R00135